RESOLVE

RESOLVE

From the Jungles of WWII Bataan, the Epic Story of
a Soldier, a Flag, and a Promise Kept

BOB WELCH

BERKLEY CALIBER, NEW YORK

BERKLEY BOOKS
Published by the Penguin Group
Penguin Group (USA) Inc.
375 Hudson Street, New York, New York 10014, USA
Penguin Group (Canada), 90 Eglinton Avenue East, Suite 700, Toronto, Ontario M4P 2Y3, Canada
(a division of Pearson Penguin Canada Inc.) • Penguin Books Ltd., 80 Strand, London WC2R 0RL,
England • Penguin Group Ireland, 25 St. Stephen's Green, Dublin 2, Ireland (a division of Penguin
Books Ltd.) • Penguin Group (Australia), 250 Camberwell Road, Camberwell, Victoria 3124, Australia
(a division of Pearson Australia Group Pty. Ltd.) • Penguin Books India Pvt. Ltd., 11 Community
Centre, Panchsheel Park, New Delhi—110 017, India • Penguin Group (NZ), 67 Apollo Drive,
Rosedale, Auckland 0632, New Zealand (a division of Pearson New Zealand Ltd.) • Penguin Books
(South Africa) (Pty.) Ltd., 24 Sturdee Avenue, Rosebank, Johannesburg 2196, South Africa

Penguin Books Ltd., Registered Offices: 80 Strand, London WC2R 0RL, England

This book is an original publication of The Berkley Publishing Group.

The publisher does not have any control over and does not assume any responsibility for author or
third-party websites or their content.

RESOLVE

FIRST EDITION: November 2012

ISBN: 978-0-425-25773-9

An application for cataloging has been submitted to the Library of Congress.

PRINTED IN THE UNITED STATES OF AMERICA

10 9 8 7 6 5 4 3 2 1

Tomorrow sees undone, what happens not today;
Still forward press, nor ever tire!
The possible, with steadfast trust,
Resolve should by the forelock grasp;
Then she will ne'er let go her clasp;
And labors on, because she must.

—JOHANN WOLFGANG VON GOETHE

Blessed is the man who perseveres under trial.

—JAMES 1:12

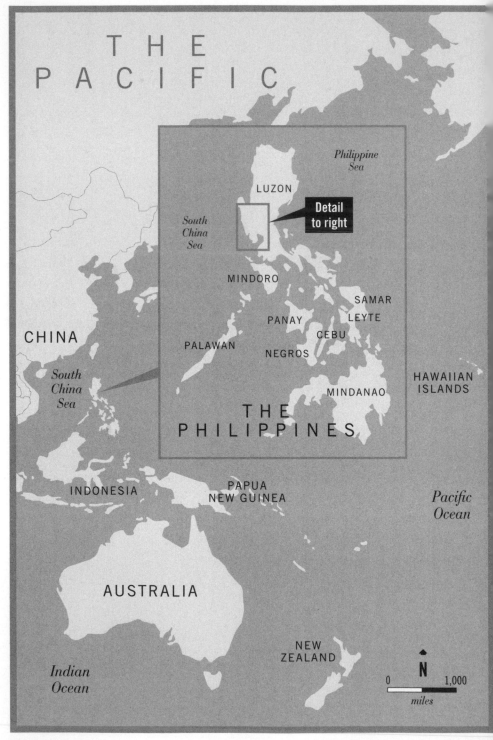

Map by Tom Penix

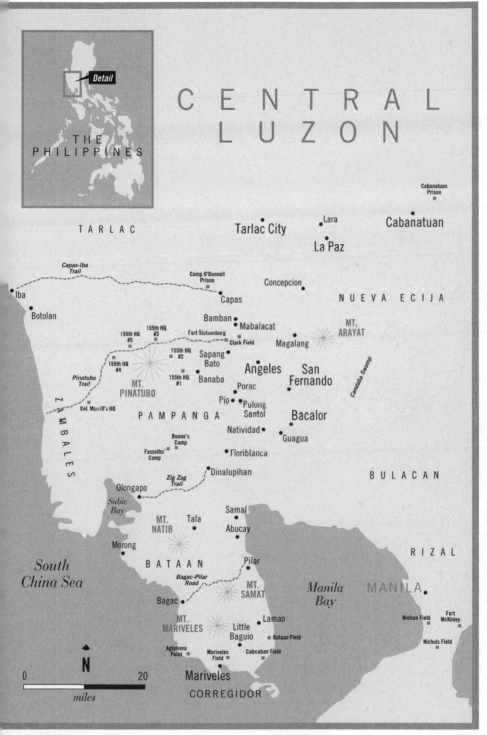

THE PHILIPPINES

Detail

CENTRAL LUZON

Cabanatuan Prison

TARLAC

Tarlac City

Lara

La Paz

Cabanatuan

Capas-Iba Trail

Iba

Botolan

Camp O'Donnell Prison

Capas

Concepcion

NUEVA ECIJA

Bamban

Mabalacat

MT. ARAYAT

159th HU #5

155th HQ #3

Fort Stotsenburg

Clark Field

Magalang

155th HQ #2

Sapang Bato

155th HQ #4

Pinatubo Trail

MT. PINATUBO

155th HQ #1

Banaba

Angeles

San Fernando

Cantaba Swamp

Col. Merrill's HQ

Porac

Pio

Pulong Santol

Bacalor

PAMPANGA

Natividad

Guagua

Boone's Camp

Fassoths' Camp

Floriblanca

Z A M B A L E S

Dinalupihan

BULACAN

Zig Zag Trail

Olongapo

Subic Bay

Samal

MT. NATIB

Tala

Abucay

Morong

RIZAL

South China Sea

BATAAN

Pilar

Bagac-Pilar Road

MT. SAMAT

Manila Bay

MANILA

Bagac

MT. MARIVELES

Little Baguio

Lamao

Nielson Field

Fort McKinley

Bataan Field

Nichols Field

Aglaloma Point

Mariveles Field

Cabcaban Field

0   N   20

miles

Mariveles

CORREGIDOR

ap by Tom Penix

CONTENTS

PART IV: PERSEVERANCE 161

PART V: PEACE 241

FOREWORD

A WHILE AFTER the *Band of Brothers* HBO series came out, I was in a Wal-Mart in my hometown of Salem, Oregon, wearing my "Easy Company" jacket, when a young man rushed up to me.

"You're . . . you're . . ."

"Don Malarkey," I said. "Now, you'd better take care of your shopping cart, son. Move along."

The attention that's been heaped on us "Band of Brothers" has been gratifying; I can't deny it. But, hell, it doesn't make us any better than any of the other soldiers who did the same kind of things we did in World War II: rolled up their sleeves and won a war, whether it was in the frozen forests of Bastogne or in the humid jungles of the Philippines.

Which brings me to my cohorts who fought in the Pacific Theater—and, in particular, to Clay Conner Jr.

I never knew the man. But after hearing his story from the same author, Bob Welch, who helped me write my book *Easy Company Soldier*, I think the two of us would have hit it off great.

Like me, Conner had a certain renegade spirit in him that I can't help but admire. It's not as if we didn't have respect for military rules; it's just that, at times, it seemed we had to take the bull by the horns and get the job done our way. (That said, I'm not sure Conner would ever have done anything as stupid as trying to grab a souvenir pistol off a dead soldier in the heat of battle, which, of course, I did at Brecourt Manor in Normandy.)

Like me, Conner was a university man, a fraternity man, a Sigma Phi Epsilon at Duke. I was a Sigma Nu at the University of Oregon. He appreciated good literature: Shakespeare, Emerson, and Thoreau. I loved the poetry of William Ernest Henley, such as "Invictus," and Kipling's "Gunga Din."

We both left girlfriends back home when we headed overseas. Both of us had a thirst for adventure. Both made friends in war who would stay with us the rest of our lives, some only in our memories.

I'm not saying Conner and I would have been like twins; there were plenty of differences, too. I was a West Coast kid; he was an East Coast kid. He seems to have grown up in a pretty supportive family; mine wasn't that way. I parachuted out of airplanes and went after the enemy; he lived in a jungle and tried to keep the enemy from coming after him.

In some ways, I might have enjoyed his experience in the Pacific; after all, as a kid growing up, based on a series of books I had read, I fashioned myself as "Bomba the Jungle Boy." I imagined myself swinging from tree to tree on vines.

Hell, Conner *was* Bomba the Jungle Boy. In April 1942, after the Fall of Bataan, his future depended on his finding a way to adapt to that native environment, build bridges to the natives who lived there, and elude an enemy that was continually after him. Not to mention eluding the snares of those Mickey Mouse Communist outfits that only complicated the mix.

I'm ninety years old—and feeling every bit of it. Conner died younger. But I'd like to think that if we'd ever met, we'd have had great fun sharing stories of our experiences. Were we heroes? Well, some people seem to think so; Conner was never part of a ten-part HBO series, but he did appear on a popular show called *This Is Your Life*—and the host said no single story they'd ever done triggered such positive response.

I like to think of us as a couple of guys who got thrown into a mess called war and found a way to help win it, survive it, and, later on, tell stories about it.

Whatever theater of war we fought in and however we fought it— land, sea, or air—the thing that bound us together as Americans in World War II was something Henley refers to in my favorite poem, "Invictus." Something that Clay Conner Jr. must have had in spades: an "unconquerable soul."

DON MALARKEY
SALEM, OREGON
JANUARY 2012

IN THE PHILIPPINE jungle, the soldier ran with the panicked zeal of a hunted animal. He sloshed through rice paddies, splashed across muddy drainage canals, and threaded his way through leaves the size and thickness of B-17 props. His lungs heaved. His uniform, bleached by the sun since he'd first plunged into the Luzon jungle nearly a year before, was matted to his skin with a seal of sweat. His legs bled; the bamboo hedges had shredded his pants.

It was the morning of March 15, 1943. Clay Conner Jr. fell to his knees, hidden in chest-high cogon grass. From inside, the malaria gnawed at his spleen; he shivered despite the morning's growing heat. He heard a vehicle and the crunch of more boots. Machine-gun fire chattered, playing ominous percussion to his panting. His stomach lurched. He vomited.

When surprised by the raid in the barrio of Lara in Tarlac Province, Conner and three other American soldiers had run straight into a camouflaged cluster of Japanese soldiers, dropping a handful with pistol fire then bolting for a bamboo thicket. There, they had discarded their musette bags, knowing the baggage would only hinder any hopes of escape. Conner was about to pluck from the bag Junko, the silly but sentimental stuffed monkey he'd known all twenty-four years of his life, when bullets shredded bamboo stalks around him. The four men scattered. There was no time to save Junko.

With Japanese troops entrenched to the north, the men headed east. Moments later, Conner saw Bob Mailheau and Eddie Keith pinned down in a ditch some fifty yards away. Its banks were coated in mud, and the two were trying desperately to claw themselves out but getting no traction. Conner raced back, unloaded at the Japanese gunners half a magazine of fire from his .45-caliber pistol, reached down, and helped the two out. Mortar rounds exploded. Shots peppered their feet. "I'm hit!" someone yelled. "I'm hit!"

It was Frank Gyovai (GUH-Vay), the last member of the ragtag foursome and Conner's closest pal, the "gentle giant" who had carried the disease-racked Conner on his back the night before because Clay could not walk. Conner saw Gyovai get up and start running. He figured Frank must be all right and so began running, too. A mile. Two. Finally, after four miles, he dropped in exhaustion when finding the cover of the white-tasseled cogon grass. Now on his own, it was a question of endurance, of wills, of resolve: Conner's and the enemy's.

His pistol, Conner figured, had a single bullet left in it. Based on the glut of soldiers he'd seen as they left Lara and on the volleys of fire he'd heard since, he figured the enemy had dozens of men—perhaps scores of men—with rifles, machine guns, and mortars. What's more, they had a seemingly inexhaustible bent to flush out, kill, and otherwise humiliate their American enemies. Why else would they have gone to the trouble to do what they did next: set the field on fire to flush him out. All this for one enemy soldier. One.

Conner instinctively crawled to the field's middle, where he'd seen a small stream and knew the grass was greener and less likely to burn. He lay still the rest of the day, even when smoke drifted over him and tempted him to cough. The sun filtered through the grass to sear his already leathery skin. When darkness fell, he slipped through the scorched grass and found the coolness of a canal partly full of water; he heard Japanese soldiers on the bank above. Someday, he vowed, if he survived this ambush, he would return to Lara and get revenge on the Filipino mayor who had betrayed him and his men by tipping off the Japanese.

Before sunrise, he made his way into a cane field to hide during the day, unsure which was worse: the threat of being killed by the Japanese or hours of being driven nuts by mosquitoes and flies that dove on him like crazed kamikazes.

The fever beckoned him to stay still, but Conner knew he must keep moving. Before light on the third day, he repositioned himself in the muddy upper banks of a creek that wound through the field. Around him, reeds stretched skyward. Suddenly, voices. Japanese soldiers. And, worse, the ominous rumble of a half-track, its front wheels matting down the grass, its caterpillar tracks clanking through the mud with an occasional metal-on-metal squeak. In back, soldiers scanned the grasses for the enemy, one occasionally tossing a gas-soaked torch into the fields. The Japanese were still trying to burn him out.

He looked around. There was nowhere to run without being seen. And nowhere to— *Wait.* He remembered the lone bullet in the pistol's chamber; perhaps he should just end it the way Japanese soldiers sometimes ended it when their only other choice was surrender. Conner began digging frantically into the mud like a man digging his own grave. Given what the Japanese sometimes did with the bodies of Americans, why would he want to be found?

The patrol closed in. The day got lighter. Conner's mind flashed to stories he'd heard about U.S. soldiers being killed and their heads hacked off and hung from marketplace palms to trumpet Japanese superiority. Not for him. No such humiliation for a recent college grad who had a mom and pop and girl waiting for him back home.

No, he would end this game with no help from anyone else, particularly the guys who'd already claimed far too many of his buddies. Beyond, more cogon grass whooshed into flames. Conner stuffed his Bulova watch into his pocket. He wiggled into the body-sized trench like a human clam and began dragging mud over himself, holstered gun on his leg. Moments later, the half-track lumbered toward the spot where he lay. Right next to the spot. Finally, well beyond the spot.

Then, as if suspicious, the patrol returned. The half-track and its men moved slowly one way, then the other, almost as if they *knew.* The soldiers talked to each other in staccato bursts. Torched more grass. Smoked more cigarettes. And waited—as if to prove that their resolve was stronger than Conner's.

Finally, at about 5 P.M., the soldiers left. Darkness descended. The area grew quiet. That's when it happened: A single reed in the bog twitched slightly. Beneath it, the sun-baked mud quivered just a touch: a crease here, a crack there. Moments later, the man breathing through that reed, Clay Conner Jr., lifted his darkened head as if he were a charcoal mummy coming slowly to life.

Everything under control.

PART ONE

PARADISE

ONE

The Call

August 31, 1918, to November 1, 1941

ON THE FIRST day of November 1941, drizzle shrouded San Francisco Harbor like wet smoke, the weather mirroring the nation's mood beyond. By now, the prospect of America entering World War II wasn't a question of "if" but "when" or "where." A disquieting certainty had settled in, a collective queasiness that portended the inevitable retching to follow.

Indeed, if Joe DiMaggio's fifty-six-game hitting streak had provided an "I don't care if I ever get back" escape from the heaviness of the world, a summer of baseball and picnics and vacations had given way to the gnawing anticipation of war. As Japan and Germany battled elsewhere with guns and grenades, friction between those countries and the United States ground like oceanic plates on the bottom of the sea: nothing visible, but, at some point, something certain to send shock waves far and wide.

Only the day before, President Franklin Roosevelt had faced the press in Washington, D.C., while wearing a black armband, his symbolic mourning for the crew of the *Reuben James*, which, earlier that day, had become the first U.S. Navy ship sunk by a German submarine. Most of the 159 men on board were dead, their bodies scattered on the chilly veneer of the North Atlantic Ocean.

More than a million soldiers had died since Germany declared war on Poland in 1939 and surged into Russia. Japanese armies were ravaging China with a horrific disregard for civilians. By now, the United States had been drafting soldiers for a year—the first-ever military draft in a time of peace. And as war became an increasing probability, the Department of Justice, on October 11, had announced that Japanese-American and Japanese civilians were being targeted for "evacuation" from the West Coast because of fear they might aid the enemy.

Against such a backdrop, soldiers' boots drummed a mournful sound across the gangway of the SS *President Coolidge* on this Saturday morning. Among the men: Second Lieutenant Henry Clay Conner Jr., a twenty-three-year-old army air force officer from East Orange, New Jersey. Conner and the others were part of the 27th Bombardment Group (Light), more than a thousand men who'd spent the last few weeks saying good-byes or breaking up with girlfriends or closing checking accounts or getting married or selling cars or getting sauced in San Francisco's Chinatown—the things soldiers do in the sliver of time between here and there, peace and war. Then, they had converged at Fort McDowell on nearby Angel Island before ferrying to Pier 45 for departure on this bleak morning.

The loading continued, the mood among the soldiers a mixture of anticipation and angst. Meanwhile, friends and family who'd shown up to bid the troops farewell hardly beamed with confidence when a boxcar waiting to be placed on the *Coolidge* broke loose and slid into the bay. Nor were such onlookers likely sold on America's military might when, after the container was retrieved, the items inside were spread out to dry on the dock. Among the cargo? Golf clubs, one set belonging to Clay Conner Jr.

THE DOCK WAS a clutter of order and disorder, the melding of intricate planning and woeful inexperience; the United States had not been at war for more than two decades. Secrets were virtually impossible to keep—like where the ship was headed. On essentially every box, crate, and piece of equipment had been stamped the acronym PLUM. If most men didn't realize it was code for "U.S. Army in the Philippines," they had at least heard rumors that they were headed for this group of islands in the Western Pacific Ocean. Which, of course, only encouraged the 27th's black humorists, who suggested PLUM stood for "Places Lost Unto Man" or said the entire ship was headed "PLUM to hell."

By the time the ship sailed, 1,209 men would be aboard the *Coolidge*. The 654-foot vessel had once been among the largest and most lavish ocean liners in the world, but now soldiers had replaced vacationers: men seeking adventure and men fearing it. Older men leaving families behind and those—some teenagers—who'd lied to their recruiting sergeants about being the minimum age of eighteen. For the most part, they were young men in their early twenties, among them Conner, who, along the rail of the passenger deck, now scanned the send-off crowd below. His cousin, Marge Pamphilion, and her husband, Max, had hoped to see him off; they lived in nearby Berkeley.

Conner was five-foot-nine and about 150 pounds. If he looked a touch like a young, wavy-haired Spencer Tracy, he was more like Fred Astaire in talents: a great dancer who'd taught professionally. He was Indiana-born, New Jersey–reared, and Duke University–schooled, his degree in economics but his heart in history. "The war was coming on, and I was fascinated by things that were happening in Europe," he later wrote. He had enlisted on February 24, 1941, with the idea of becoming a pilot, but when color blindness shot down that idea, he had become a group communications officer. He spent a seven-month stint at the Air Corps Technical School at Scott Field in Illinois, then five weeks at Savannah Air Base in Georgia.

Now, less than two years since graduating from college in the tweedy environs of Durham, North Carolina, Conner was lost in a mass of tethered testosterone, a single drop of water in a vast military watershed. In the last year, the draft had helped build an army of nearly 2 million men.

The draftees and enlistees had trickled forth from no-stoplight towns, joining streams of men from big cities and merging into rivers of training camps across the country, a tributary from which was now emptying into the mighty Pacific.

Most had arrived by train, but not Clay Conner Jr. No sir. With permission, he and two pals had driven his '40 Ford convertible: cream-colored with red leather upholstery. The buddies were a couple of other guys in the 27th Bombardment Group whom he'd met at Savannah: Second Lieutenant Leroy Cowart Jr., a twenty-year-old pilot from Atlanta, Georgia, and Second Lieutenant William Strese, a twenty-seven-year-old pilot from Durand, Wisconsin. Why waste a great adventure, Conner figured, by sitting on a train like so many head of cattle, when you could be zipping down the open highway? When you could, as he did in Albuquerque, New Mexico, stop to buy a cactus lamp for the mother in New Jersey who doted on you, her only child? When you had plenty of money to blow, thanks in part to receipts from an under-the-radar Coke-and-candy business you'd established at Scott Field the previous spring? (OK, so he'd gotten busted, but his commanding officer still let him split the stash.)

Conner was a mercurial young man who blended that free-spiritedness with a sense of pragmatism that leaned toward safety and survival. He looked ahead, saw the obstacles, then determined a plan to overcome them. It's one of the reasons he earned an economics degree at Duke in only three and a half years. Sure, there was time for a few fraternity pranks, but the goal of school was to learn and to graduate and to go off and be a success. Sure, he had driven his car more than twenty-five hundred miles to board a ship, but, with the help of his cousin's husband, Max, he had promptly sold it to a San Francisco used-car dealer. "It was," he later wrote, "like losing my best friend." Sure, his girlfriend at Duke, Mimi, had talked of marriage, but if Conner hadn't broken off the relationship, he had at least nixed the idea of tying the knot before he shipped out.

He was no fool. He had no idea what he was getting into or when he might be coming back, but he was braced for the worst. On the more whimsical side, Conner had tucked his lifetime companion, a stuffed monkey named Junko, into his duffel bag, but he also had developed a code for letters home so he could update his folks on his status without giving away military secrets.

If Conner, in his olive-drab uniform, looked essentially like every other soldier in this regulated sameness; if, like so many others, he was leaving a girl behind; if he was headed for the Philippines, some seven thousand miles away in Southeast Asia; if he had a somewhat distant father who was outwardly proud of him but silently pained; if he had a mother who was already praying for his safe return; if all this, he was nevertheless different from—and destined for an adventure unlike that of any other man on board.

CONNER, ONE OF eighty-two officers on the ship, glanced at his watch. The hands on the new Bulova his folks had given him before he'd left had long since swept past the ship's noon departure time. Finally, at 1 P.M., the ship's whistle blasted from the bridge. Some soldiers muffled the sound with hands over their ears. Lines were cast. And with tugs at her side, the *Coolidge* left the safe hold of America to the occasional cheers and whoops of soldiers in winter coats and well-wishers ashore huddled under umbrellas, Conner's cousin and her husband among them.

Once safely away from the pier, the ship steamed beneath the arches of the Golden Gate Bridge, the span's orange vermillion muted by the dankness of the day. Soldiers waved hats and hands in farewell to the motorists above. To America. To times that would never be recaptured, places that would never look the same, moments that would be gone forever—such as a trio of freewheeling soldiers zipping down Route 66 in a convertible, the wind in their faces, their futures stretching as far and wide as the rose-colored desert beyond.

As the ship sliced through the Pacific swells toward Hawaii, what frothed in her wake was certainty—and with good reason, history would show. Of the 1,209 men aboard the *Coolidge*, only 240 would return. One in five. And of the soldiers in that convertible flying west toward the rest of their lives, only one in three.

TWO

The Heritage

November 2, 1941, to November 26, 1941

THE *COOLIDGE* PLIED the Pacific en route to what would be its lone stop before reaching the Philippines: Hawaii. With Cowart and a new pal, Damon "Rocky" Gause, Conner shot craps, played cards, chewed the fat like the rest of the guys. But unlike many others, he also had a more contemplative side. Despite some light seasickness, he finished one book, A. J. Cronin's just-published *The Keys of the Kingdom*, about an unconventional Scottish priest's lifelong challenge to prove himself worthy.

"[Cronin's] book had a very good lesson I thought, and expressed a philosophy which everyone would like to follow but few can," he wrote in a letter home. "Too bad more people, including myself, don't have a little more of Father Chisholm in them." He hoped to soon begin a 1,176-page tome, Marguerite Steen's *The Sun Is My Undoing*, about the early slave trade shipping between England and the Ivory Coast in Africa and a couple with an interracial daughter.

On his fourth day at sea, from the state room he shared with three other officers, Conner wrote home. "Dear Mother & Dad," the letter began. Obviously, his intention was for it to be read by both parents: his father, Henry Clay Conner Sr., forty-seven, and his mother, Marguerite, forty-five. And yet by the second sentence, Clay Jr., had already tipped his hand about to whom the letter was really intended. "I am glad I got to say goodbye once more before I left the other night," he wrote, "and I was sorry Dad was not there."

Conner loved his father. Drew insight from him, particularly regarding sales, which was Clay Sr.'s vocation and Clay Jr.'s passion. Played golf with him. In many ways, admired him greatly. But while he was growing up, particularly in Clay Jr.'s younger years, the family had been more of a twosome than a threesome. As Conner Jr. suggested in his letter, his father was often "not there." Instead, he was on the road, selling coupon books.

In 1925, when Clay Jr. was seven and the family lived in Indianapolis, his father went to work for John Allison, president of the Allison Coupon Co. and a longtime friend of Marguerite's, whom Clay Sr. had met at the couple's wedding in Indianapolis in 1917.

Allison commanded respect. He hailed from one of Indianapolis's regal families; his grandfather, Noah, had started the business in 1888, supplying merchants with prepaid coupon books that businesses offered to their customers to ease credit problems. John's uncle, James, was the cofounder of the Indianapolis 500 and counted among his friends President Warren Harding and automotive magnate Henry Ford.

Clay Conner Sr., meanwhile, was a grinder, a traveling salesman who, in the 1920s, went through shoes and tires like most people went through packs of cigarettes. His territory was Maine to Florida and New York to Minneapolis. One man. One car. Roughly five hundred thousand square miles of responsibility, more than one-eighth of the continental United States. At age thirty-one, Conner Sr. would be gone for literally months at a time. His car broke down. Tires exploded. Hotel life lost its luster.

After two years, Allison agreed with Clay Sr. and Marguerite that the job was too demanding, and he offered Clay Sr. a more urban region, the company's Eastern territory: Maine to Virginia, New York to Pittsburgh. The family moved some six hundred miles away, to Hartford, Connecticut, even if Marguerite was reluctant, her roots planted deeply in the

Indiana soil. But Hartford didn't ultimately solve Clay Sr.'s on-the-road dilemma either. He hated big-city traffic, of which the East Coast had plenty.

Clay Conner Sr. believed a man could be happy if he loved God, cheered for the St. Louis Cardinals, paid cash, stayed out of debt, and was loyal to both the United States government and the state of Kentucky, where he was born and reared. But not if he lived in Hartford. So the family moved to Harrisburg, Pennsylvania. By the time he was ten, Clay Jr. had lived in eight different houses or apartments. He made few friends. But he won something of a consolation prize for life with an often-absent father: He learned to rely on himself.

He learned to ride a city bus. He began hawking magazines door-to-door: *Liberty, Colliers,* and *Women's Home Companion.* Five cents a pop. His sports coat, smile, and slicked-down, parted-on-the-left hair didn't hurt his cause, nor did the fact that he was eleven and housewives found him precociously adorable. Within a short time, he had the largest route in downtown Harrisburg.

Meanwhile, his mother became Clay's closest friend. She never liked Harrisburg and missed her husband; letters and telegrams did little to compensate for the man's absence. Her escape from loneliness became watching movies and following the lives of movie stars with compulsive fascination. Hollywood had erected its hillside shingle in 1923, and by the end of the decade, movies had become a $2 billion industry; nearly a thousand films a year were being released, some even with sound. Marguerite watched, and read about, the likes of Greta Garbo, Gary Cooper, and Mickey Rooney, vicariously living their exciting lives through her less scintillating version.

At times, with Clay Sr. gone so much, she would buy and wrap a Christmas present from "him" to her. But if she hurt, she put on a good face, even when her spinal meningitis—a lifelong challenge—flared up. Friends described her as a more obscure version of Gracie Allen, the zany partner and comic foil of husband George Burns, with whom the actress had a dynamite radio act. Quirky. Funny. Pushy.

With Marguerite's husband seldom around, the person who shared her movie wonder was Clay Jr. Marguerite never learned to drive, but by bus, taxi, or subway, the two went to theaters together, shopped together, ate out together. It was a relationship steeled by the absence of a man they both loved. For Clay Jr., his mother became his security; for Marguerite, Clay Jr. became more than just the little boy who could fetch another soda to feed her Coca-Cola addiction and buy her the latest issue of *Modern Screen* magazine at the drugstore they lived above. He became her purpose. She encouraged him, defended him, protected him.

When, in 1930, the family moved to Irvington, New Jersey—New York City, twelve miles away, had become Clay Sr.'s golden egg—the Depression was leveling huge swaths of America like an economic tornado. But for Clay Sr. it spawned a huge demand for credit, meaning, of course, a huge demand for coupon books. Every personal loan required such a book, and there, on the ready to meet the increasing demands, was Clay Sr. If his competition was stiff, his dedication and high valuing of relationships won him accounts such as General Motors, the National City Bank, and Fidelity Philadelphia Trust. He became among the top salesmen in the industry.

Clay Jr., meanwhile, resumed his door-to-door career. With an ignorance-is-bliss attitude, he even tried selling a competitor's toothpaste at the home of a family named Colgate, who politely declined, saying they had enough of their own, thank you.

His father, for the first time, reached a place where he could work the city during the day and take the train home to Irvington in the evening. The family began eating meals together. They gathered around the radio in the evenings to listen to *Amos 'n' Andy*, Lowell Thomas, and Bing Crosby. Joined the Disciples of Christ Church and, in 1932, the Maplewood Country Club.

Clay Jr. remembered these as the happiest years of his childhood. He not only caddied for his father, but occasionally tried to match strokes with the man. Sometimes, they'd take the train into New York City to watch a show. In the summer, the family vacationed at Asbury Park, New

Jersey, on the Atlantic Ocean. Occasionally, they'd return to Indianapolis and stay with their good friends the Thomsons, who had a little girl, Elizabeth, an only child who was nine years younger than Clay.

The irony, of course, was that the opportunistic Clay Sr. managed to turn hard times into good times. That the relationships he'd built—the trust he'd earned—had, in the end, helped him avoid the jungle of despair that had claimed so many others. And that, in so doing, he had brought together, and protected, those people closest to him. All lessons that, as the *Coolidge* steamed southwest, would soon serve his son well.

INDEED, IF THERE was a Conner trait that had endured the generations, this was it: a passion to survive. "He was educated in five different states," his mother would later write of Clay Jr. "He seems to have a natural inclination and ability to adjust himself to any surroundings and to make friends wherever he goes. [He had] that old urge for adventure. 'Get out and see what makes things tick.' That [was] his slogan."

He wasn't the first Conner with such gumption. Clay Sr.'s German-born great-great-grandfather, Phillip Haman, had eluded death, disease, and starvation in the Revolutionary War. Afterward, the man had moved to Kentucky, where Clay Sr.'s folks, Richard Conner and his wife, Sarah Ann Hanks, had endured the ravages of the Civil War, the postwar depression, and the hardship of life in the mountains of Powell County.

You are a part of all this, Clay Sr. told his then-teenage son. *Never forget that.* Clay Sr. had his son join him on a trip to Kentucky to see the old log house where Clay Jr.'s grandfather, Richard Conner, a farmer, had once lived. To meet aunts and uncles. To hear the family stories, including ones about how he, Clay Sr., was born in 1894 and was named Henry Clay Conner for Henry Clay, the hawkish Kentucky senator.

Richard, Clay Jr.'s grandfather, had been an elder at Antioch Christian Church, and a man for whom integrity was paramount. Once, he found a glove in his barn after some of his chickens had been stolen. He placed the glove on a shelf at Harry Lincomb's store on Locust and Queen. When a man claimed it, Richard Conner notified the sheriff. After committing a more serious theft, the man wound up in jail.

Zack, Richard's brother and Clay Jr.'s great-uncle, favored a less diplomatic approach to wrongdoing. Once, his own son, Howard, got drunk with some buddies in Winchester and was randomly firing his gun. When his father confronted him, the boy bristled. "I'm tired of you telling me what to do," he said, and reached for his gun. Zack shot his son's hand seemingly before the gun cleared the holster.

"Zack Conner," a family friend told them, "was the fastest man with a gun I'd ever seen. He could shoot the eyes out of a squirrel before the critter could see him draw."

Such a skill would seem to be all but obsolete in the more refined decades of the 1930s and '40s, particularly for a man like Clay Conner Jr., who'd lived his life not in the backwoods of Kentucky but in cities and on golf courses and amid an architecturally rich Duke campus known as a "Gothic Wonderland." Yet as the *Coolidge* churned toward Hawaii, his world was about to turn considerably less refined and would get worse before it would get better. Meaning that a quick trigger finger could be a legacy well worth inheriting.

For now, beyond slight sea sickness, Conner wrote to his parents that life on the ship was good, the meals "swell."

"Everything is under control with me and hope you are both feeling fine," he concluded the letter. "Love, Clay Jr."

IN HAWAII, WHICH Clay would later tell his folks was "absolutely the most beautiful place I have ever seen," soldiers got one day of leave. He and one of his Route 66 travel mates, Leroy Cowart, took in the sights like shoppers on a one-minute spree. Waikiki Beach. The Upside Down Waterfall. The Royal Hawaiian Hotel. Finally, the Trade Winds Bar, whose lack of walls and doors intrigued Conner. "The atmosphere made me feel like I was Bing Crosby in *Road to Singapore*," he later wrote to his parents.

Soldiers drank, ate, caroused, swam, got sunburned, and returned to the ship that night with flowered leis around their necks. As the *Coolidge* sailed for the Philippines, the USS *Louisville*, a heavy cruiser, flanked it. "Which is a great comfort," wrote Conner. "There is nothing to worry about."

He had, from a young age, been a glass-half-full guy. When doing door-to-door sales, he could get turned down at ten straight houses and be absolutely convinced that the eleventh would buy big. His ambition was unbridled. Though no honor-roll student, Conner graduated early from Irvington High School in New Jersey, in January 1937, and, instead of waiting until fall, enrolled immediately at Duke, a proper Southern school handpicked by his Kentucky-bred father.

Clay Sr. drove his son to Durham, North Carolina, where the two shared a round of golf together before parting ways. Clay Jr. joined the Sigma Phi Epsilon fraternity and roomed with future Pro Football Hall of Famer George McAfee. He wasted no time starting an in-house laundry business to make spending money, and he made the golf and cheerleading teams as a sophomore. That, of course, wasn't enough for Conner; with fraternity brother Bob Stivers, he hatched the idea to also sell sandwiches at Duke Stadium on football Saturdays. The two pooled their profits to buy a car whose deficiencies included a loose connection in the right headlight. On occasion, Bob would drive while Clay lay on the fender to hold a wire in the headlight socket, at least once while wearing a tuxedo.

As graduation neared in the spring of 1940, Clay's steady girlfriend, a young woman named Mimi, pushed for marriage. She might have been the right girl, Clay thought, but this was the wrong time. He graduated with a bachelor of arts degree in economics and returned to New Jersey, the relationship left with neither a promise nor a permanent parting.

He was far more certain about this: leaving some mark on the world, even if he expected it to happen without much effort on his part, as if the captain of a collegiate cheerleading team would be, upon graduation, automatically imbued with greatness. On June 3, 1940, the Commencement Choir's last note of Lutkin's "The Lord Bless You and Keep You" had barely faded from Duke's graduation ceremony when Conner mentally bolted into the post-college world like a bull out of a rodeo chute. Alas, he quickly found, reality was far more mundane.

Conner's father granted his son two days' vacation, then ushered him into a job working on the press that printed the Allison Coupons in Indianapolis. Clay stayed with close family friends, the Thomsons, with whom the Conners had once been next-door neighbors on Broadway Street. A few months later, Clay tired of the printing-press job; making coupons offered none of the challenge that sales did—trying to convince somcone they needed what you had to offer. He moved back home to New Jersey. By day he sold Fuller brushes in Newark's mansion-studded Montclair area and, by night, worked as a dance instructor at an Arthur Murray studio. If the jobs enabled him to buy a 1938 Ford convertible— he later upgraded to a '40—his morning-to-midnight days got old fast.

"I had always thought that once I was out of college the world would somehow recognize me as something special," he later wrote, "and would elevate me into a position of recognition and responsibility whereby I could express my talent and energy. None of this seemed to happen."

WITH ISOLATIONIST AMERICA nevertheless gearing up for war, what Conner really wanted to do was fly airplanes, a dream that vanished when he learned he was colorblind and, thus, ineligible for the cockpit. The consolation prize? An offer by the War Department, as a single man and college graduate, to become an air corps squadron communications officer. Clay enlisted. This wasn't the "something special" he had in mind, but if it lacked the kind of honor and adventure he was seeking, at least it was *something*.

World War I was history. His generation pined to make a difference. "We were naive about the horrors of war," he said, "but we were enthusiastic about saving the world for democracy. Old men dream dreams, as they say, and young men fight wars."

At Scott Field in Belleville, Illinois, he was instructed in the basics of radios, marching, and properly wearing a uniform; discipline was strict, the school demanding. On a hundred-point scale, his "final rating" was 84.1. If he learned about transmitters and receivers and antennas, however, he learned virtually nothing about combat.

However, he did find a way to funnel his entrepreneurial spirit into running a covert Coca-Cola operation, selling up to 180 bottles of pop per day, plus candy. It was vintage Conner. When his commanding officer found out about it, he made Conner turn over half his profits to a "cadet fund," though Clay still walked off with about $300 profit in his wallet.

In June, after his graduation from aviation cadet school, Conner was assigned to training at Savannah (Georgia) Army Air Base. First, he headed east to see his folks in East Orange, New Jersey. Both had been experiencing heart problems, not serious enough to dread the worst but worrisome to Clay. When his mother snapped a photo of father and son on the sidewalk in front of their apartment building, the two men appeared remarkably similar: medium builds, good posture, uneasy smiles.

MEANWHILE, ACROSS THE Atlantic Ocean, Germany invaded Belgium, Luxembourg, and the Netherlands. On June 22, Germany quickly brought France to its knees, a move which convinced a once-reluctant Congress to appropriate $1.5 billion for a fortified air force.

Conner became part of the 27th Bombardment Group (Light or L), the latter indicating the unit used planes—dive-bombers–equipped with small bombs dropped in close support of ground troops: single-engine Northrop A-17s, twin-engine Curtiss A-18s, and twin-engine Douglas B-18s. As a communications officer, Conner's job was to help those planes get out and back safely.

If Conner's Scott Field experience seemed well removed from war, the Louisiana experience was far different. In August, he became part of the Louisiana Maneuvers in Lake Charles. They involved more than 350,000 soldiers and 50,000 vehicles spread over 3,400 square miles, the largest U.S. military "war game" in history. Seventeen soldiers died in the first week of exercises alone. Two men Conner knew died of bites from coral snakes. Meanwhile, rumors about the 27th shipping out hovered like the Savannah base's dust.

This, Conner realized, was not the fun and games of Duke. Like a chess player planning the next move, Conner's mind went to work. When Stiver, Conner's fraternity pal, came for a weekend visit, the two of them not only schemed about how they could someday clean up on the sugar market, but devised a code so Clay could keep his parents informed without revealing any secrets that an enemy might discover. He would use a letter's complimentary close to indicate his status. For example:

> *Your son—means everything is under control and we are just maneuvering.*
>
> *Your loving son—means we are living in a backwoods tent area.*
>
> *Affectionately your son—means we are living in a new expanding base.*
>
> *Lovingly your son—means we are on an old established base.*
>
> *Your only son and heir—we are moving to another island.*
>
> *Your son and heir—we are moving to the continent of Japan.*
>
> *Your boy—we are winning.*
>
> *Your loving boy—we are losing.*

Beyond snakes, Savannah meant summer heat, humidity, chiggers, and mosquitoes. It was, for Conner, a first step into real adventure, highlighted by his letting a buddy, Zeke, talk him into riding in the Plexiglas nose of an A-20 that his friend was ferrying to San Antonio. En route, the plane ran low on fuel. From the cockpit, Zeke signaled for Clay to bail. Clay refused. He signaled again, but again Clay refused. Ultimately,

Zeke brought the plane down on a country landing strip in Brackettville, Texas, that wasn't much more than a cornfield. Conner was a lump of sweat.

When the two returned to Savannah, they were greeted by plenty of back-slapping laughter regarding their harrowing landing and by well-supported rumors: The 27th was headed for duty. Destination: the Philippines.

Now, nearly three weeks after leaving San Francisco, Conner stood at the port rail and saw the manifestation of such rumors. It was November 21, Thanksgiving Day. The Philippines—a sprinkling of seven thousand islands—stretched between the South China Sea and the Philippine Sea as if God had flung a handful of sand on a plate of shimmering blue. They represented the world's second largest island archipelago, extending north and south roughly the length of the United States' Pacific Coast. Luzon, where they were heading, was roughly the size of the state of Ohio, the largest island and the northernmost in the string among those of any size.

A sergeant considerably older than Clay nodded at a pollywog-shaped island, a mass of rock called Corregidor in the entrance to Manila Bay. "The impregnable rock of the Orient," he said. "The guns there defend this entrance to the bay. No ship can get under those guns."

After weeks at sea, Conner's eyes widened. Beyond, he saw the Bataan Peninsula. "It looked like nothing but uninhabited jungle," he later wrote. The peninsula was named for the Bata, the small, dark Negritos who'd inhabited it since deep into the reaches of time.

The sergeant pointed to a particular area. "Up there is where Frank Buck caught the largest living python in captivity," he said, referring to the worldwide animal collector.

Conner shook his head in measured amazement.

"See that mountain?" said the sergeant, pointing to a peak that rose regally from the peninsula's southernmost point, a cloud hovering above it. "That," he said, "is Mount Mariveles. That cloud is always over that mountain. In fact, it was written up in *Ripley's Believe It or Not* not too long ago. You'll never find that cloud leaving that particular place. It's always there."

In time, Conner would come to know the mountain well. Would come to know the Negritos well. And would make one of the most pivotal decisions of his life based on those ever-present clouds.

THREE

The Good Life

November 27, 1941, to December 7, 1941

UNTIL RECENTLY, IT had been a daily tradition. At Fort McKinley, seven miles south of Manila, a cannon fired each afternoon at 5 P.M. All traffic on the base came to a halt. Men stopped what they were doing and turned their attention to the forty-eight-star American flag. A bugler played "To the Colors." And as the flag was lowered in the tropical breeze, all military personnel snapped a crisp salute.

If the ritual was a call to patriotism, it was also a call to something else that had proven extremely meaningful to those on the post: the cocktail hour.

In many ways, a United States military assignment in the Philippines—known as the "Pearl of the Orient"—had been an assignment in paradise. The softest prison sentence in the service. To this tropical land came a collection of eager young officers and deadwood vets, many of whom had served in World War I more than two decades ago and were biding their time while waiting for retirement.

But, oh, what a place to bide and wait. Palm trees swayed against skies that turned from coral blue to pink to black as the sun set on Manila

Bay, the mountains of the Bataan Peninsula then sharply silhouetted before blending into the night. Tropical birds flitted from tree to tree. Along the roads, pink hydrangeas splashed color amid the urban setting and white butterfly orchids grew among the coconut husks.

Even Fort McKinley—an infantry post that was established in 1901 during the Philippine-American War—was, in Conner's words, "a beautiful base." Conner's air corps unit was supposed to have been stationed at Fort Stotsenburg, about fifty miles north of Manila, but since its "ships" hadn't arrived yet, McKinley became the 27th's temporary headquarters. Conner was amazed at the neatness of the infantry post, the parade grounds, the "discipline and dignity" he saw in the elite Philippine Scouts who were out for inspection. "Everything connected with them—their attire, their tent set-up, their field equipment—was immaculate, perfect," he wrote of such units, which had been authorized by Congress in the 1920s and were part of the American Army. "Everything was in place."

General Jonathan Wainwright welcomed the 27th with a speech that some found odd: Thirty minutes of what would happen if they didn't wear crisp, clean, proper uniforms. A scolding of how the Filipino soldiers wore their uniforms in more proper military fashion. And a lecture on how to behave in the tropics. "Not one word as to any island defenses or our part in any movement of the sort," wrote one soldier. This from a man who was commander of American forces in the Philippines and yet somehow found the time and inclination to serve as the scorekeeper at local polo games.

Meanwhile, Conner's amazement with McKinley continued. He saw wide porches wrapped around one-story buildings, screened to keep out mosquitoes. Streetcars ferrying people to a pool, bowling alley, and golf course. In a place that could wilt in heat, shade abounded. So did servants. "Shortly after we arrived, we were approached by several Filipino families who were interested in selling us the services of their daughters," wrote Conner, who lived in officer quarters with six others. "They were called *lavanderas*. Three and five pesos a week, five pesos being about two-

and-a-half dollars. For that amount, the girl was to wash our clothes, shine our shoes, make our beds . . . and keep everything in tip-top shape."

IF THE RELATIONSHIP between Americans and Filipinos had a hint of master-slave to it, there was history behind it. In the late 1800s, Filipino revolutionaries fought to gain independence from Spain, which had controlled the country for centuries. Enter the United States, ostensibly to protect the Filipinos and free them from the yoke of the evil Spaniards. But the U.S. role in the 1898 Spanish-American War, say most historians, was far more self-serving, an international extension of Manifest Destiny. America entered the fray, wrote Filipino historian Teodoro Agoncillo, "not as a friend, but as an enemy masking as a friend."

Indeed, if Americans and Filipinos had been allies against Spain, the United States formed a partnership with the European country and became more intent on suppressing the native insurgents than waging traditional war against the Spaniards. At the end of the ten-week war, neither country recognized the Philippines' independence. Instead, in the 1898 Treaty of Paris, the Spanish government ceded the Philippines to the United States as an unincorporated territory for $20 million.

"Not one competent witness who has actually known the facts believes the Filipinos capable of self-government at the present," U.S. President Theodore Roosevelt said. He called the Filipino freedom fighters "a syndicate of Chinese half-breeds" and said to allow them self-government "would be like granting self-government to an Apache reservation under some local chief."

Buried beneath more honorable U.S. history—and unknown to many—were years of mistreatment of Filipinos at the turn of the century. American soldiers basically replicated the same atrocities that Spain had thrust on Filipinos—and that the United States had used as justification for entering the fray in the first place: widespread torture, concentration camps, and the killing of disarmed prisoners and helpless civilians. In the bloody Philippine-American War that ensued, U.S. soldiers killed more than three hundred thousand Filipinos, more civilians than soldiers, according to James Bradley in *The Imperial Cruise*. It produced a far higher body count than in the preceding Spanish-American War.

"This shooting human beings is a 'hot game,' and beats rabbit hunting to pieces," wrote one soldier, Anthony Michea, of the 3rd Artillery. "We charged them and such a slaughter you never saw. We killed them like rabbits; hundreds, yes thousands of them. Everyone was crazy." POWs were, per U.S. official policy, killed, some after enduring a form of water torture akin to being drowned.

Some Americans—notably William Jennings Bryan, Mark Twain, and other members of the American Anti-Imperialist League—strongly opposed America's takeover of the Philippines. Roosevelt, meanwhile, looked past such atrocities to a nobler end, "the bravery of American soldiers" who battled "for the triumph of civilization over the black chaos of savagery and barbarism." He called it "the most glorious war in the nation's history."

After more than a decade of campaigning by the Philippine government, Congress, in 1933, passed the Hare-Hawes-Cutting Act, which promised the country independence after ten years. It provided for the United States having several military and naval bases and for imposing tariffs and quotas on Philippine exports, but still granted the Philippines what it had shed considerable blood for against Spain and the United States: the chance to govern itself.

IN THE MEANTIME, however, U.S. officers such as Second Lieutenant Clay Conner Jr. lived like little kings. The duty was light, the idea of war easily ignored. By early afternoon, most, after fulfilling whatever drills or duties were on tap, retreated to the local golf course, tennis courts, polo fields, beaches, or—in nearby barrios—brothels.

Officers were allowed off post virtually every evening. Men in white suits sipped drinks at the Army and Navy Club, which, perched on the east shore of Manila Bay, exuded the regal feel of a country club. For less refined socializing, others headed downtown to lounge at the Alcazar Club, the Manila Hotel, or if in a betting mood, the Jai Alai Club, known for "bets, beers, babes, and [ending up] broke."

Soon after arriving, Conner grabbed a car from the motor pool and, with Leroy Cowart and Rocky Gause, headed north on Dewey Boulevard to downtown. Conner, with a fascination of history, marveled that the hulls of Spanish ships, sunk in the Spanish-American War of 1898, still protruded from the sands and waters of Manila Bay to the west. The trio, en route to Manila, poked around Santa Anna, a melting pot of pilots, artillerymen, submariners, marines, and women from around the world eager to connect with them—and take their money amid the beat of honky-tonk music.

Downtown Manila pulsed with more eclectic energy, made more frenetic by a noticeable lack of traffic signs or signals. *Carretelas*—coaches pulled by ponies—clip-clopped along the pavement, trying to dodge the more dominant taxicabs and cars. A cacophony of "buy, buy, buy" come-ons littered the air from Filipino hawkers working carts and wagons filled with food and wares. Children begged for money. Soldiers searched for bars and whores.

In a country of 17 million people, Manila was, in 1941, home to 684,000, roughly a quarter of the population of Los Angeles at the time but still a thriving metropolis. If downtown was rough and poor and brazen, it was also the rich dressed in all white; the now-touristy "Walled City," built centuries before by the Spaniards to protect them from the "savage natives"; massive acacia trees lining Taft Avenue; the Juan Arellano–designed Manila Metropolitan Theater; and the upscale Jai Alai Club.

The government-operated club, which had opened only the previous year, represented the most striking architecture in the country: four stories accented with glass and anchored by a cylinder-shaped entry that not only evoked the velocity of the fast-paced game played inside, but spoke of the future, of possibilities, of everything an independent Philippines might be. True, it was designed by an American, Welton Becket, who had done the Los Angeles Airport and homes of Hollywood screen legends. But the elegant building nevertheless had emerged as a playground for those pursuing the good life, which plenty of U.S. soldiers were in hot pursuit of in the fall of 1941.

The building featured courts for jai alai, a Basque-based game involving white-suited players who whipped a rubber ball against a wall using a *cesta*, a long, curved wicker scoop strapped to a player's right arm. The game, which was bet on heavily, fascinated Conner. Filipino boys in white coats ferried bets to the windows, expecting, of course, tips, perhaps even part of someone's winnings. Over drinks, Conner, Cowart, and Gause made such bets, nibbled on food, and looked around the expansive room with a sense of awe. They were a long way from home—and from war.

Sure, they had gone through all the motions on the trip over: closing the portholes at night, not smoking on deck, small mistakes that might tip off their appearance to the pilot of an enemy observation plane. "We thought it was like maneuvers all over again, but we went along for the gag," wrote Conner. "We obeyed the rules, but we didn't think much of them." The troop buildup in the Philippines was only precautionary, right?

Then Conner, as he scanned the bar, noticed something missing. He'd seen women of all sorts of races but virtually no Caucasians. American women. Officers' wives. Where were they?

"Shipped home," said Gause, who'd been in the army ten years before becoming a pilot.

"Shipped home—why?" said Conner.

"War, Clay," said Gause. "War."

It turned out, officers' wives, along with their children, had been sent home in May, five months before. At the club, more drinks arrived. The night deepened. The jai alai players leapt in the air and balls bounced off walls and bets were made and exotic-looking women swept through the room like tropical breezes; it was all almost enough to make Conner forget that the U.S. military thought trouble was imminent enough that it had sent officers' families home.

Almost.

IN NOVEMBER 1941, the 27th Bombardment Group (L) was the only combat-ready dive-bomber unit in the U.S. Air Army Corps, which was transitioning into the Army Air Forces. All it needed was airplanes, which were supposed to be arriving by ship soon. Some members of the 27th believed that the *Meigs*, a transport ship carrying the much-needed dive-bombers, had been only a couple of days behind the *Coolidge* and would arrive any day. Meanwhile, to keep some of its pilots sharp—they hadn't flown in nearly a month—the 27th got a reluctant loan from the 19th Bomb Group of four obsolete B-18s that were seemingly held together by model glue and twine.

The United States awakened slowly to the idea that Japan was prepared to wage war against it. With one eye already affixed on Germany's rampage through Europe and Russia, the United States overlooked the might of a country smaller than California that had been fighting China fruitlessly for a decade. In short, the military was overconfident and unprepared; cavalry units may have had a long and storied history in U.S. military operations, but a regiment of Philippine Scouts on horses—admittedly, a small piece of the American defense forces—would likely prove little resistance to Japanese tanks.

In the world's political chess game, the Japanese needed control of the Philippines because of oil reserves in the Dutch (or Netherlands) East Indies to the south of it. In 1941, the Dutch East Indies and the United States supplied 90 percent of Japan's oil. Japanese strategists knew the U. S. presence in the Philippines would be a threat to Japan's flanks as its troops sailed south to the oil-rich East Indies they hoped to conquer. They also wanted the Philippines as a means to facilitate air and sea travel between the new acquisitions and Japan proper. And, of course, they knew Manila itself had an ideal deep-water port.

When, on July 26, 1941, President Roosevelt had frozen Japanese assets in the United States, the British and Dutch followed suit with similar restrictions. The moves amounted to an oil embargo that U.S. leaders figured would either force Japan to drop its aggressive strategy in Southeast Asia or to seize the Dutch East Indies for oil, a move that, in essence, would mean war. Japan hadn't blinked.

It was no coincidence that on that same July day, a man who had previously been in command of the Philippine Army was called back to duty in the U.S. Army and given command of the United States Armed Forces in the Far East (USAFFE). His name was Douglas MacArthur. A valedictorian at West Point. A brigadier general on the Western Front in World War I. A winner of seven Silver Stars and two Distinguished Services Crosses.

Since World War II had begun in September 1939, the United States had been hesitant to get involved, still stung from lost sons in World War I. Meanwhile, though, its military leaders weren't naive; for decades, they had considered what to do with the Philippines in case of war with Japan. Large and home of the capital city of Manila, Luzon would almost certainly be the first island attacked, though MacArthur wasn't expecting that until April 1942, five months in the future.

MacArthur favored stopping the invaders at the beach, most likely at the Lingayen Gulf to the north, whose harbor and gently sloping beach emptied to relatively flat plains leading to Manila. It wasn't a popular decision among much of the brass. Given a Lingayen landing, others favored what was called War Plan Orange, falling back south to the mountains of the Bataan Peninsula. There, U.S. forces could stall the south-headed enemy for months awaiting reinforcements of men, weapons, food, and equipment from the fleet moored at Pearl Harbor.

AT TWENTY-FIVE, MACARTHUR had become the army's youngest major general. Now, hardened by time and war, he was being called on again at age sixty-one. In the Philippines, he commanded an army of 130,000 men, about 31,000 of whom were U.S. Army troops and the rest Filipinos. Of the latter, about 12,000 were elite Philippine Scouts—the soldiers Conner had seen training so efficiently at McKinley—and the remaining 90,000 to 100,000 troops were members of the Philippine Army.

Many of those troops had been hurriedly drafted into the army as November became December and hadn't even fired a rifle. In civilian life most had been simple farmers. They disliked unfamiliar tasks. Their weapons were often obsolete. Language barriers made it even more difficult; in 1941, fewer than a third of the general Filipino troops spoke the English that their American officers used. That said, what also made assimilating Filipino troops difficult was an American attitude of superiority—or so wrote Lieutenant William Gardner Jr., of the 31st Infantry (Co. L) and part of the army for nearly twenty years.

> The lure of the Orient prior to the war seemed to be a selfish one. Americans usually built a barricade that insulated themselves as thoroughly as possible against the Philippine Islands (or any other country of the Orient they happened to occupy). In Manila they were "big fish" in a small pool. They would complain continuously about petty inconveniences and berate the "miserable natives."
>
> The ideal situation was to have two barefoot Filipinos in white waiting on them. Some also had their yard boys, chauffeurs, and Chinese Ameh. They were members of the Polo, the University, and the Wack Wack Country Club. They organized mahjongg parties at nine o'clock in the morning, played golf, tennis, and badmitten [sic], and signed "chits" all over town.

If the battle-tested Gardner was critical of his fellow American officers, it may have come from his looking at life as a non-white person himself. He was an Apache.

> The average American who resided in the Philippines at the start of the war . . . knew very little about the Filipino people, limiting such knowledge to "the irritating habits of their servants," and of this cared

less. He had his Army and Navy Club, his Manila Polo Club, his Elks
Club, and a variety of other clubs where he had excluded Filipino
patronage, or membership.

Such attitudes couldn't have helped strengthen the American-Filipino
military alliance. And American arrogance, some contend, also mani-
fested itself in the military's underestimation of Japanese forces. "From
chairborne warriors at Olympian heights in Washington to the humblest
KPs and latrine orderlies, it was taken for granted that any piece of American equipment must be of better quality and construction than its Japanese counterpart," wrote Lieutenant Robert Lapham of the 45th Infantry,
among those officers in the Philippines, "that U.S. soldiers were naturally
superior as well, that Japanese pilots were shortsighted and lacked a sense
of balance, that soldiers from an authoritarian society lacked the intel-
lectual flexibility of defenders of democracy, that (presumably) some
celestial source had decreed Yankee ingenuity to be the unique property
of Americans forever." At its roots, he contended, was what he called "one
of our national shortcomings: lack of interest in and consequent ignorance of other peoples."

"Bring on the slant eyes, we'll take them," said Private Leon Beck of
the 31st Infantry Division. "There was no way they could stand up to the
U.S. Army. If our navy doesn't sink them, we will."

If officers, particularly older ones, arrived in the Philippines with a
sense of entitlement, the soldiers beneath them often came with chips on
their shoulders. "The feeling of American superiority had a strong hold
on each of us," wrote Edgar Whitcomb, of Indiana, one of those young
soldiers. "Since childhood we had been taught that American planes,
American equipment, and American men were superior in quality to all
others on the face of the earth."

In 1941, the average enlistee was "a youth of less than average education, to whom the security of pay, low as it was, and the routines of Army
life appealed more than the competitive struggle of civilian life," said a
U.S. Army report. The report said the men resented their officers, found

training rote, and had little esprit de corps, a moral force binding them together in common purpose.

All of which made this new life in this tropical outpost perfect for the Americans. Life in his anti-tank company, Beck said, "was almost paradise. Bunk boys made our beds, picked up our dirty clothes, shined our shoes every day. We got pedicures and manicures once a month. . . . Steak fries and beer busts. We got out on the beach somewhere and [had] a company picnic. As I said, life was real easy." The closest his unit had gotten to combat was shooting staples at each other to pass the boredom or having slingshot fights with Filipino kids in the Walled City.

"The activity on the base was slow," wrote Conner. "And although the weather was hot and humid, it was kind of nice to be there. It was a thrill, a new experience. Everyone in our group was happy."

Given such tropical ease, ignorance was, indeed, bliss, though some contend that it wasn't common among younger officers. "Some charge that the slackness extended all the way to the top, to MacArthur himself," wrote Lapham, a twenty-five-year-old lieutenant like Conner. "Such contentions are hard to evaluate. In regard to the middle and lower levels they are unjust. . . . Higher up, sadly, the allegations contain some truth."

As December deepened, nobody in Conner's 27th seemed particularly concerned about the Japanese or about the bomb group's yet-to-arrive planes, which, on the morning of December 8—December 7 in Hawaii because of the Philippines being west of the international dateline—were some five thousand miles away. The aircraft—fifty-two A-24 dive bombers—were in the *Pensacola* convoy, steaming toward the Philippines from Pearl Harbor as a far-flung lifeline, if necessary.

But it was a lifeline that was more than eight sailing days away. Meanwhile, the men's minds were elsewhere. On December 6, a buddy took a photo of Conner teeing up his driver at a Fort McKinley golf course. Years hence, the scrapbook caption was simple: "There was always time to play golf."

PART TWO

PERIL

FOUR

Paradise Lost

December 8, 1941, to December 23, 1941

SOUTH OF MANILA, at Fort McKinley, Conner threw off his mosquito net, rolled out of his bunk on a screened porch, and headed for the showers. He heard the news from a handful of other officers who were huddled around a radio, not that it particularly sunk in. Conner, Cowart, and Gause had spent the previous night at the Jai Alai Club, as usual, and Conner's mind was still partly cloudy. He nonchalantly waved his towel as he passed by the others. Not until he was in the shower did the words hit home, like a dud firecracker that suddenly explodes.

"Are you kidding?" he said.

"No," said another officer. "Pearl Harbor was bombed!"

"I looked at the faces of those men who were gathered about the radio, and you could almost tell what they were thinking," Conner later wrote. "Fear. Insecurity. Were they really involved in a war? Would they get out of the Philippines? How long would it last? The expressions were deep. You could see little emotion, but you could see that every one of those men [was] completely occupied with this new thing called war."

On the radio, all army air corps personnel had been told to report immediately to their units. Conner dressed with the speed of a firefighter. He packed a bag with clothes, and tossed in Junko at the last minute. He rushed toward the officers' club, where the air-warning headquarters had been established.

In the fifty- by one-hundred-foot room, scores of similarly dressed men zipped here and there with the urgency of hummingbirds. With others, Conner gathered around a map of the Lingayen Gulf that had been spread across a table. Far East Air Force (FEAF) officers sat on stools behind the map and, with wooden sticks like pool cues, pushed model airplanes around. The indication? Japanese planes from the north were already over the gulf, apparently headed for Fort Stotsenburg or Manila, maybe both.

Men poured into the building, looking for orders. A Colonel Davies spotted Conner. "Gather all radio equipment from the air corps units and take it over near the firing area, the target-practice area," he said. "Establish a communications depot there. They want you on the air in three hours."

Conner nodded unconvincingly. Davies wasn't through. "Establish your position, quarter your men, and get your transmitter hot. Now."

Conner was just naive and brash enough to question the order. "Colonel," he said, "you know that's impossible to do in three hours."

"It may *be* impossible," said Davies, whose eyes widened as if to suggest he nevertheless wanted it done—now. And hurried away.

Conner's thirty men were scattered all over the post, and he had no idea where, exactly, all the equipment was. He headed out the door, bumping into his buddies Cowart and Gause. With permission, the two joined Conner on the scavenger hunt. Gause, in particular, was a godsend to Conner because of his experience and demeanor. He was tough. He knew radios. And, unlike Conner-the-former-cheerleader, he wasn't afraid to inspire clueless enlisted men with butt-chewing rhetoric.

"Get out of here and get that damn thing organized," he said to one group. "Don't you realize there's a war going on?"

Rocky headed out to find the equipment, Conner to find the men, and Cowart to get the supplies. Conner pulled some men off the golf course in mid-swing, others out of the sack. Most hadn't heard the news; some who had weren't buying it. But once they were all together, Conner was surprised at how quickly they snapped to the task, largely because of Rocky's leadership. "He was an inspiration to all of them," Conner wrote. "If you gave that fellow two tubes and a hunk of wire, we could contact America from Australia. He could make the most out of anything."

Such ingenuity would soon be in great demand for both men. For now, thanks to Rocky, it got the transmitters on the air long before the three-hour deadline.

HOURS LATER, THE sunlit planes flickered like tinfoil in the sky. Conner, outside with Rocky and some others, counted seventy-two of them, the fact that he took time to do so pointing to an innocence that would quickly pass. The planes' collective drone was ominous, like the deep bass of a viola playing a note of suspense. But Conner, as when hearing the news of Pearl Harbor, was slow to understand the threat. "I thought," he later wrote, "the Navy must be out. I didn't think that these could be Japanese planes." To believe that was to believe that he was about to be the target of the bombs of such planes, and his mind wouldn't let him go there. To believe that was to believe he could die, and you just can't go from golf and the Jai Alai Club to death overnight, can you?

Then the air began to break. "I heard this screaming, chilling, sickening sound of the bombs as they began to drop," he wrote. He dove to the ground. "I tried, as I pressed myself into the earth, to cover myself somehow with all of the dirt around me. I wasn't actually making a move, but the pressure within my body to confine myself to the smallest space seemed to be exerting itself with great force."

The sky crackled with what sounded like dry timber being snapped. The ground trembled with each explosion that pounded home. "Then the singing of the shrapnel as it ricocheted through the area, and tore through the roofs of the buildings," wrote Conner. "They say you never hear the bomb that actually hits you, but every time one would hit, I'd wait for the next one to hit. And yet, nothing seemed to happen. And then it was over."

Conner got to his feet, brushed off the dirt, and looked around. Others were doing the same. In their faces, Conner could see the same expression on each man: Release. Joy. Thankfulness to be alive. "They were," he wrote, "running about, kind of like children, all shaking hands and slapping each other on the back and saying, 'Boy, we got through that one, didn't we?' And then we saw the Jap planes as we looked up in the air disappear in the distance. And we began to hate them."

The Japanese raid consisted of 252 aircraft flown from Formosa, some four hundred miles north of Luzon. The U.S. Army Air Corps had roughly half that number on the island—and half of those had been destroyed by noon. Many never got off the ground. The Japanese pilots expected fierce in-air retaliation at Clark Field north of Manila; instead, initially at least, they found delicious targets, planes parked wing-to-wing on the ground. American soldiers at the base were inside eating lunch. In a five-day period, Clark Field would initiate no fewer than thirty-five air-raid sirens. Coal-black smoke roiled on the horizon from fuel dumps taking direct hits. Here and there: chaos.

When American pilots finally got planes in the air from Clark and other bases, they encountered all sorts of problems: false alarms, non-functioning communication systems, many P-40s in which no oxygen-tank adapters had been installed. Meanwhile, the Americans' antiquated three-inch antiaircraft guns couldn't reach Japanese planes bombing from twenty thousand feet. And America's P-40s were no match for the Japanese Zeros when it came to maneuverability.

"We were vulnerable as hell," said Private Bob Mailheau, with the 24th Pursuit Group. "And just plain scared."

TWO WEEKS AFTER the Japanese air attack, forty-three thousand Japanese ground troops splashed ashore from the Lingayen Gulf, one hundred miles to the north, and headed south for Manila. It was December 22. Though outnumbered two to one, Japanese troops battle-hardened in China quickly overran resistance from a half-trained Filipino Army; the invaders broke through American lines like water pouring through a dynamited dam. Only a handful of U.S. fighter planes were available to challenge Japanese air superiority; a report that the 27th's new A-24s had arrived in Manila Bay proved false. So one-sided was the assault that thousands of Japanese troops headed from the Lingayen Gulf to Manila— on bicycles. Within a day, MacArthur abandoned his stop-'em-at-the-beach plan and realized the Americans' only hope was what many had suggested in the first place: War Plan Orange, a retreat to the Bataan Peninsula to hold off the enemy until the Pacific fleet could come to the rescue. An enemy that, a day after landing north of Manila, also began surging toward the city from the southeast, at Atimonan, virtually uncontested.

Meanwhile, for the next week, the earth shook in and around Manila from relentless Japanese air attacks. Air-raid sirens wailed. Civilians fired pistols into the sky. Craters pocked once-tidy Fort McKinley, but Clark Field, north of Manila, was hit far harder. Its oil tanks blazed. Most of its buildings were destroyed, its men living on a rifle range next to it—that is, if they weren't dead or hadn't been hauled off, injured, to a field hospital.

Many suffered from concussions, having dived into holes and ditches during the raids and then had the earth shudder around them. Their faces were lacerated with cinder burns and blown dirt, some of them blinded. By mid-afternoon of the first attack, doctors and nurses at nearby Fort Stotsenburg pleaded for help from Sternberg Hospital in Manila. It only got worse. By week's end, with the hospital out of beds, the wounded were placed on canvas cots outside on lawns and tennis courts, the symbolism of then-and-now lost in the medical staff's frantic attempts to save lives.

To the south of Manila, at Fort McKinley, damage was less but morale was sinking. What few planes available were now tangled wrecks, courtesy of Japanese bombs. Conner got orders from a general to move his unit to a wooded area on nearby Nielson Field. It was the second time in days that he'd been asked to do the impossible. But he saluted, turned around, and walked out.

Conner turned to one of his men. "Bring back five trucks. That's what it's going to take to move this outfit."

"But how—"

"I don't care how you get them, just bring them back," he said. "We've got a job to do, let's get it done."

THE MOVE TO Nielson—specifically, to occupy the airport's tower—was a move into an even more dangerous area; the Japanese dive bombers had feasted on the base—and were coming back for seconds and thirds. The field had been ravaged. Planes were ablaze. Hundreds of men were already dead. "I don't think we could have had a hotter assignment," wrote Conner. "[It] was like being at ground zero. If the Japs were to hit anything, [this] would be it."

Nevertheless, those in command thought it would be an advantage if Conner's communications group could use the tower for air/ground control and to pick up reports from up north. But just as Conner and his men arrived, Japanese planes dove and dipped, their machine guns spitting bullets that peppered the dirt near the men. Some guys were so desperate for cover that they splashed into what turned out to be a sewage ditch. When the attack ended, the sight of men covered head to toe in crap triggered a rare burst of laughter.

They laughed because to not was to sink deeper into desperation. Likewise, when Conner and his boys realized that the 27th Bombardment Group seemingly had but one plane doing battle against the Japanese, flown by a guy known as "Buzz" Wagner, they turned him into sort of a cult hero. "He'd come in there at Nielson Field, set it down, and we'd always wave to him as he'd take off and come in," wrote Conner. "We'd yell out, 'Keep flying!' [He] was our Air Force," a joke not far from the truth. In actuality, only a handful of the 27th's pilots ever got into the air in the weeks after the attack. Most were digging slit trenches and foxholes and learning how to be ground soldiers, having been issued 30-06 rifles left over from World War I that hadn't been fired in years.

One day, the one-man air force, Wagner, was taking aim at a host of bombers from the sky when bullets shattered his windshield, blasting glass into his face. He managed to land, but his face looked like a splattered tomato, his skin gouged with glass. Thus ended the 27th's air force. Wagner was later shipped out to Australia, his face scarred for life. Nobody was laughing anymore.

The bombs kept coming, day and night. Nobody slept much; the tropical heat and the Japanese weren't letting up. The men tinkered with radios in the tower, sending out and receiving whatever communications they could before the next attack, then, when the sound of planes returned, racing outside to find shelter in the rice paddy dikes across the road.

A runner came to Conner with a message. The air force had lost a ton of B-17s at Stotsenburg, but one such plane was still available. The plan was to pack as many pilots into it as possible and get them the hell out of there, to Australia, where the air force could regroup. Conner's job was to see to it that the B-17 got into, and out of, Nielson Field safely with the pilots aboard. He climbed into the tower.

The four-prop beast—one of the few B-17s still in one piece—landed on schedule. Soon, the pilots arrived and clamored aboard. The radio squawked with an alert: Japanese planes were coming in from the north. Conner radioed the plane, which he could see about three hundred yards north of the tower, sitting sideways to Clay. After a quick exchange between Conner and the pilot, the radio went dead. Clay hadn't even had time to warn him. He tried, again and again, to do so. No luck.

Conner and a few others had only one choice. They raced out on the runway, waving arms and yelling, but the plane's props were whirling, the noise deafening. Suddenly, the Japanese Zeros dropped out of the sky like runaway elevators. Conner and the others hit the dirt. Enemy fire crackled from the direction of the plane. It had been hit. The plane was on fire.

After the Japanese planes left, Conner's group rushed to the B-17 to see if any of the pilots could be saved. The plane was empty. They'd been able to get out on the opposite side of the fuselage that Conner could see from the tower and race to shelter in a building. Not a man was lost.

"Guess it just wasn't our time to leave the Philippines," said one to Conner.

Many never would. One plane did manage to get twenty-three pilots from the 27th flown to Australia, where the group's long-awaited A-24s had been rerouted from Hawaii following the attack on the Philippines. But most of the pilots not on that plane would never leave the ground. Instead, they would be buried in its dirt.

FIVE

Leaving Manila

December 24, 1941, to January 1, 1942

ON THE DAY after Christmas, 1941, Conner and a handful of his men bumped along in a command car across a U.S.-built airfield on Bataan. The mountainous peninsula jutted, like a giant thumb, into the waters west of Manila, forming one of Luzon's forty-eight provinces.

Conner, at the wheel, saw them first: Japanese bombers dropping toward the airfield like sharks diving for bottom prey. He jammed on the brakes. He and the others piled out and hit the dirt. One man bolted from the vehicle and sprinted away. "No, don't run!" Conner yelled.

But the man kept going, heading for the edge of the runway and jungle foliage. "You could hear the screaming, singing noise of the bombs as they began to drop, cutting the air as they fell," Conner later wrote. "And then the jolt, and vibration, and explosion as they hit the ground."

Conner shut his eyes. Each bomb seemed to come closer. When the blasts seemingly stopped, he wondered if the attack was over. "I opened [my eyes]," he wrote, "to see one of those fifty-pounders hit right where this boy was running, and as it exploded, he disappeared in the dust just as if he'd been swallowed up. And after the raid was over, and the planes had returned a couple of times to strafe, we got up out of the dirt and went to the edge to find him and see what had happened, and it was impossible to find even a trace of him. He'd just completely disappeared when the bomb hit him."

Conner stumbled away, buckled to his knees, and retched. "How could this be?" he wrote. "One minute, a happy, singing, living, breathing human being. The next minute, nothing. Absolutely nothing."

AS MANILA FELL to the Japanese in the waning days of 1941, the landscape in and around the city was a study in contrasts: Here, two Santa Clauses walked along the Escolta River as palm trees swayed; there, the roads out of the city thickened with refugees leaving for their native villages. Here, women in evening gowns arrived for a dance at the palm-framed Manila Hotel overlooking Manila Bay; there, Rocky Gause helped Rita Garcia, a young Filipino woman, to the hospital after she'd been injured in an air raid. Here, the opulence of the Jai Alai Club; there, uncollected garbage and plumes of smoke from the oil tanks at Pandacan, to the east, staining the sky. "Let it be known," reported NBC correspondent Bert Silen, "that our Christmas Eve was the darkest and gloomiest I ever hope to spend."

Conner's was arguably worse than that of any hotel-billeted reporter's, but his telegram home didn't indicate any such thing. "Feeling wonderful," he told his folks back in New Jersey. "Merry Christmas."

On the day before Christmas, 1941—"Black Christmas" some were calling it—orders had been given for all U.S. military personnel to evacuate Manila. On the day after, MacArthur declared it an "open city," meaning that the United States was abandoning all defensive efforts and that the Japanese Army would, thus, be expected to not bomb or otherwise attack it, but to simply march in.

On Christmas Day, MacArthur slipped out of his Manila Hotel penthouse and was taken to a safer location, a giant tunnel burrowed deep beneath the rock of Corregidor, the island guarding the bay.

It was the hottest Christmas Day most of the Americans had experienced. In Manila, as bombs pounded to earth, patients at all area hospitals ate their Christmas dinners under their beds. If that wasn't chaos enough, American nurses were being evacuated to the Bataan Peninsula; soon, they would become the first U.S. military nurses sent into a battle zone for duty. By New Year's Eve, nearly all eighty-seven army nurses were gone from Manila; only a few remained, though they, too, would soon flee to the peninsula.

Either the Japanese did not get MacArthur's "open city" declaration or they chose to ignore it, because while troops closed in on the city from the north and the south, the sky above Manila was, on December 27, rife with bombers trying to take out port installations and buildings in the Walled City. Meanwhile, U.S. forces burned off fuel supplies at surrounding airfields. A day later, Gause picked through the bay-front wreckage in search of signal supplies "beneath a rain of enemy steel."

For decades, Manila had been a bastion of energy and, in places, elegance. Now a few thousand American civilians packed clothes and essentials for expected confinement in a makeshift internment camp. Looters picked through vacated stores like seagulls working the beach after a storm. The hulls of partially sunken ships littered the waterfront. Atop the five-story Manila Hotel, where MacArthur had once scanned the bay as if from a crow's nest: empty rooms.

Cars and trucks jammed the streets, trying to get to the port. With the Japanese plunging south across Luzon's central plains, the fallback was what many other American officers had favored in the first place: hunkering down on the Bataan Peninsula with hopes of creating a stalemate until a naval rescue arrived. With the change in plans, ripples of confusion only added to an American force already in disarray. The bay front was a cacophony of chaos as troops poured into any still-floating craft to be ferried across Manila Bay to Bataan. Soldiers commandeered whatever civilian cars, trucks, and buses they could grab. The ragged units of the North Luzon force had blown some 184 bridges, which slowed the Japanese pursuit south, but time was running out.

IF THE MILITARY'S formal protocol had not gotten lost in the shuffle, it certainly had been relaxed. Conner would get his revised orders while sitting at the bar of the Army-Navy Officers' Club across from the Manila Hotel. The windows were blacked out, the room lit by candles, the air thick with cigarette, pipe, and cigar smoke. More than a hundred men were stuffed inside, some already thick with beards, their 100 percent cotton uniforms having long lost any crispness in the tropical heat.

The bar, Conner realized, was tinted with a touch of fear, the usual five-beer bravado replaced by resignation, weariness, and worry. Conner connected with his commanding officer, Captain Lassiter Mason of the signal corps. "He looked tired," Conner remembered, "and I could tell that although he wasn't upset, he was definitely concerned."

Mason, like many of Conner's superiors, was far older than Clay. He instructed Conner to get his men to Pier 7 and board whatever barge, ferry, or ship they could and cross the bay to Bataan. He rolled out a map on the bar and showed Conner their destination: "Little Baguio," a place so small it wasn't even on the map—and named, by the Americans, because it reminded many of the Philippines' cool, green summer capital, Baguio.

On the map, Conner looked at Bataan, about thirty miles long and twenty miles wide, a thick stretch of land between the South China Sea to the west and Manila Bay to the east. Mountains spiked Bataan's north-south spine, most of the peninsula shrouded in thick jungle. Little Baguio was only about four miles from the southern tip of the peninsula, not far from the island of Corregidor.

By 2 A.M., Conner and his men were in trucks at the end of a long line stretching from the pier. Conner got out and hurried to the water-front. Was this really the best they could do? He was asking an MP about alternatives—and had been told to buck up and live with it—when the siren blasted.

Air raid. The men piled out of their trucks and scattered toward buildings. Others slid into spaces between oil drums stacked outside. The bombs pounded home around them. Concrete, brick, and mortar crashed down. The barrels tipped over.

"Look out!" yelled Conner.

The rolling barrels crushed a handful of his men, eventually killing them all. "I heard them cry out for help," Conner wrote, "and then their voices kind of died away."

After the bombing stopped and daylight arrived, Conner wasn't out to prove anything. But as he saw ships and boats on fire in the bay and saw, in the distance, Japanese Zeros strafing others as the crafts motored toward Bataan, he was out to find a safer way to get to Little Baguio. "The idea of getting on some small craft and being out in Manila Bay seemed to me like setting ourselves up for [being] ducks in a shooting gallery," he wrote.

Conner pulled his car out of the line, drove back to the officers' club, and found Captain Mason. Things were terribly jammed up and dangerous, he said. "What are the chances of us going by road?"

Mason spread out the map again. It would be a longer trip and riskier, with the Japanese advancing, but, yes, said Mason. Go by land if you want.

CONNER INFORMED HIS men of the change of plans, then told them to fan out and collect any abandoned vehicles they could. If it was Conner's first eyebrow-raising order, it wouldn't be his last. The men commandeered thirteen vehicles. Conner and Gause drove a 1940 four-door Ford sedan and Cowart a similar car. No map. No directions. And, Conner quickly realized, all but no room on the lone road to Bataan; plenty of other units were going by land.

Darkness descended. The road was clogged: civilians on foot, soldiers in an array of vehicles, and ox carts twined in a desperate surge to safety.

Mothers carried children. Old men—the younger ones were in military uniforms—balanced jig-poles on their shoulders with a sack on either end. Unlike when the soldiers had arrived on Luzon, nobody flashed them the "V" for victory sign.

The noise was as loud as the road was crowded. Children cried. Women hollered for kids lost in the shuffle, fighting a flow of people who seemed unconcerned about the mothers' plights. "You could see the pain in [their] faces," Conner wrote.

Soon, the thirteen vehicles had gotten beyond the rush, and the road was solid cars carrying military personnel and Filipino civilians. The setup was ripe for Zero pilots, the men who flew the long-range fighters that had been strafing Americans without much resistance. But Conner made sure his men's vehicles kept their lights off as they crept along.

When the unit had cleared San Fernando and headed down the peninsula, the driver of a bus behind Conner and Gause got impatient and started honking his horn and flashing his lights. Rocky yelled at him to turn off the lights and quiet down. No luck.

"If you don't put those lights out," said Gause, "I'll shoot them out."

The lights went out. Conner was impressed. Gause was only five-foot-five, but a tough Georgia boy who, as a teenager, had favored boxing over studies. He had quit the University of Georgia after a year to join the Coast Guard and, after an honorable discharge, spent some time on an oil tanker bound for South America before joining the U.S. Army Air Corps.

A few minutes later, however, the lights clicked back on. Gause grabbed his Browning Automatic Rifle, walked back to the bus, and, with two squeezes of the trigger, made good on his promise. Conner was even more impressed.

In the darkness, the sight of the fleeing civilians touched Conner. "Evacuation like this," he wrote, "is a terrible thing. People hungry, sick from exposure, and many of them carrying too much and, as a result, had lost everything."

But nearly one hundred thousand people—sixty-five thousand Filipino troops, fifteen thousand U.S. troops and the rest civilians—managed to reach Bataan, the military among them digging in to build a defense against the approaching Japanese. At dawn, Conner's convoy hit the southern tip of the peninsula, where the Mariveles Mountains all but dropped into the sea. The men drove out on a wooden pier. To the south, the island of Corregidor rose from the water like a haystack made of rock. Overhead, Japanese planes dove and rose, dropping bombs. Conner and his men watched the anti-aircraft fire from the island and cheered when they'd see an occasional plane turn to smoke and plunge into the ocean.

About the only thing that reminded him of home on this Christmas Day was meeting a soldier named Ed Whitcomb. He was Conner's contact to establish a communication center behind Cabcaban Field, where their signal reach was occasionally to Australia but more often only to the island of Mindanao, in the southern stretch of the Filipino archipelago. Whitcomb hailed from North Vernon, Indiana, not far from where Conner had spent his early years, in Indianapolis. The two talked for hours while setting up a ramshackle communications system, as if, Conner wrote, "we were kindred spirits."

Later, back at Little Baguio, a tented mess hall had been put in place. The Christmas Day menu for Conner and his thirty men was simple: hardtack—hard, saltless biscuits—and water. Prison food, in essence. The men tried to laugh about it, but after nearly a week of similar rations at Little Baguio, four miles inland, Conner, Rocky, and Cowart talked of the grimness of the situation. Not only did they not have enough food, but they didn't have enough tents. A few dozen men were packed into one. The Japanese were still some distance north of the peninsula, radio reports said. So the trio decided to take a chance before the enemy arrived: return to Manila and raid the quartermaster corps. Get whatever they could. It might be their last chance for resupply. Cowart would stay with the men. Rocky and Clay, with a group of seven men, would take a truck.

The roads were clear this time; the men had no problem getting into Manila. At a dockside warehouse, they started loading up food. As they did so, Conner and Rocky saw abandoned trucks parked nearby. The idea struck the two of them almost simultaneously: Soon, they'd rounded up a few Filipinos to be drivers, and secured another ten vehicles to pack with food. They even found some stowed-away radio equipment and supplies that were hidden in a Santa Anna cabaret.

It had been a long day. The convoy was to head back an hour before dawn. Along Escolta Street, Conner and Rocky heard the voice of a Filipino woman. It was Rita Garcia, the woman whom Rocky had helped to a hospital a few days earlier. She thanked Rocky again for his kindness. Would the two like to join her at a New Year's Eve party?

It made no sense whatsoever. It was 9 P.M. The Japanese Army was closing in on Manila; on December 30, the advance from the south had reached a point only five miles away. And Conner's men had a long and bumpy ride to Little Baguio ahead of them. The two smiled at Garcia.

Why not?

CONNER AND GAUSE walked into the velvet-walled Empire Room like a couple of rogue party-crashers. Pistols hung from their hips. Whiskers darkened their faces. Their long-sleeved chino shirts and button-fly trousers were well rumpled by long, hot days and no wash. The two were among the few soldiers in a less-than-packed room sprinkled with Filipinos and at least one U.S. nurse, Helen Summers. Still, the orchestra played lively, the drinks went down fast, and a few couples danced. With most of Manila's bars long since shut down, the Empire Room was essentially the only game in town, a final burst of brightness from a lightbulb about to go out. It was New Year's Eve.

Earlier, the two had swung by Rita's place, a Spanish-style house in one of Manila's better sections; she would meet them later, coming with a friend. Her father was already off fighting. She and her mother feared the arrival of the Japanese Army, which, while at war in China and Manchuria, had killed, tortured, and raped hundreds of thousands of civilians. Already, reports abounded from north of Manila regarding similar atrocities. Would the men be willing to take her mother and sisters to Bataan so they would be safer? Rocky and Conner exchanged glances at each other. They would like to, Rocky had said, but it was against regulations. Now the two felt a touch sheepish as they waited to meet Rita at the Empire Room.

Outside, Manila was dark. Lifeless. And though the Empire Room was putting on a good face, it was nothing like it had been before. No bar fights. No tangle of arms and legs on the dance floor. No shifty eyes and muted conversations about what troops were where, whispers of "Fifth Column" spies. Such snitches were pro-Japanese Filipinos trying to learn all they could about the enemy, the name stemming from a 1936 radio address by Nationalist General Emilio Mola during the Spanish Civil War. The four columns inside Madrid would be supported by a "fifth column" of supporters, he had said, working to undermine the government from within. Nothing Conner understood now, in the haze of a lounge's cigarette smoke, but something he soon would.

A Filipino waiter placed plates in front of the men. "Will you give the Japanese as good service as you have us?" Rocky asked, only half-kidding.

"Oh, but I will not be here then," the young Filipino said. "I am staying only until there is no further need of me tonight. My gun is ready in my room. By dawn I will be on my way to Bataan."

"You might do better if you stayed here," said Rocky. "It isn't going to be any picnic on Bataan. And you don't have to fight, you know."

The waiter was only about five feet tall, but he arched his back in a touch of pride. "Sir, my brother was killed five days ago in northern Luzon. My father is in the hills, fighting with his old outfit. My mother and sister have gone to care for the wounded. We will fight, all of us, to the end."

Perhaps to impress Rocky, Conner decided to play a little devil's advocate. "But the Japanese say they are bringing you freedom," he said. "They may treat you well."

"The Americans have promised us freedom," he countered. "It is their kind we want. We will never forget what they have done for us. And the Japs we will always hate."

Not much got to Rocky Gause. But his expression, Conner noted, changed slightly at the words, as if inspired by the young man's pride.

Moments later, when Rita arrived with a friend, she looked stunning: long, black hair framing sparkling eyes and cameo-like Spanish features. A deep, red evening dress studded with sequins. Hardly the young woman Gause had pulled out of the debris earlier in the week. As Gause explained what he'd been doing lately, leading convoys, destroying radio setups before the enemy arrived, and the like, she couldn't understand it. "But you are a pilot," she said.

"Yes," he said, "but a pilot with no plane."

As the evening deepened and the drinks flowed, Gause and Conner danced with Rita and someone else she knew. The band played "The Beautiful Blue Danube." Conner ran into a couple of guys from the 27th, Bert Bank and Ollie Lancaster. He chatted with Summers, the army nurse, one of the few who hadn't already left for Bataan. She had a boyfriend, a lieutenant named Arnold Benjamin, somewhere out there on the peninsula; she didn't know where. They hoped to marry soon.

As midnight and 1942 approached, it was as if those at the Empire Room were trying hard to embrace some semblance of traditional, year-end revelry and yet realized that it just wasn't the same. "You could tell," wrote Conner, "there was a cloud over the whole place. A cloud of unrest; a cloud of uncertainty."

They were seven thousand miles from home, clinging to the edge of the unknown. Midnight came and went with muted celebration. For three more hours, Conner and Gause partied with friends; by this time, drinks were on the house. Finally, Conner looked at his Bulova. They had to get going. Rocky agreed. The two said their good-byes and, along with Rita Garcia, left. The orchestra was playing the Philippine national anthem. "We were," Rocky later wrote, "the last Americans to set foot in the famed hotel before the arrival of the Japanese forces."

The three found a blue Hudson that Rocky had used before. They lit cigarettes and drove through the dark, lifeless streets, Rita sitting between the two men. Shortly before they arrived at her house, Conner felt her shoulders shaking slightly and noticed her head tilted down.

She was, he realized, crying uncontrollably.

The Flag

January 2, 1942, to January 26, 1942

CLAY CONNER WOULD come to believe the Philippine Scouts were "the finest soldiers in the world." One of them, in particular, would come to impress him. He was part of the hard-riding 26th Cavalry—comprised mainly of Filipinos—that had been charged with defending a village called Demortis, on the Lingayen Gulf, when the Japanese ground troops splashed ashore December 22. His name was Sergeant Gaetano Bato. He had been part of the U.S. Army for twenty-three years when World War II broke out.

With forty-three thousand seasoned soldiers, the Japanese onslaught proved overwhelming; the United States had twenty-eight thousand men in northern Luzon, only a small percentage trained to fight. As the rear guard of the northern Luzon force, the 26th fell back with the rest of the troops. MacArthur established his main line of defense from Abucay to Morong, across the north end of the Bataan Peninsula. *"Banzai! Banzai! Banzai!"* Left and right, men of the cavalry went down. Horses, too. Their ranks were thinned, their spirits waned, but they kept fighting. The horse of a Sergeant Mojo, the regimental flag bearer, galloped beneath the wind-whipped colors of an American flag.

On January 16, the 26th thrust forward into the Japanese-occupied town of Morong, on Subic Bay. For four hours they fought, ultimately pushing the Japanese troops out of Morong. But a machine-gun bullet felled Sergeant Mojo. He tumbled headlong from his mount to the ground. Dead.

Sergeant Bato swung his horse to the scene, picked up the flag, and rammed it into his saddle's leather flag pocket. He would, he vowed, defend that flag with his life, doing whatever it took to preserve its honor for America, for the Philippines, and for the men who had fought beside him—and would fight beside him in the future. Among the latter, it turned out, would be a young lieutenant—now some twenty miles away, in Little Baguio—who did not yet have the courage that coursed through Bato's veins on this historic day, the last time a U.S. cavalry unit would ride horses into battle.

The lieutenant's name was Clay Conner.

FINDING LEVEL GROUND on the Bataan Peninsula was like finding a soldier who didn't smoke. The interior part of the peninsula rose to mountain ridges whose peaks fell off into rugged craters, canyons, and cliffs, most of them thick with jungle foliage. In spots, ridges among the Zambales Mountains to the north and the Mariveles to the south looked like the jagged spine of a stegosaurus. Between steepness and dense foliage, many places were virtually impassable. Whatever lowlands existed ran along Manila Bay, to the east. Their presence was so overshadowed by the mountains in between that, from the air, Bataan looked to pilots like a witch's hat—all slope, little brim. Because of the mountains, the only north-south roads followed the lowlands flanking Manila Bay and the South China Sea. The only east-west road wound its way between the double knuckles of Mount Mariveles and Mount Natib midway down the peninsula, from the town of Pilar on the east to Bagac on the west.

On Bataan, most Filipinos lived in the lowlands, where they farmed land usually owned by someone else. They lived clustered in thatched huts in barrios, the equivalent of small American towns, or in towns, which were larger. A province was similar to an American county; Bataan was one of forty-eight such provinces on Luzon.

It had been roughly a month since the Japanese landed at Lingayen Gulf, one hundred miles to the north, and surged down Luzon's central plains and through Zambales, Tarlac, and Pampanga Provinces to Bataan. Meanwhile, other Japanese troops were also approaching through the rocky, heavily forested western flank of the Zambales Mountains that rose sharply above the South China Sea. It was the beginning of a two-front push that, they hoped, would allow them to eventually attack the Bataan Peninsula from both front and side.

By January 26, 1942, the Japanese Army's farthest advance was roughly midway down Bataan's peninsula, about ten miles north of Conner's communications group. The area flanking the Pilar-Bagac Road was, for now, no-man's-land—a litter of battles come and gone. Conner realized as much after taking a few trips up and back to the front lines to check communications installations. The once-thick tropical forest had been chopped to bamboo stubs by machine-gun fire. Shells of burned-out and sometimes overturned trucks smoldered along the road. Bodies of soldiers lay scattered, a few tangled in barbed wire as if they were scarecrows. Flies feasted. The area stunk of death, the one thing, Private Leon Beck would later observe, that war movies could never convey.

To the northwest, the tattered jungles also cradled the remains of horses killed in battle—if they hadn't already been butchered and eaten by starving soldiers. Whatever surviving soldiers or civilians who were once in these combat areas had retreated deeper into the jungle, partly for protection, partly for sanity.

The air hung in suffocating stillness. Each day, the jungle heat wilted Conner and his men as if they were in a sauna. Temperatures sometimes hit triple digits. The heat hurried the unseen—but easily smelled—process of jungle rot along the floor, an invitation for mold, flies, leeches, mites, and mosquitoes. At night, men sometimes shivered in their tents as coolness came with the dark.

THE INEVITABILITY HUNG over Conner and his men like jungle humidity. The next day. The next week. The next month. Nobody knew when, but they all knew that, at some point, the Japanese Army was coming for them, even if they secretly hoped some fleet of navy ships would arrive for a miraculous rescue. Making it worse was their utter lack of experience as infantrymen, a fact that wouldn't bode well against a regular army, much less an experienced one that had fought for years in China and, now, for weeks in the Philippines.

After their trip to Manila for food and supplies, the group had been the last convoy out of the soon-to-fall city, Gause later wrote. The convoy had returned without incident. Back at Little Baguio, where a command post had been set up, the fresh supplies provided days of relative splendor. More food. More equipment. More tents. "We were," wrote Conner, "living like kings." Word, of course, got around and men began pouring into the area to beg, borrow, or steal whatever was on hand. Conner guarded their stash with diligence.

At a higher level, plans were hatched to have a ship anchor in the bay off Bataan and ferry a group of pilots to Australia. But days later, some in the 27th saw that ship. Its carcass lay forlorn in the bay, its masts barely above water, the victim of two direct hits from Japanese planes. For the Americans, it mirrored a morbid truth: Not only could they not win this battle on Bataan, they could not escape it.

Within a week, Rocky Gause was transferred out. He was heading for the front lines to the north to establish radio contact between the artillery, the infantry, and the operations post, and link it with the 27th's makeshift headquarters carved into the southeast flank of Mount Mariveles. Conner watched him leave. Same old Rocky, he thought. Stocky. Tough as nails. Officer's cap on his head. Cigar in his mouth. "OK, boys," said Rocky, "keep 'em on the air. I'll be in touch with you."

Leroy Cowart, Conner's other close pal, who'd driven with Clay and Bill Strese from Georgia to San Francisco, also got orders to move out.

He was assigned to beach defense, taking a handful of guys with small radio receivers and transmitters to warn of any Japanese invasions from the South China Sea to the west.

Cowart was the opposite of Rocky. Quiet. Slender. And he faithfully wore his helmet rather than a hat. He was from military stock. Went by the book. And Conner respected him, even if he was drawn more deeply to Rocky's Hollywood-esque swashbuckling. In Manila, Clay had come across an old campaign hat, the kind worn in World War I and by park rangers and the like, a round hat in which the creased ribbing on top looked like a citrus juicer.

Rocky was gone, Cowart was gone, but Clay would one day embody the style of both: Rocky's devil-may-care looseness. Cowart's more measured approach, born of legacies passed on to him. For now he replaced his officer's cap with the new hat, and carried on.

SEVEN

Beginning of the End

January 27, 1942, to March 30, 1942

EVERYTHING UNDER CONTROL LOVE TO MIMI
AND YOU

—WESTERN UNION TELEGRAM SENT HOME
BY CONNER MARCH 4, 1942

BY MID-FEBRUARY—MORE THAN two months since the Japanese attack—war and the half rations demanded by MacArthur January 2 had whittled soldiers to wisps of their former bodies. Faces were gaunt, sleep rare, malaria and scarlet fever common.

Conner, though gaining a few notches on his belt, was more than happy to be headquartered well behind the front lines; he and his men were far from the approaching fray. But he realized that they were going to run out of food long before he'd originally figured. The situation worsened when his unit was told to move its headquarters near a munitions dump and a makeshift hospital that had been established in an old building. Conner had already inherited more men. Now, after relocating, soldiers from other units began slipping into the chow line and poaching grub. Virtually every American soldier on Luzon had been stuffed onto a peninsula not even half the size of Rhode Island. Meanwhile, however, much of their food had been left in Japanese-occupied Manila during the hasty evacuation.

The unit's radio, housed in a truck-trailer rig, squawked with military chatter from Australia, China, and Honolulu, none of it particularly promising. Monkeys chattered from treetops as if protesting the intrusion. At first light, the bent-toed geckos chirped, the jungle's version of the barnyard rooster. And, from the nearby hospital, soldiers screamed in pain when frenzied docs hadn't allowed enough time for the Novocain to take root while treating burns or shrapnel wounds. Such were the sounds of Clay Conner's war, even if, for him, it was still war at arm's length.

Upon the men's arrival, the quiet fear among them was tree snakes or pythons. But something else bothered them more: rats, which came out at night. Once, Conner's men heard screams from a nearby field hospital. Some thought this was it: The Japanese bayonets had come. No, they later learned, just a nurse awakened in terror by a rat nuzzling her neck.

Still, Conner had it better than most—and he paired his physical well-being with enough mental rationalization to convince himself that guys up front could somehow stave off the Japanese invasion. "Ignorance," he later wrote, "is bliss." A Filipino soldier had offered his carpentry skills to build an officers' shack for Clay and Captain Mason, with whom Conner was bunking, using materials from a bombed-out building in Mariveles, four miles away. Not that a particular provost on duty approved of the acquisition. Conner had taken the wood when the provost had gone to check out Clay's story that Captain Mason had ordered him to clear the stuff out.

On another trip to Mariveles, Conner picked up a redheaded soldier named Edwards who was often hitchhiking in for Sunday morning church services. Clay hadn't been to church since he was a kid—and that was only under the threat of a parental court-martial.

"Here, I want you to have this," Edwards said to Conner one day and handed him a brown-covered pocket New Testament. "It's a present I got from my mother and father before I left home."

"I don't want your book," said Conner.

"That's all right," said Edwards. "You need it. Keep it."

"I don't need it."

"I want you to have it as a present," said Edwards.

Christ, thought Conner, it was easier to take the thing than to refuse it. "OK, if that's what you want," he said.

UNLIKE THE SOLDIERS on the front lines, the danger factor was low for Conner and his communications men. He moved around a lot, coordinating radio setups. A wizened U.S. colonel in Mariveles, the commanding officer of a quarantine station, enlightened him regarding the natives of the peninsula. He showed Clay around the outpost, which was primitive, rough, and, to Conner at least, intriguing. "It fascinated me because I had never experienced this life before," he wrote. "I was thrilled by it all."

He got to know some of the Filipinos who lived along Bataan's southern tip. The boys would take him and others out to "The Rock"—the island of Corregidor—on their outriggers for skinny-dipping, warning them, in broken English, about sharks. At noon, he'd watch the daily cockfights. Then he'd get on with his business, hopping from airfield to airfield—Bataan, Cabcaban, and Mariveles—to check on communication setups. The air fleet was small: two P-40s at Mariveles, to the southwest; two at Cabcaban, to the southeast; and one at Bataan Field, just up the Manila Bay coastline from Cabcaban.

At one point, the Japanese landed an additional few thousand men on Bataan's western shore. They rushed inland, camouflaged themselves, and waited for the Americans to slip by them, then opened fire. In the rare cases where they were defeated in skirmishes, it was not uncommon for them to feign surrender, then, when being taken prisoner, pull the pin on a grenade, killing themselves and their capturers. "More banzai, more suicides, all for the emperor," wrote Conner. "It was a hard way to fight a war."

Near a town named Agloloma, Conner came across an American tank whose interior chilled him. The Japanese had killed the crew, chopped their bodies up, filled the insides with dirt, and placed the heads atop the pile, so they were the first thing Conner saw. "A ghastly sight," he wrote.

Indeed, if his short trips allowed for some fun and fulfilled a sense of curiosity, they also proved unsettling. Several times he visited a jungle hospital—technically, "Hospital #1"—where he saw some of the nurses he'd gotten to know in Manila. The hospital wasn't much, just hundreds of irons beds or cots scattered beneath the jungle canopy, most with T-bar supports holding up mosquito netting. Beds on which lay wounded soldiers—even a few Japanese POWs—or those suffering from an array of diseases such as malaria, beriberi, and dysentery. When the breeze was just right, it smelled of diesel fuel; nearby, motors chugged away to feed generators for water and electricity. By now, the rattan-vine stretchers soldiers had fashioned were moist with blood upon blood upon blood. In the tropical heat, the wounded lay stacked next to one another like trout in a fry pan. Men whose wounds went beyond the body to the soul were relegated to what was known as a shock tent, home of the proverbial "thousand yard stare." "It was," wrote Conner, "pitiful."

The nurses worked day and night; six weeks into the war, more than ten thousand soldiers were recovering—or dying—in aid stations and field hospitals on Bataan. At night, nurses with flashlights went soldier to soldier, lifting mosquito netting to check on their condition. To give the women a break, Conner would take a few with him to the beach when he was checking on Lieutenant Cowart's communications setup. "When we'd return, I would walk around with them, from one bed to another, while they'd check to see what was going on," he wrote. "I had no conception of what it meant to be sick, having never been sick a day in my life." Empathy was not a Conner strong suit. "I didn't appreciate the suffering that these men were going through."

As February became March, the hospital intakes swelled. More American units from the north, flushed out by the approaching Japanese, retreated to the jungle near Conner and his men. Again, more mouths to feed. When canned food ran out, quartermasters slaughtered carabao—water buffalo—and more of the cavalry's horses, at night. Mango, banana, and coconut trees had been picked clean. Some soldiers resorted to cooking grass and leaves to spice up their rice.

One day, Conner complained about the food himself, something usually reserved for the men under his command. "They'd taken some rice and they'd watered it down to where it was practically mush, and they'd served it to us with some of the meat of the cavalry horses," he wrote. After his outburst, a few of the men, in essence, told Conner: *If you don't like it, then get us something better. You think there's a problem? Fix it.* They hammered home their seriousness by brandishing guns. "They blamed me for their hunger," he wrote.

Weeks passed. Tempers rose. Stomachs growled. One night, Mason invited Conner to ride with him to Mariveles, where the captain was meeting with some military brass, including General Spencer Akins of the signal corps. On the way in, Conner shared with Mason how his men had turned on him. Later, as Conner waited outside the tent where the officers had gathered, he could hear the conversation.

The American and Filipino plight was hopeless. The Americans could, like a caged lion, keep fighting back, but no food, supplies, or ships were en route for the men of Bataan. MacArthur had, on March 22, left for the safety of Australia. For the first time, Conner faced a new truth: He and the others could become prisoners of war—or wind up like the soldiers whose decapitated heads he'd seen in that tank.

On the bumpy ride back to Baguio, Conner turned to Mason, a man for whom he had developed great respect and who, in a sense, had taken on at least the semblance of a surrogate father. Clay asked what their options were.

"We just go ahead, day to day, and take it as it comes," said Mason. "That's the way it is with a soldier."

The more he thought about it, the angrier Conner got about MacArthur's decision to leave. "It would seem that he left us behind," he said. "If it was right for him to go, how about us?"

Mason let Conner's anger cool a moment. "Maybe you don't know the big picture," he said. "Maybe you're not acquainted with all the facts."

The words stung; Conner had had great respect for Mason since the day the two had met in the bar in Manila for his evacuation orders.

"Lieutenant," Mason continued, "are you responsible for the men in your outfit being hungry?"

"Of course not," said Conner. "You know better than that."

"But you're receiving the blame, aren't you?"

"Yes."

"Why are you receiving the blame, Clay?" asked Mason.

"You know why. Because they don't understand. They think that I'm getting more food than they are, but they just don't know the whole story."

"So," he said, "you're being falsely accused."

The words hung in the air like dust kicked up on a windless day. Mason didn't need to say another word, nor did Conner. The two drove on in silence, the truck's headlights illuminating but a sliver of the vast darkness beyond.

DAY BY DAY, as food supplies dwindled, worry roiled deeper in the guts of the Americans. At Hospital #1, rumors rippled down the rows of beds that the nurses might be taken to Corregidor; the brass didn't want women around when the Japanese broke through, not after their troops' rape-filled history in China, Manchuria, and northern Luzon. Morale among Conner's men sagged like wet hammocks, equal parts boredom, hunger, and fear. Fear because men realized they were stuck between a literal rock— the island of Corregidor—and a hard place, the latter the Fourteenth Imperial Army, which was squeezing them like a vise.

Fights broke out over food. When Japanese Zeros splintered an outdoor eating area, Conner left his food and dove into a foxhole with the rest of the men. Afterward, a private in his outfit used the opportunity to swipe some of Clay's rice. The private bristled when Conner called him for it.

"The way I see it, Lieutenant," said the man, "if you haven't got guts enough to protect your own food, and you have to run and get in a fox-hole every time you hear the sound of a motor, you don't deserve it."

Conner was speechless. Not because the man was out of line, but because, as Clay would later write, "I agreed with him." He had to face it: Since the Japanese had attacked, he'd been more observer than participant. Standing safely on the sidelines, a military version of the Duke cheerleader, not the guy taking the hits on the field. He was the lieutenant living in custom-built quarters made of materials he'd basically stolen, the guy skinny-dipping off "The Rock" and driving nurses around, not the dead soldier wrapped in that barbed wire up north. The guy in charge of dozens of men and responsible for communication, but who freely admitted, when it came to radios, "I didn't know one tube from another." Blame it on a doting mom or lack of siblings to share with, but Conner had always lived with a certain sense of privilege. Now the private calling him out had stripped him of whatever delusions the bars on his collar had hidden. He was a coward.

As others watched, Conner's shame quietly melted into anger, then embarrassment. His emotions were exacerbated by the fact that he was as starved as the rest of these guys, his clothes far too large for the shriveling body on which they hung. When more machine-gun bullets peppered the makeshift mess hall from the air, the private who'd taken him to task used the opportunity to grab some sugar that wasn't his. On a second strafing he dropped it and scurried behind a tree. Conner hadn't moved. He walked over, looked at the man, and placed his boot on the sugar. He ground it into the dirt.

"I notice your guts aren't made of iron either," he said, then walked off to the transmitter station.

MAYBE IT WAS fear of the approaching enemy, maybe shame at his lack of guts, but, for whatever reason, Conner began retreating deep into the jungle with his .45 pistol, the gun he had never fired. Until now, that is, the waning days of March 1942. He would pick targets, draw the pistol from his holster, and fire it. Over and over. Day after day. Week after week, honing his skills in the jungle hollows.

Meanwhile, one moonless night, Conner shared with Mason and the other men what he'd seen at Agloloma: the dead men inside the tank whose bodies had been hacked up. The group spent the rest of the evening talking about why MacArthur left, about when the Japanese might come, and what would happen when they did. The stories of torture and muti-lation had sifted through the ranks and settled in the men's minds like jungle rot. Soldiers grew edgy; nobody hit his bunk until 2:30 A.M.

Conner hadn't even closed his eyes when a shot rang out, singing right by his hut. He rolled out of bed, hit the floor. More bullets splintered the night. Could this be it, the moment they'd all feared? "Cease fire!" Conner yelled. "Cease fire!" Finally, the bullets stopped.

Outside, Conner heard footsteps. A Japanese soldier? The private who'd called him out? No, instead, up walked a Sergeant Robert Boboski with a sheepish look on his face. He'd gone to sleep with his rifle across his bed. A monkey had fallen out of a tree and startled him; instinctively, he'd started firing. The monkey had been killed.

Conner shook his head, then exhaled. "Take the monkey to the mess hall," he said. "We'll need it for breakfast."

AS DAYS PASSED, Conner continued his daily retreat into the jungle to practice more with his pistol, driven by a newfound need to be prepared and, he had to admit, a sense of adventure. "I practiced thinking that some day I might need that advantage, but I also think my admiration for the old western [movie] stars had something to do with it," he wrote. The ones he'd seen on the silver screen with Mom, growing up in New Jersey. "I appreciated their talent, and their accomplishment, in the art of fast-draw and fire." Whatever his motive, the practice was paying dividends. He was, he discovered, becoming a damn good shot, a regular Uncle Zack, his great-uncle who—as it was once said—"could shoot the eyes out of a squirrel before the critter could see him draw." Soon, Conner had developed a newfound confidence in his ability to defend himself, a skill that a man who was about to surrender probably wouldn't bother honing.

Back at camp, fear of the inevitable increased like sweat-house heat. Hunger, a growing lack of purpose, and a fear of capture were taking their toll. One morning, Conner awoke early and, as usual, went to a trailer unit to check on the receivers. Another man, one of Conner's best, was on duty, sitting at the desk. A message squawked from one of the Hallicrafter radios. Conner poked the man to suggest he acknowledge the transmission. The man didn't respond. Conner said something to him but, still, no response. Conner waved his hands in front of the man's eyes. The guy kept looking straight ahead, eyes open, alive, but as if frozen by some unseen force of evil.

A doctor said there was nothing they could do for him. The man was taken outside and propped at the base of a palm tree, with banana leaves tucked behind him for padding. He never moved a muscle. Just stared straight ahead, knees bent, as if he were still in the chair, even as men walked by and looked at him. Day after day.

A week later, he would be in the same place and in the same position when the Japanese soldiers descended like screaming locusts.

EIGHT

The Fall of Bataan

April 3, 1942, to April 9, 1942

March 31, 1942

Mrs. Clay Conner,
174 North Grove Street,
East Orange, N.J.

My dear Mrs. Conner:

I have received and appreciate your letter of March 21st.

I wish that it might have fallen to my lot personally to meet your son, Lieutenant Clay Conner Jr. so that I could give you first-hand information about him. Unhappily, I did not run across him and can, therefore, only report to you that our soldiers are doing a wonderful piece of work on Corregidor and in Bataan. America owes to you, parents of sons there, a great debt of gratitude.

Faithfully yours,
Francis B. Sayre
United States High Commissioner to the Philippine Island

═══════

ON APRIL 3, all hell broke loose on Bataan. Some one hundred Japanese aircraft and far more pieces of ground artillery hammered American and Filipino soldiers, turning Mount Samat into a virtual inferno in the process. After a rugged battle, the "rising sun" flag now fluttered atop the mountain, an ominous sign suggesting that the Japanese now controlled the Mariveles Mountains and that the U.S. garrison on Bataan could not hold out much longer. And it didn't. By April 8, the American lines had been broken more than once.

The wounded and weary trickled south into the Little Baguio area where Conner was, first dozens, then hundreds, escaping the pursuit of the Japanese Army. Men who'd seen too much. Bloodied. Hobbled. Some without weapons, their ammo having been depleted long before.

Meanwhile, a buddy of Conner's was among a group of men ordered to fly the air corps' final four planes off Bataan and to the safety of the nearby island of Cebu. Conner hurriedly gave the man a three-word message to have sent home by telegram: "Everything under control."

Conner was ordered to report to Mariveles. Once at the town on the southern tip of Bataan, he heard the familiar thrum of plane props above. In seconds the bombs exploded right and left of him. Five navy men dove into a huge foxhole that had been dug next to one of their buildings. When a bomb landed nearby, the concussion caved in the trench, burying all five alive. Conner helped dig out their bodies.

He gathered with other officers for the hurried briefing. General Jonathan Wainwright had, that morning, ordered three battalions of infantry—about three thousand men—to Corregidor. In addition, he wanted the medical corps sent, too, including all nurses. As a result, the port town of Mariveles churned in chaos, the air thick with diesel exhaust and dust. Trucks, buses, and cars rumbled in from points north, unloading soldiers and nurses. Civilians begged for spots on boats. Children cried. Soldiers dragged bags, equipment, and whatever resolve they could muster, the black, volcanic-ash beach littered with equipment.

All this played out to the unsettling thump of bombs, which echoed and re-echoed off Mariveles's finger-like cliffs in deafening blasts. Amid the commotion, as if frozen within the frenetic madness beyond, a young nurse in army fatigues sobbed. It was Helen Summers, who had spent time with Conner and Rocky in the Empire Room on New Year's Eve. Only moments before, aboard a bus to Mariveles, another nurse, Hattie Brantley, had come to where Summers was sitting. A chaplain wanted to see her.

"Helen," he said, "I'm Chaplain Preston Taylor and I've just come from the Battle of Mount Samat, and—"

"Yes, Chaplain?" said Summers.

"And I met this young lieutenant named Benjamin."

Her eyes brightened. "Yes, *Arnold* Benjamin," she said. "We're going to be married!"

"He's dead, Helen."

The news hit like a hand grenade.

"Oh, God, no," said Summers.

Taylor bowed his head slightly.

"Yesterday, during the battle for Mount Samat."

Brantley put her arms around Summers and hugged her near.

"He wanted to leave you these," said the chaplain.

From his pocket he pulled out a gold watch, a key chain, and a college ring.

Amid the late-afternoon chaos at Mariveles Harbor, nothing suggests Conner saw Summers, who, after boarding a PT boat, managed the faintest of smiles amid a face streaked with tears. But seeing the nurses loaded onto boats to begin a desperate trip to Corregidor stunned Clay. Who, he thought, was going to take care of all these men? "This was it," he wrote. "The higher command realized that it was only a matter of hours."

AT LITTLE BAGUIO, Captain Mason ordered Conner to prepare his men to destroy all equipment when the final word came: cars, trucks, radio equipment, everything. That night, a nearby munitions dump was purposely blown. The blast was so intense it blew Conner flat on his back. Smaller blasts, like firecrackers, snapped and popped nearly all night; the sky fluttered light and dark like a strobe light. The air was stained with the smell of burned powder. Nobody slept much.

The next day, April 9, after Conner headed out to scrounge food, he heard the squawk of the receiver in the trailer. Immediately he recognized the voice of a Captain Bert Bank, a fellow 27th Bomb Group officer who, Conner later wrote, "sounded like a mad man."

"We are retreating from the front lines!" Bank said. "The Japanese have broken through! They are scattering west and east of the main road. The Japanese are almost to Bataan Field. Pull back! Pull back!"

Bank repeated the message over and over. Conner was convinced. He raced to the message center where Captain Mason and a Colonel Gregg were.

"What are we going to do?" Conner asked.

"There's nothing we *can* do," said Mason.

By now the stragglers from the Japanese pursuit to the north had thickened. Thousands of soldiers were arriving at Bataan's southern tip; there was nowhere else for them—for anyone—to go. Conner got the combat men whatever rations he could find and showed them where they could sleep. Gradually, the stories came out. About thousands of Japanese troops pouring through a hole in the American line, bayonets fixed, eyes ablaze. *"Banzai! Banzai! Banzai!"* Crazed soldiers wanting to die for the emperor. "And as they, in droves, ran forward into the barbed wire," Conner wrote, "they formed human bridges of dead bodies as they would project themselves . . . into the face of machine guns. And then the ones behind would climb over the dead bodies of their own men. And finally, they were such an obstacle that the Japs moved their tanks in and crushed the bodies so that more men could come through."

The Japanese had expected to take Luzon in fifty days; the Americans and Filipinos had held out for four months. "But there was nothing left to fight with," wrote Conner. No ammunition. No strength. No energy.

Captain Mason hastily reversed his orders. Now the high command *didn't* want the equipment destroyed. They figured, wrote Conner, that the cars and trucks would be used to "transport us to prison camps, and that the valuable radios and transmitters would be used to relay information to the States concerning our [status]. They figured by turning their equipment over to the Japanese, they would treat us with greater consideration."

Not everybody wanted to be so concessionary. A Captain Bernard Anderson was drumming up support for a flee into the jungles. Anderson, a reserve officer and pilot, had been cobbling together a civilian airline business before war broke out, and he knew Luzon well. The Japanese, he pointed out, were funneling nearer to them on Bataan's main north-south road, along the lowlands stretching to Manila Bay. His plan was to evade capture and, instead, head north into the mountains and avoid the Japanese troops that were heading south. The plan was to link up with a Colonel Claude Thorp, who had established a "spy station" in the Zambales Mountains near Clark Field and Fort Stotsenburg.

Few of the men seemed interested in the idea, least of all Captain Mason and Colonel Gregg, who were older than most of the men and didn't like their chances in rugged terrain that would be crawling with the enemy. Men were tired. Stomachs, empty. Spirits, dead. Some talked of surrender as the only means of surviving; The Geneva Convention, they said, mandated that the Japanese treat prisoners civilly. And how long could it be? Six, eight months in captivity? That wasn't bad.

But Anderson's idea was more intriguing to Conner, the same Conner who had zipped across America in a convertible rather than take the train like everybody else, who had so deeply admired the rogue spirit of Rocky Gause, and who had just had his courage questioned by one of his men.

When the gathering broke up, he walked off with Anderson and peppered him with questions. Thorp, Anderson told him, had been commissioned by MacArthur himself back in January to escape through the front lines with ten men. If successful, they were to establish a headquarters in the Zambales Mountains, from a perch where they could monitor the planes at Clark Field, near the Japanese's main garrison in Fort Stotsenburg. They were to organize guerrilla forces to harass the Japanese. And be prepared to help when the troops returned. Anderson was anxious to join them.

Without the Philippine Scouts the idea was suicidal, said some men. Forget the friggin' enemy; some guys had gotten lost just going to and from Little Baguio's latrine. How were they going to survive a jungle that was one mountain after the next, with ridges as steep as the sides of skyscrapers? If the idea piqued Conner's sense of adventure, he also had great respect for Mason and Gregg—and felt that to leave them would be an abandonment of sorts.

At approximately half past noon, Major General Edward King, after a meeting with Japanese military leaders outside a house in Bataan, removed his .45 pistol and set it on a table. It was official. The United States was surrendering. Meanwhile, as if on autopilot, Conner found himself climbing a flank of Mount Mariveles. He sat on a knoll, looked into the sky, and saw the ever-present clouds that the sergeant had told him about on the deck of the *Coolidge*, as they'd entered Manila Bay. As Conner watched, the winds were shaping and reshaping the white puffs. In moments, their splendor captivated him, pulled him far away from war and fear and—

Wait. The clouds seemed to be forming something that looked familiar. Bataan. It was as if Conner were looking at the island on a fluffy map, as if it were offering—as maps do—direction. Finally, the clouds began breaking up from inside, leaving distinct blue sky in what appeared to be the upper reaches of the Bataan Peninsula. Of course! The Zambales. The place where Thorp and his men had gone.

Clay Conner had never followed much beyond his mind's compass; he was a pragmatist. You need money, you go sell Fuller Brushes. You see the boats on fire in Manila Bay, you go around the bay. "I was no 'sign reader,'" he said. But this was different. It was as if something—someone? God?—were telling him: *Go. Here. Now.*

CONNER SCURRIED DOWN the pitched slope. He desperately favored an escape attempt, but first he tracked down Captain Mason. He needed approval—no, something deeper than that: a blessing. He found Mason in their makeshift headquarters, already sweating hard in the morning heat. The sound of rifles cracked in the distance, occasionally overlaid with machine-gun chatter.

"Would it be all right," he asked with a sense of urgency, "if I wanted to go with Captain Anderson? Would you object?"

If the stakes weren't a tad higher, he might as well have been asking his dad back in Jersey if he could borrow the car.

"No," said Mason. He looked tired. "No, I wouldn't object. It's every man for himself now. General [Edward] King has already been taken by the Japs. We just got word and, officially, you're on your own. You're no longer under the command of the United States Army."

Conner's edgy spirit grew even bolder. Mason bowed his head and placed his hands on his face.

"We've been taken," the captain said. "We're through." He looked up. "But let me tell you this. I've been in Bataan for many years, on maneuvers, Clay. And if you want my advice, don't try it."

It was as if someone had pulled the plug on a juke box. "What do you mean?" asked Conner.

"You don't realize how rough, how rugged, how many places that are absolutely impossible to get through in those treacherous craters and canyons and jungles of Mount Mariveles," he said. "You'll never make it. It's impossible."

Conner didn't want to hear any more, but Mason had more to say. "The front lines are mined, and the Japs are there. They'll be all through the area. Your chances are one in a million."

"But what about the way we've already seen the Japanese treat some of our men?" said Conner. "What about the severed heads in that tank? They'll kill us."

"It's safer to stay and be captured with the rest of us," said Mason. "Remember, there's safety in numbers. They can't kill us all."

Much as he respected Mason, Conner couldn't bring himself to bend to the man's will, as if what he'd seen in the clouds above Mariveles had a stronger, insurmountable pull.

Anderson arrived. "I've gotta grab some gear and round up a few others," he said. "I'll swing by to see if you're going."

Conner tried to rouse some support for the idea of going it on their own. "Boboski," he said to one of his men, "do you want to go?"

The sergeant shook his head no. "I was leery," he later said, "because I thought the chances of survival there were very slim, if any chance at all." Conner looked to another. "D'ya want to—"

"No."

Others looked down or away; not one of Conner's men dared to follow. "They didn't have any confidence in me," he wrote later. "I was twenty-three. We were heading up a mountain full of pythons and wild boar and savages. Why would they go with me instead of going with 15,000 to surrender?"

Anderson had hardly left when the men heard it: the grinding of tanks to the east, on the Old Highway. The muted cries of "*Banzai!*" The screaming zing of bombs from above, which, with the tropical forest now drying out, roiled flames through the jungle like dragon's breath. Hundreds of shells pounded down, the noise like the climax of a Fourth of July fireworks show back home. Clouds of acrid smoke hung in the air. Men scattered for cover. Vaguely, through that smoke, Conner saw them: American and Filipino soldiers waving anything they had that was even remotely white—rags, T-shirts—on the end of bamboo poles. Whatever said: *We surrender*. Here and there, soldiers frantically dug holes and buried rings and watches. To hell with that; more cynical soldiers flung their valuables into the thick jungle, knowing they were never coming back here—or, for that matter, back to anywhere—but not about to let the conquerors get their possessions.

In the distance, the machine-gun fire intensified. The ghostly silhouettes of Japanese soldiers emerged from the jungle haze. Mason leaned against a tree with a white undershirt in his hand. He was about to become part of what history would remember as the greatest defeat ever suffered by a U.S. force in the field: seventy-five thousand men surrendering to the enemy. Conner nodded a thank-you to his mentor. Mason extended a hand to shake. "Good luck, Clay," he said.

Conner scurried to the ramshackle headquarters. In his musette bag he madly stuffed seven cans of C rations, two pairs of socks, a couple of handkerchiefs, bandages, iodine, a blanket, a mosquito net, and, of course, Junko. He strapped it all together and threw it on his back.

He met up with Anderson and five others. "Move out," said Anderson.

They slalomed through the jungle and soon were traversing the steepening eastern flank of Mount Mariveles. Conner was running on adrenaline. His chino shirt and trousers were soaked with sweat, which drew mosquitoes like a dinner bell. Last in line, he stopped to slow the panting, then continued on. Nobody said much of anything. Just the sound of footsteps in the jungle tangle, of breathing, and of leaves being thwacked from side to side.

At nightfall, the seven bedded down atop a small hill. They wanted to start a fire and cook, but the flames would be a dead giveaway. Conner tied the four corners of his mosquito net to bushes and spread out his blanket. Exhausted, stomach aching for food, he crawled beneath it. Not exactly the sleeping porch at the Sigma Phi Epsilon house or even the tattered headquarters the Filipino boy had made for him. But, for tonight, home.

In the distance, the roar of bombs and machine guns had given way to the silence of surrender. In some ways, the quiet carried with it a more sinister sound than war, the emptiness giving breath to the imagination's darker side. In the night, rain began falling. "I woke up," wrote Conner, "with a sense of panic." Until training in Georgia, he had never even camped out. "I was a concrete New York cliff dweller," he later wrote. "I lived in the upper floor of an apartment most of my life. You can imagine what I knew of guns or anything else. My adventure was in a convertible at Duke University." He was, in essence, exactly the kind of American soldier the Japanese highlighted in their propaganda: inexperienced, not particularly courageous "mama's boys," allegations hard to refute. Now he was challenging a jungle that the famous animal collector Frank Buck had called the densest in the world.

If leaving San Francisco on the *Coolidge* had been leaving a semblance of certainty—if fleeing Manila had been fleeing an approaching enemy, at least the going had been done en masse. Comfort in numbers, as his men had said earlier in the day. Now Conner lay in a jungle with six strangers, one of them already snoring like a muffler-busted chain saw. Whatever traction in life he'd once had was gone. The challenge had initially been a far-off war that, when seen from a distance, evoked more thrill than threat; then, at Manila, a case in which he at least knew who and where his enemy was.

Now everything had changed: The terrain. The numbers. The mission. The men around him. The supplies. And Conner's very identity; officially, he was no longer under the command of the U.S. Army. But what had changed most was the enemy, which was now not only an almond-colored man with a rifle, but something even more threatening.

The unknown.

He closed his eyes on a day that ultimately would define much of his life. A day of doubt. A day of decision. A day that began his quest to see if Colonel Mason's concerns would prove prophetic or if Conner were, indeed, that one in a million.

NINE

Into the Wild

April 10, 1942, to April 20, 1942

May 14, 1942

Mrs. Clay Conner
174 North Grove Street
East Orange, New Jersey

Dear Mrs. Conner:

I wish to thank you for your kind letter of May 9th. I am sorry to say that I have no information regarding your son, Lieutenant Henry Clay Conner Jr.

Sincerely,
John D. Bulkeley,
Lieutenant, U.S.N.

IN 1930, A large American lumber company scrapped its logging and milling operations on Bataan, driven out not by the peninsula's steep,

thick-foliaged terrain or Negrito warriors, but by disease—and the mosquitoes that carried much of it. Dengue fever, dysentery, skin fungus—the
Bataan jungles were breeding grounds for all sorts of microscopic enemies
whose attacks could, at best, make life miserable for a man and, at worst,
kill him. If it wasn't mosquitoes carrying malaria, it was flies spreading
dysentery, one minute feasting on an open-pit toilet, the next minute a
corpse, then winding up on some poor soldier's C rations.

Conner awoke the next morning suffering from just such an attack—
or so it seemed. At sunup, as the group of seven headed out, his stomach
rumbled like the chop of a wind-whipped ocean. He began the day second
in line to Anderson, but frequent stops to discharge the diarrhea soon
forced him well to the back. It wasn't enough that he was sick; he was
sick while trying to keep up with desperate, fast-paced strangers with
whom he was making a lousy first impression. Men in no mood to even
joke about slapping on a pair of diapers and hurrying his butt up. Men
who, when he asked them to slow down, simply ignored him. Conner
hadn't even been gone a full day and Mason's "every man for himself"
line was already proving true.

By nightfall Conner was too tired to even set up his mosquito net.
The other men ate and talked quietly. Conner had no appetite, little
energy, and only tenuous connection with them. He offered up his C
rations; the others gladly took the tin-can concoctions of meat and beans,
or meat and potato hash.

Anderson decided to break the men into three groups to expedite
travel: Conner was paired with a private, Ernest Kelly, a 27th Bomb Group
guy. Rugged. Outdoorsy. Even had a compass, which was more than
Conner could claim. And, best of all—from Clay's standpoint—Kelly
was willing to put up with a guy who'd quickly become the group's walk-
and-squat straggler.

As the day wore on, the hiking only worsened Conner's condition,
which he'd initially thought was simply diarrhea but later realized was
dysentery. The more he sweated, the thirstier he got. The thirstier he got,
the more water he drank from streams. And the more he drank, the more

aggravated the condition got. Finally, Kelly had no choice but to move on without him, at least for a while.

Conner was alone in the jungles of Luzon.

JUST LIKE THAT. A Jersey boy seven thousand miles from home, a kid who could tie a tennis sweater around his neck but didn't know a bowline from a half hitch. Now alone. "I was afraid," he wrote. By itself, that would not doom him; a healthy amount of fear often translated into necessary caution. But what might doom him was wrong thinking. "Whether with a group or alone, you will experience emotional problems resulting from fear, despair, loneliness, and boredom," said *The U.S Army Survival Manual*. "In addition to these mental hazards, injury and pain, fatigue, hunger, or thirst, tax your will to live. If you are not prepared mentally to overcome all obstacles and accept the worst, the chances of coming out alive are greatly reduced."

Conner pressed on. Long days. Longer nights. He couldn't keep any food down. What's more, he realized his pack was far too heavy and making a bad situation worse. He jettisoned extra socks, medicine, bandages, blanket, and more. With his knife, he sliced his mosquito netting in half. All he had left, basically, was the net, a few odds and ends, and Junko. Whether it was a good luck charm, habit, or his last reminder of home, he could not part with the stuffed monkey.

The terrain, Conner realized, was everything Mason had said it would be—and more. As if that weren't bad enough, he decided to stay high, in the steeper stuff, to avoid detection by Japanese soldiers who, he assumed, would be prowling for escapees. The pattern became as monotonous as it was difficult: up the south side of a one- to three-thousand-foot ridge, down the north. Across a stream. Repeat. No trail. Tangles of vines. Fighting through jungle leaves that could be like brushing back wet canvas. All while skirting gorges that fell off as decidedly as the side of the *Coolidge*.

On the third day, his canteen was empty, and in lower elevations, he resorted to drinking water that had collected in carabao footprints from the last downpour. Meanwhile, the slow going forced him into a potential trap: When darkness hit, he was nowhere near water and high up on a razor-sharp ridge. But he had to stop; he was spent. The night was moonless. In the inky blackness, Conner found himself on his hands and knees, moving along almost as if he were a snake. Knowing he couldn't go any farther for now and sensing he might be on the edge of an abyss, he slid his musette bag's strap through a hole in what felt like a dead tree trunk, wrapped it around himself, fastened it, and promptly fell asleep. In the morning, he awoke and looked down: He had slept on a live tree trunk that extended out over what looked like a five-hundred-foot-deep canyon. Gingerly, he shinnied back to solid ground.

Then he saw it: smoke from the bottom of the canyon. Someone had a fire going. Conner figured that someone was a group of Americans. He worked himself down a less-steep pitch of the ridge. It was, Conner soon realized, Anderson and the six others, including Kelly.

"Hey, up here!" Conner yelled to them, then scurried down to their camp.

"Look, Conner, these jungles are full of Japs," said Anderson in whispered rage. "Every time you go hollering around like that you're asking for all of us to get killed. Now get this: The next time you pull that, you're on your own."

The scolding wounded Conner, but also awakened him to the realization that the terrain couldn't be his only concern. Nor could his own pathetic health, which, by this, the fourth day, was improving. Much as the warning hurt, Anderson was right. He had to be more attuned to Japanese soldiers, lest he wind up a prisoner as thousands of others back in the lowlands undoubtedly had.

One of the men shared his breakfast with Conner. Kelly said he'd hike with Clay again. All in all, the brief reunion refocused and reenergized Conner, even if, as they continued on, Kelly was still clearly more at ease with thwacking his way through this jungle than Clay was. The two other groups were far ahead; Kelly and Conner followed. By now, the routine had been worn into them: Trudge forward. Climb ridges. All this while listening for the enemy—scurrying iguanas fooled them more than once—and while being careful not to get lazy with foot plants on slopes. "Every step," wrote Conner, "could have been our last. The cliffs dropped off for hundreds of feet underneath us."

In the afternoon, they reached a vantage point that afforded them a view east of Manila Bay. If it was uplifting to finally gain perspective, it was discouraging to see what that perspective actually meant: In four days they hadn't traveled much more than ten miles. And the going wasn't getting any easier. Kelly managed to get through a steep slope of loose shale—a gorge gaped below—but when Conner crossed the same swath of rock, it gave way, triggering a small landslide that slowly took Clay with it. "[Kelly] just stared at me," Conner wrote. "I could see he wanted to reach out, but it was no use." Conner's only hope was to cling to the shale-sided slope like a suction cup on a window and slowly slide his way down to safety.

He did so. But when the two reunited at a stream at the base of the gorge, he told Kelly that was it. Cramps were knifing his stomach every few minutes. His legs and hands were bloodied. The two had made less than a mile for the whole day. "No more mountains," Conner said.

Kelly agreed. It was the first time since Conner had left that anyone had landed on his side of any issue. But when the pair headed east in an attempt to skirt another mountain, they encountered something for the first time: a Japanese patrol. Panic surged through Conner's veins; he had never seen the enemy up close like this before. Maybe thirty men, Conner figured, all "jabbering" as they walked single-file through the jungle. Had even one of them glanced in the direction of Kelly and Conner, the two might have been seen.

That night, they agreed on having a small fire for the first time, to heat some C rations. Kelly built it. Meanwhile, Conner walked to a nearby stream for cooking water. A few minutes later, Kelly, too, headed for the stream—at the same moment Conner saw a ten-man Japanese patrol crossing the water just downstream. He couldn't warn Kelly; all he could do was hope he wouldn't break into conversation or make undue noise. Kelly did neither. He, too, saw the men and froze in his tracks.

One afternoon, two close calls. The pair had now been at this for a week—it was April 16, 1942—and found themselves at what had been the front-line area stretching to either side of the Pilar-Bagac Road. Conner had seen a different section of this weeks before: no-man's-land, ground zero for the worst of the fighting that came and went. Bodies tangled with the foliage of the jungle floor. The deserted trenches ghostlike in the jungle quiet: Here, the contorted corpse of an American soldier, draped on a splintered mango tree; there, the bodies of two others sprawled in a trench strewn with cans, blown-to-bits radios, scattered paper, and more. Buzzards picked at corpses, the silence of death watched over by giant maniknik trees, guardians of the killing grounds.

What kept Conner going was his belief that MacArthur and his men would be back soon. Three weeks, he figured.

AMID PALM TREES decapitated by heavy artillery fire, the two rummaged through the trenches the Americans had been in, looking for anything they could use, particularly food and ammunition. They even resorted to going through the pockets of the dead. "The stink was almost unbearable," wrote Conner. But the hell of war was that they got used to it. They had to stay; it was daylight, and to move across this no-man's-land in daylight was to set themselves up for being killed or captured. So they waited for the darkness and moved on, narrowly avoiding a couple of Japanese trucks and soldiers that came down the road.

Eventually, they hoped to link with an outfit headed by Colonel Thorp, somewhere in northern Bataan or southern Zambales or Pampanga Province. Across the road, they came to the Japanese trenches. "Filth from top to bottom," wrote Conner. Not only had the soldiers slept, ate, and fought in these trenches, but they had used them for latrines. The two found sacks of rice, but mosquitoes, bugs, and flies hovered in a cloud. Conner's stomach lurched. He and Kelly looked at each other and, without a word, kept moving north. Only this time, faster, an occasional burst of machine-gun fire or crack of a rifle in the distance.

Conner endured a sleepless night, his mind lost in delirium. In the morning, the two continued on. Conner again lagged behind. First, ten yards. Then a hundred. Then a quarter mile. He lost sight of Kelly every once in a while, then stopped and braced himself against a bamboo tree, fighting for breath. "The thought going through my mind," he wrote, "was, 'I've got to go on. I've got to take another step. I'm going to die if I don't.'"

At this rate, he thought, death at the hands of the Japanese was less likely than death by starvation or sickness or exhaustion. "There had been nothing in my education at Duke University to cover jungle craft such as I needed now," he wrote.

Finally, he caught up to his waiting partner. They ate. And, before darkness descended, Conner pulled out the New Testament that Edwards had given him. Strangely, the words soothed him. "I found a peace in them," he wrote.

Not that there was much time for spiritual reflection. The two slogged northward, the relatively flat land now giving way to the kind of mountains and ravines that had marked their earlier days. There was not always a "lowland choice." Up they went. Morning cool gave way to afternoon heat, dry shirts to wet shirts. Eventually, they found a river and headed down it with trepidation; Kelly pointed out that rivers almost always led to civilization and, in their case, the probability of Japanese troops.

By morning, Conner and Kelly were in rolling hills. Orchards. Fruit trees. Conner was starved—his 150-pound frame now carried what he figured was less than 100 pounds—but soldiers had picked the banana and guava trees clean. Soon, Conner and Kelly came upon a house of Filipinos, who, it turned out, were friendly and spoke English. Had the two men, the Filipinos wanted to know, escaped from "the death march"?

"No," said Conner. "What's the 'death march'?"

The Filipinos told them that several days before, thousands upon thousands of Filipino and American prisoners of war had been marched north up the Old National Road out of Bataan. They had seen the men, in the town of Abucay, as they trudged by, baked by the sun, bayonet tips at their backs. Thousands had died, some having been stabbed, starved, or tortured. "They had been forced to walk all day on the hot roads without water," wrote Conner, "and at night they had been jammed into small barbed-wire enclosures, forced to sleep on one another. Those that couldn't walk, were chopped up with machine guns and left on the side of the road for the dogs to eat."

SERGEANT BATO, AFTER the surrender at Morong, had eluded capture. He packed the tattered American flag in his musette bag and headed for the high country. In days marked by hunger, exhaustion, and thirst—water was rare up high—Bato climbed up and over the Zambales Mountains, a few days' walk from where Conner was now. He threaded his way through pockets of Japanese soldiers and finally reached his family in the barrio of Sapang Bato, near Fort Stotsenburg, having traveled some forty miles to the lowlands north of the Bataan Peninsula. His story of saving the flag touched his wife. Without delay, she put it inside a pillowcase that she placed in the family chest.

Soon, Japanese soldiers rifled through the barrio on a raid. Bato was captured and, with thousands of others—Filipino and American—forced to nearby Camp O'Donnell, a Philippine Army camp that the Japanese had taken over. For decades, it had been an obscure military post. But in time, it would gain notoriety for being one of the gruesome last stops on the death march.

The Enemies Within

April 21, 1942, to September 1942

Time in the jungle since the Fall of Bataan:
Two weeks to five months

Aug. 30, 1942

Nurse Quarters
Mitchel Field, Long Island

Dear Mrs. Conner:

Although I only met your son once, I believe I can tell you a little about him.

First of all, even though the cablegrams were addressed from Cebu, it didn't necessarily mean he was there. You see, Cebu was the only place we could send cablegrams from, and the air corps officers flew down there [when] they went to Cebu for quinine.

Clay was introduced to me by a girlfriend of mine on Bataan. If I remember correctly, it was on New Year's Eve [1941]. Although I didn't know him before the war, he looked well and was very cheerful. I don't recall meeting him again after that.

I'm sorry I can't be of more help to you.

Sincerely,
Helen L. Summers

CONNER WAS TRAVERSING the side of a steep ridge when he saw it dug into the foliage: a sniper's position that left him in fear and awe. He'd seen toeholds chiseled into mountainsides where he didn't think a toehold was possible. And an eagle's-nest howitzer placed on such a precarious perch that he marveled at how it had gotten there. The Japanese, it had become clear, had used these same mountains while battering American positions before the surrender. And had obviously done so with great skill and agility. "Each time I came across these signs, a new panic would grip me and I would plunge ahead a little faster," he wrote.

During one such plunge, on April 21, Conner tripped over a vine and tumbled to the bottom of a small ravine. As he got up, he saw a young Filipino man staring at him. No shoes. No shirt. A gunnysack over his back, a straw hat on his head, a smile on his face, and a hand extended in friendship.

"You are sick," he said in broken English. "You had better come with me."

His name was Margarito Silva. Conner, hailing the nearby Kelly, accepted the offer; after all, if the young man had been the enemy, wouldn't he have just killed Clay? "I have several Americans living with me, and I'm supporting them," said Margarito in poor man's English. "I have just been to the lowlands, and I have gotten food for them. We will be glad to have you."

For men who had barely eaten in two weeks—and whose bony bodies showed it—the offer was inviting. Conner and Kelly followed him on a trail to a spot near the Orani River. Margarito crossed the river with an ease that amazed the weary Conner, as if the young Filipino were a human skipping stone. Behind a wall of underbrush five little thatched-roof huts nestled deep in the forest green. They had been built by the Filipinos to escape the killings, the confusion, the mistreatment from Japanese soldiers, whom Margarito said he hated.

It would be the pair's first stop on Bataan's "underground railroad." Two Americans were already there—beyond the Anderson group, the first Americans Conner and Kelly had seen since their seven-man party had left Little Baguio: Ray Schletterer, twenty-eight, from Galton, Pennsylvania, and Hayden "Larry" Lawrence, twenty-five, from Buckeye, Louisiana. Both were out of the 17th Tank Ordnance.

The four shared stories about what they had in common: the trip over from San Francisco, the Japanese attack, their escapes. But Conner was tired. And still sick. Silva gave him a little rice and a handful of sugar, and led him to one of the shacks, where Clay slept. He'd been in the jungle for two weeks. "For the first time since the escape, I had somewhat of a peaceful feeling," he wrote.

Hours later, noises in the jungle snapped him awake. Footsteps. Labored breathing. Getting louder. Getting closer. Conner reached for his pistol, then saw two men: a tall, raw-boned young man drenched in sweat from carrying a bloodied-to-the-bone man on his back. Americans. Best he could, Conner helped set down the semiconscious man, and then he extended a hand.

"Clay Conner," he said.

"Frank Gyovai," said the newcomer, pronouncing his last name Gu-VAY. "Got one more. I'll be back."

Conner looked at the wounded man. "He was so weak he could barely talk," remembered Conner, "and was delirious. All he could talk about, when he did open his mouth, was how the Japs had beaten him." He had escaped the march and Gyovai had come across him. Apparently, this kid, Gyovai, had kept two other guys from dying.

When Gyovai returned with yet another all-but-gone American, he and Conner had a chance to talk. Gyovai was out of the 17th Tank Ordnance. He'd quit high school in Red Dragon, West Virginia, to work with his Hungarian-born dad in the coal mines. One of those rangy, tough kids who looked like he could whip a water buffalo one-handed. About six-foot-two and 185 pounds. And easy to like. If Conner was a thinker, Gyovai was a doer. But despite their differences, they would soon be bound by things far deeper.

A FEW OTHER Americans wandered into the makeshift camp: Pierce Wade, from Georgia, and Eddie Keith Jr., of Gary, Indiana—all six-foot-five inches of him. Both, like Schletterer and Lawrence and Gyovai, were from the 17th Tank Ordnance. So was Jim Boyd, from Sweetwater, Texas. The newcomers were rounded out by a Filipino, Jimmy Espino, and a guy named Alvin Ingram, who had escaped the death march. Gaunt. Hoarse. Literally speechless, his eyes fixed in the proverbial thousand-yard stare. A spark would pop in the fire, and while lying on his side, the man would scurry like a spooked cat. Nobody knew the name of the first soldier Gyovai had brought in.

In the days to come, whatever relief and encouragement this gathering had provided gave way to troublesome realities: The place wasn't big enough for all of them. Lawrence, Conner realized, despised any man in officer's insignia, which didn't bode well for Clay, the only officer in the bunch.

Kelly left on his own. So did Gyovai, Pierce, Keith, Ingram, and the other beaten man. Conner was still too listless to move on. Day after day, Lawrence complained about officers, muttering about how they had hoarded food before the surrender. Sounded familiar to Conner. One day, he overheard Lawrence telling Schletterer that "Conner is a yellow belly" and threatening to kill Clay.

Conner—weak, hungry, and facing the growing reality that he'd contracted malaria—had had it. From inside his hut, he opened the flap on his holster and checked to make sure he had a bullet in the pistol's chamber, then slipped the weapon back in. He buckled the belt around his waist and tied the holster to his leg. He walked outside, a bravado-fueled

Bataan version of all those on-screen western stars whose "fast-draw and fire" Clay so admired, though this one so fever-racked he could hardly stand up.

"Were you talking to me?" he said, looking at Lawrence and his scruffy red hair.

"Yeah."

"What do you propose to do?" Conner asked.

"Kill you."

Conner was so tense he thought he'd wet his pants, but he couldn't back down.

"Then you better get the job done."

The two stared at each other, then Lawrence got up and walked away. Conner turned to the few men left. "Do all you feel the same way about officers?" he asked. "Do you feel that same way about me?"

Nobody spoke. Conner had his answer. He nodded his head slowly, then gathered his gear and headed out. He'd rather be alone in the jungles of Bataan then be with men who didn't trust him—and whom he didn't trust. He climbed a hill and lay down. Despite the afternoon heat, a coldness clinched him like a vise. Soon, Espino approached and offered to move north with him.

"No," said Conner, "I don't think I can, Jimmy. I'm in pain right now. I've got chills or something—maybe sunstroke."

Espino left. Conner was again on his own.

THE DEATH MARCH may have been over, but it left disease in its bloody tracks. The Japanese had blown up dams and dikes in the swampy area, leaving stagnant water everywhere. Winds blew south down Luzon's mid-section, bringing with them clouds of mosquitoes—and, thus, malaria and other diseases. Thousands of refugees clustered in camps without shelter, often without food. Germ-laden mosquitoes hopped from person to person, then drifted eastward, whipped by thermal winds headed for the hills. And, once again, for Clay Conner.

It was here, on May 1, 1942, where Conner found refuge in the barrio of Tala on the lower flank of a mountain, near the top of the Bataan Peninsula and about five miles inland from Manila Bay. It was here that two Filipino brothers, Francisco and Agado, invited Conner to stay as he faced another bout of malaria. By now, death and disease visited daily. The unknown man who had escaped the death march died, the Filipinos told him. Francisco was laid low by malaria; so, too, were two of his children.

Agado helped get water for his brother and for Clay; food, once again, was not agreeing with Conner. But if he appreciated the help, Conner tired of Tala's commotion. Francisco shook incessantly from the effects of malaria. His four-year-old son babbled all day, apparently suffering from some sort of cerebral palsy. "*Eyoko, eyoko,*" he'd repeat over and over. ("I don't like it, I don't like it.") The noise made it nearly impossible for Clay to sleep; malaria may have been his biggest challenge, but that was just one problem amid many: exhaustion, diarrhea, exposure, and hunger.

Finally, Conner drew a picture in the dirt for Agado—Clay spoke none of the Tagalog language that the Filipinos did—in an attempt to say: *I need to be alone.* Agado motioned for Conner to follow him. He led him on a long trail, at the end of which was a grass hut. "Here," Agado said. He patted Clay on the shoulder and left. Conner tied his mosquito netting to the four posts anchoring the hut, a small task that nevertheless exhausted him. He filled his canteen from the nearby stream, drank, took off his pistol belt, and, using his holster for a pillow, fell fast asleep. He awoke in the night and lay there, beneath the moon, wondering what he should do. What he could do. In the morning, he tried to get to the stream to cool off—he was on fire—but his legs would not hold him. He could hardly lift his head. His skin wrapped around his bones like cellophane; his estimated weight was about seventy-two pounds. "I was done," he wrote.

Conner's mind was a tangle of jungle roots, his thoughts flitting from food back home to the trip over on the *Coolidge* to Mason's words, which now threatened to prove true: *You'll never make it.* And then he was suddenly back at the forested pathways of Duke.

"I wondered how two worlds could exist on the same earth, and be so far removed, one from another," he later wrote. "Duke with all its happiness and freedom and life; and this. This was confining, filled with sickness, rot, decay, and death. It was almost impossible for me to believe that these two situations existed at the same time."

Conner stopped himself. He was, he realized, languishing in his own pity. After hearing a stirring in the underbrush, he was greeted by "the beautiful friendly face of Agado." Never mind the man's teeth blackened because of his appetite for betel nuts, a peppery-tasting seed from a certain type of palm trees, Clay found him a welcome sight. As much as he wanted to be alone, Conner had, in his self-imposed exile, felt forgotten. Now Agado, in broken English accompanied by hand signs, reminded Conner that suffering wasn't Clay's alone. Of the three thousand people in the nearby town of Samal, two-thirds had already died of disease. "These people were already hardened to war," Conner wrote.

We are, Agado seemed to be saying, *in this together*. "Come," he said, knowing Conner couldn't survive on the hillside by himself but also allowing the American to realize that on his own. Agado took down Clay's mosquito netting, gathered the rest of his stuff, put his arm around Clay, and slowly walked him back to the village. Agado showed Conner to a bamboo lean-to. For the most part, Agado and his family left Conner alone, as he'd originally wanted, though they brought him water and bananas. Clay was riper than jungle rot. Agado's wife, Maria, washed his clothes, leaving him under a blanket until she returned from the river hours later with crisp, dry pants and shirt. It was a small gesture, but the clean clothes buoyed Clay's spirits considerably. Still, by midday the chills returned. His muscles tightened. The fever sent his body into rages of sweat. Conner again drifted into delirium. When he awoke, he made out the blurry outline of a man unlike any other Conner had seen: a Negrito, he would later learn. Black. Short. Mysterious. And wearing only a loin-cloth. He had come at the request of Francisco and Agado.

He squatted in front of Conner and grunted a few times. Then he brewed an herb called dita, and offered it to Clay to drink. Conner had nothing to lose. He drained the cup. And later he took some more that the little man had left him. For two days Conner threw back the bitter liquid. On the third day he awoke and no longer felt like a man on fire one minute and on ice the next. The fever and chills were gone.

Conner gained strength and, as he did, a new perspective. It was the same squalid gathering of humanity around him—and the same worn-to-the-edge Clay—but now, for some reason, Conner saw this place not as nuisance but as necessity, not hellhole but haven. "It was a thrill to see the life of those little children now," he wrote.

Somehow, he was alive. All because of this Negrito who had vanished as suddenly as he had appeared.

CHILLS. FEVER. AFTER weeks of better health, a new strain of malaria was eating away at Conner. By now, Tala was like a jungle-draped hospital of which Conner seemed to be a permanent patient. One night, at dusk, a colonel stumbled into the camp in a state of near shock. Clothes torn and dirty. Starved. He'd been traveling the highest country to avoid being caught, but had finally been driven down because he was out of matches and couldn't start a fire. Others in Tala were no less desperate, including Harry Porter, a beanpole from Kentucky, where Clay's grandfather had lived. The two had much in common. The Kentucky connection. The flight to the mountains just before the Japanese arrived. And the malaria, which had leveled them both.

Though clean shaven, Porter's face had the skeletal bent of a man four times his age. He had perhaps 110 or 115 pounds on his lanky frame, Conner estimated. Not much, even if it was 20 to 25 more than Clay had on his.

Conner welcomed Porter to the lean-to; it wasn't much, he pointed out, but enough to cut down on the jungle cold at night. Porter gladly accepted. To stay warm they slept under burlap sacks. "It was hard to sleep, night after night, as skinny as we were because [the] bones of our hips, and elbows, and backs and shoulders were all sticking through our skin," Conner later wrote. "Sleeping on that hard bamboo was almost like sleeping on a torture bed. Every few minutes we would have to roll over to let another place on our body take the beating."

When a young, English-speaking Filipino offered to fetch them medicine from the lowlands, the two parties struck a deal. But though the young man returned with the medicine, he refused to give Conner the change—and demanded Conner's Bulova watch. The one his folks had given him, the one that was now so loose that he had to wear it well up his arm to keep it from slipping off.

"No, I can't do that," said Conner.

"You might as well, sir," said the Filipino. "It isn't going to do you any good. You're going to die anyway."

It was bravado born of the realization that neither Conner nor Porter had the energy to sit up, much less walk or run should they want to give chase. Conner looked at the boy, then at Porter to divert the young man's attention. In a flash, he pulled the gun from his holster so fast the young man's eyes bulged in panic. Conner got his change—and the medicine, Atabrine. It was something that Conner had taken before the surrender and that had kept away the disease. He took four tablets and gave the other four to Porter.

After nearly a week, Conner called for Maria and Agado. He felt good enough to try walking: Would they bring him some bamboo poles to use as canes? At first, he lurched forward and almost fell. But, slowly, he found his balance. Each day for ten days, he practiced, at times with the help of Jimmy Espino, who had returned. Each day, he walked farther, his biggest worry not that he would fall down but that his pants would, his body now skin on bones.

And yet for the first time he found himself happy. His appetite returned. He began learning Tagalog with Francisco, whose malaria was dissipating, too. Maria brought pencil and paper to help with the language. He began thinking about the possibilities of somehow getting to Australia and out of this mess. By June 1, he could tell the Filipinos—in their own language—that he was hungry, tired, feeling better, whatever the case might be.

"For the first time [since hitting the jungle] we were learning to think for ourselves," he wrote. "If we were to live, it was not going to be because somebody was doing our thinking for us." They pored over maps of the country and read every book Jimmy could get for them. "The Bible, too, came in for some serious discussions," Conner wrote. "I read it myself eight times, and had scores of questions I wanted answered by some competent authority."

The brush with death had steeled him to a deeper purpose. "No longer was I thoughtlessly ready to jump at every chance to receive personal happiness and self-satisfaction like some inconsiderate college scamp," he wrote in a journal shortly thereafter, "but I deeply desired to take my place in the world and do something beneficial for my fellow man. I knew that if I accomplished this satisfactorily I would no longer be reluctant to meet journey's end, but be ready, with pleasure, to take my rest in eternity."

IN TALA, THE rains began June 10, about two months since the escape. Dirt became mud. Vegetation seemingly grew overnight. The Filipinos reveled in the wetness, which cleansed the village and made the fruit grow. By July, the rains were heavier—as was Conner, whose newfound appetite and better food, including eggs and fried potatoes, sent his weight to record highs before he began doing calisthenics to keep in shape. Because of his skinniness, Conner had taken off his Duke class ring and watch; now, he wore them again. For the first time there, a rhythm filled his days. He had expectations. Goals. Challenges. Even if there was a certain solemnity to one such challenge: taking care of Porter, whose health had worsened.

Conner began a journal, recording everything that had happened since he'd fled Manila for Bataan, and getting a promise from Francisco that he would hide it for him until the war was over; it would be impossible for Clay to carry it when he moved on, which he knew he must do. He continued reading the New Testament each morning when he awakened and each evening before dark. The words of that book, he discovered, were changing him in interesting ways, notably when it came to fear. "There was none left," he wrote. "I lost all fear of dying."

In a precursor to a pattern that would often repeat, other "lost" Americans found their way to camp: Gyovai, Boyd, Wade, Ingram—guys he knew—and a Captain Vinnette and a Jerry Dunlap, whom he did not. They all, too, seemed to be doing well. The Filipinos would awaken at dawn and fix coffee made of burned rice and cook other rice, placing it on banana leaves for the soldiers to eat. The natives would offer them other kinds of food: wild boar, fish, guava, bananas.

In exchange, the soldiers did tasks to help the village. The good-natured Gyovai carried water from the stream on a jig-pole and villagers would dip it out in coconut shells when they needed some. Wade helped cook, gather crops, and pound rice. Others took their turn at the mallets, too, beating the rice in a tub carved into a cup shape from the trunk of a tree. "The men," wrote Conner, "became almost like the natives. They were a friendly group."

In particular, Conner built a bond with Gyovai and Dunlap. Dunlap was a twenty-one-year-old kid from Winthrop, Iowa—Conner would turn twenty-four in August—who'd grown a little goatee. He was neat, clean, courteous—and yet, like a few others, still struggled to shake a jungle disease stuck to him like a leach. Likewise, dengue fever had hit Conner with a vengeance. Clay was soon down with a headache, fever, and muscle and joint pain. His weight plummeted again. So did his spirits. Sleep was virtually impossible. Life became the monotony of lying on his back and sweating profusely. But Wade came to Conner's camp every day to take care of him, bringing him soup. Finally, after nine days, Conner got over it.

On July 15, he was awakened by a Filipino who lived in the house where Jerry Dunlap was living. "Lieutenant Conner," he said, "my friend

Jerry has died." Conner put on his pistol belt and followed the Filipino. "[Jerry] was stretched out there on his blanket in the place where he had been sleeping the night before," wrote Conner. "And he was peaceful. All the pain was gone."

A grave was dug on the brink of a hill, overlooking Manila Bay. A handful of men carried Dunlap's body to the resting place. This was a first for the men: a funeral. A first for Conner, a kid whose hands, which not long ago had been wrapped around the steering wheel of a convertible zipping across America, now had dirt beneath the fingernails from digging a friend's grave. Nobody knew quite what to do, Conner among them. But he reached into his pocket and pulled out his New Testament, opened it at random and began to read. "And all the Americans stood there, looking down at [Dunlap]," he later wrote. "They turned and walked away. And I stayed while they covered him over."

Jimmy Espino was heading farther out to the lowlands, where food was more plentiful because the flatness lent itself better to farming: Did Clay want to join him? Conner declined the offer. Dunlap's death had shaken him. He felt weak. He needed to think and write. And, as it turned out, he needed to take care of Porter, who continued to get worse. Porter wanted Conner to read him the Bible. "It was interesting the passages that would seem to be important," wrote Clay. "I remember only one vividly. It was in the epistle written to the Romans by the apostle Paul, in the tenth chapter, the ninth verse: 'Confess with your mouth, the Lord Jesus, and believe in your heart, God raised him from the dead, and you will be saved.' He liked to hear me read that. And he liked the parables, where Jesus had forgiven the sinners for the things they had done wrong."

A few days later, on July 27, Agado awakened Clay with the news. Porter was dead. "I got up quickly and ran over to the big house, and there he was with his eyes still open," wrote Conner. "His mouth was kind of half open. His hair was mussed, and his body was still doubled up. And his fists were clenched closed."

He went to Agado and asked where he might find some thick, heavy wood. The Filipino fired quick orders to boys who soon returned with a couple of flat pieces of wood about three feet long and a foot and a half wide. Conner took a mallet and chisel and etched the soldiers' names, home towns, serial numbers, dates of birth, and dates of deaths into the wood. Grave markers for Porter and Dunlap.

Again, the men stood on the hill. Again, Conner read from Romans, the tenth chapter, the ninth verse. "We looked up into the heavens," wrote Conner. "And again I checked the faces of those men there, and we wondered who would be next."

PART THREE

PURPOSE

ELEVEN

Resistance

September 1942

Time in the jungle since the Fall of Bataan:
Six months

THE HOUSE BELONGED to Jimmy Espino's uncle, Pablo Aquino. It was tucked into the palm-fronged town of Samal, which lay just inland from the northwest nook of Manila Bay. The town was one of nearly a dozen on the Bataan Peninsula's Old Highway now tainted for having been stops on the south-to-north death march. But if the Japanese's cruelty toward American and Filipino prisoners had left death in its dust five months before, hope now stirred in Samal on this September night, if even only a touch of it. Inside the house, Filipino guards closed the grass-and-bamboo shutters as fifteen men—all Filipinos but two—exchanged conversation as intense as it was muted. Defiance would have to grow quietly in the Japanese-occupied Philippines. But grow it would, Conner had decided. With Frank Gyovai, it was here that their resistance to the Japanese would begin.

After the deaths of Dunlap and Porter, Conner had felt not only a loss of friends but, in days to come, a lack of purpose. Despite reading, poring over maps, and learning Tagalog, something was missing. "I needed something *more*," Conner wrote. Action. And the formation of a guerrilla unit seemed like just the thing.

Higher-ranking officers, Captain Vinnette among them, were too diseased to help galvanize any such movement. So, when Espino mentioned that his uncle, Pablo Aquino, was a political leader in a nearby town and staunchly pro-American, Conner seized the opportunity. Maybe Conner could unite young Filipino men and whatever U.S. soldiers were still alive to stand against the Japanese.

Espino had met with his uncle to set up the time and the place, and had been only too proud to escort the two Americans down the hill, through guava trees and banana groves and rice farms, and into the lowland town, his eyes alert for Japanese soldiers. As he'd ridden the back of carabao across a river to Samal, Conner realized that Gyovai, aboard another such water buffalo, was laughing for the first time in months. So, actually, was he.

"Where have you been, sir?" the Filipino children asked, proudly using what little English they knew. "What are you going to do, sir?" They were great questions, Conner realized. Where *had* he been? In weeks fogged by disease, it was hard to remember. And where *was* he going? For now, all he knew was that where he was going was less important than that he was going *somewhere*.

Pablo's stilted abode stood a rock's throw from Bataan's Old National Road, where the Japanese had marched seventy thousand prisoners of war north to San Fernando, from which they were herded to POW camps by rail. Now a paper or rag Japanese flag fronted every house in town, white with a red "rising sun" in the middle. To the side of each flag were the names of the people who lived in that house, the Japanese, of course, paying particularly close attention to the young men of fighting age.

The Japanese knew pockets of guerrilla warfare were popping up here and there, knew that Filipinos were organizing against them, often beneath the leadership of American officers like Conner who'd eluded or escaped the death march. A place known as Fassoths' Camp, north of Bataan in Zambales Province, had nearly a hundred American soldiers in it. In response, Japanese troops had already begun making flash raids. They would come to a town or barrio and call people outside where soldiers would contrast the names on their list with the faces in front of them. If a young man was missing from a particular house—never mind that he might only be hunting in the mountains or gone to Manila for supplies—the soldiers would kill whoever was left in that house. Men. Women. Children. It mattered not. The soldiers would then burn down the house as a warning for others not to betray the Japanese Empire. Naturally, plenty of Filipinos in Samal were spooked. And though the enthusiasm of the men meeting with Conner and Gyovai was tinted with concern, the thirteen had had enough guts to meet. It was a start.

Conner and Gyovai were greeted as if they were vanguards of a liberating force—even if most of what they knew about such operations consisted of informational morsels that filtered south on the underground railroad from Colonel Claude Thorp's camp. Conner laid out a vision to develop a guerrilla force to oppose the Japanese. Americans and Filipinos, united to fight back in quiet ways. To develop a communication system. To spy. To sabotage. And to attack now and then, but only when the numbers were few, the places remote, the odds of victory high. But, mainly, to stay alive and keep the hopes of civilians alive until they could aid MacArthur and his troops when they stormed ashore to win back Luzon, whenever that might be.

THE MEN—IN BLENDS of English and Tagalog—talked of how they could forge the lists next to the flags, removing names of young men who had joined the movement so they wouldn't be missed by the Japanese when they conducted their impromptu census. How they could work with the mayor and chief of police, staunchly anti-Japanese, to forge the records there, too. And, thus, how they could grow their shadow army. Even if not yet officially blessed by the U.S. military, it would ultimately be part of similar operations popping up across the Philippines, a sort of adjunct army to the United States Armed Forces Far East (USAFFE).

The Filipinos had weapons; after coming across the litter of war, they confiscated rifles and buried them in the ground. Conner told them to grease the rifles and wrap them in waterproof wrapping, lest they rust. The men listened. Aquino offered inspiration. "When the Americans return," he said, "we will be ready. That will be our day. Our men will be strong and they will be organized and we will get our vengeance by attacking the Japanese from the rear. But be careful. If we sow trouble for the Japanese, we will harvest only our dead men."

The Japanese soldiers prized their bayonets; the "type 30" was twenty inches long with a fifteen-inch blade, and fixed to a fifty-inch Arisaka rifle, it provided a weapon that was longer than a soldier was tall. Already, the Japanese, when suspecting a traitor, were known to roam beneath the suspect's stilted house and thrust those bayonets upward, through the bamboo floors, to pierce whatever or whomever got in the way, be it mother, father, or children. The Japanese synchronized such attacks so that one family couldn't warn another. But if the bayonet attacks deepened fears, they did something else to the Filipinos who survived: deepened their resolve for revenge.

Now, as Filipino guards at the house watched through slits in the bamboo walls for Japanese patrols outside, Conner realized the seriousness of what was happening. Never mind that, unceremoniously, he had turned only twenty-four a few weeks ago, men were counting on him. He was the highest-ranking soldier from the group. Someone had to lead. Him.

Later in the evening, a guard with his back to the house's outer wall raised a finger to his lips and nodded to the dusty streets outside: A Japanese patrol was passing. Men in the room got spooked. Conner and Gyovai climbed up a ladder to a second-floor loft. When the all clear came, it was time, they realized, to break up the meeting. After handshakes all around, Espino, Conner, and Gyovai slipped into the night to stay with a Filipino who lived about a mile from town. "Frank and I talked about the possibilities of this adventure," Conner wrote. "We were happy we'd come. It had given us new hope, new life, something to look forward to."

Guerrillas. They were becoming guerrilla soldiers. The word is Spanish, its literal meaning "little war," from the word *guerra*, "war." Not a war carried on by regular soldiers, but by partisans of one side or another, of one cause or another, fighting against a regular army, in this case the Japanese. Small, ill-equipped bands of men fighting a larger, entrenched, well-equipped enemy. War rebels, groups of men whose approach to war existed nowhere in U.S. Army doctrine and was seen by some as dishonorable. The kind of men who, after learning from Indians, had fought at Lexington. Men who, if caught, could not claim the protection of the Geneva Convention; not that the Japanese seemed to have any regard for it in the first place. Instead, these guerrilla soldiers were independent contractors fighting not for a country, per se, but for an ideal.

Freedom.

AS CONNER AND Gyovai left Samal the next morning, shots rang out. Conner recoiled as if struck by a cobra. Out of the jungle rose 101—exactly 101—men. Members of the Hukbalahap, as it turned out. Their leader stepped forward. Like most Filipinos, the man was small—five-foot-five and 165 pounds. Solid. Jet-black hair. Well groomed in a fresh khaki uniform topped with a new straw hat. Two pistols were sleeved in holsters strapped to either leg. His belt, like the flutes of a pie, was ringed with .45-caliber bullets. He reached out his hand to Conner and in near-perfect English said, "I am Julian Palad."

Conner returned the greeting, quickly sizing up Palad. He was full of energy and of himself. Brash. Forthright. Boastful. The Filipino version of Pancho Villa, a swashbuckling pirate without the ship, straight from Hollywood's big screen. Conner liked him immediately.

Along with his men, Palad had come, he said, to pick up weapons for a group known loosely as the Huks. It was an organization, he explained, similar to the USAFFE, only with a Filipino name: Hukbong Bayan Labon sa Japon, or Hukbalahap (the Huks), meaning "Army of the People Against the Japanese." The different name, he explained, would confuse the Japanese because USAFFE was already becoming too well known among them.

So did Conner and whatever men he could muster want to help Palad's outfit gather weapons?

Conner invited him back to where he was staying with Francisco and Agado in Tala. As Palad's men scattered for food and places to stay for the night, he and Palad talked for hours. Suddenly, a villager burst in and demanded to speak to Conner—alone. One of Palad's men had taken a shotgun from a villager. Conner returned and asked Palad if his men were doing that—taking arms from the natives.

"Why not?" he said. "We need all the arms we can get."

"That shotgun isn't going to do your men any good," said Conner. "Where are you going to get the ammunition?"

He said from an American named Larry, who, he'd heard, had all sorts of it. Conner knew the man well—too well. It was Hayden "Larry" Lawrence, the Louisiana private who'd defied him weeks ago. "Yeah, but it's all homemade," said Conner. "What'll you do when it runs out?"

"We'll throw the gun away."

Conner's mild agitation turned to full-blown anger. "You can't do that! This man needs his gun. It's his livelihood. They set these guns up in the woods, and they trigger them. And sometimes they are there two and three weeks before they catch a pig with them. You can't take that gun. That's the only way he can catch wild meat."

Palad's eyes squinted slightly. "What do you care about these people anyway?" he said.

"I care about them because they care about me," said Conner. "I want you to tell your men to give the gun back."

Grudgingly, Palad did so.

The first lesson Clay Conner learned about guerrilla warfare was that you were never quite sure who was friend and who was foe, and uniforms alone weren't particularly good indicators. It came down to something deeper and not easily discerned. Even as Conner and Palad shared lunch, word came that "Larry," the American soldier whom Clay had had the confrontation with weeks before, had barricaded himself in a jungle enclave some five hundred feet up the mountain, threatening to shoot anybody who came near him.

No matter how badly he wanted arms, Palad made it clear he wasn't going to confront the madman. "Do you think I'm crazy?" he said to Conner. "I don't like trapped animals or trapped men."

Palad, Conner realized, was a smart man. He told Conner he had graduated from law school in Manila and had been a police chief in the province of Tarlac before the war. He was a politician who had made a lot of money. And exuded a certain charisma that both wowed and worried Conner.

"Why don't we forget all about that fellow and relax?" Palad said. "Tomorrow, let's leave and get out of this area. My men are catching malaria down here. You'll like Pampanga Province, where I'm from. There's a lot of food and a lot of good people. It's much different than this place. And you can learn another dialect. They speak Pampangania over there. I'd like to teach you that."

Conner's mind was still on Lawrence, who, he figured, would get himself killed if he didn't learn a bit more international diplomacy. He headed up a nearby jungle-tangled hill. It was around noon and the Filipinos stopped eating and watched.

"Conner, if you come another step," yelled Lawrence, "I'm going to chop you into pieces."

Conner kept walking.

"I'll let you have it!" Lawrence yelled—and he wasn't referring to handing Conner the gun.

Conner kept walking—in fact, he didn't stop until he was just short of the hideout Lawrence had carved out of the foliage.

"Why don't you leave me alone?" he said to Conner.

"I *am* leaving you alone, but you can't get along like this. These people want to be your friends. They're organizing to fight against the Japanese, and we've got to do all we can to help them."

Conner then added something that ran against the grain of essentially every chest-puffed American who'd stepped foot in the Philippines since the Spanish-American War with his "we're here to save you" attitude. "And we need their help more than they need ours," said Conner. "Now, get up out of there and let's go find out what our job is."

The man didn't budge.

"Come on!" Conner yelled. "Let's go!"

After a few moments, Conner heard the rustling of jungle leaves. He began walking down the hill. Lawrence followed.

BACK AT FRANCISCO and Agado's to spend the night, Conner removed his pistol belt and set it aside. Later that night, as he and Palad talked in the moonlight, the Filipino picked up the belt and strapped it around his waist to check the fit. The two were the same size.

"This is an awful nice gun," said Palad. "How long have you had this?"

"Quite a while. It's the same one that was issued to me on maneuvers, in 1941."

"I'm an expert with my Colt revolver," Palad said.

"That's nice."

From there, the conversation veered away from firearms to life for the Filipinos in the lowlands and to the fledgling guerrilla outfits forming and how much Palad's people hated the Japanese since the soldiers had occupied their country the past ten months. "He told me how the Japanese would come into a town and take the young girls and then send them home pregnant some months later," Conner wrote. "This was supposed to be an honor. The Japanese said this was helping the blood of the Filipino people. It was helping to purify their race by mingling with those of the Japanese Empire. And then they would receive a letter, supposedly from the emperor, saying that he was proud that they had born a Japanese child. Well, the Filipinos weren't proud, they were ashamed. And they hated the Japanese with every ounce of life they had."

The following morning, Palad's men and dozens of Filipinos gathered to head north, but it was unwise to travel until mid-morning because the jungle was wet. As they waited, questions outnumbered answers. When, the Filipinos asked, were the Americans coming back? Had they defeated the Japanese in the southern islands? What was going on beyond the Philippines? With patched-up radios, some had picked up a little information in the lowlands, scratchy broadcasts from KGEI in San Francisco, but, for the most part, Luzon was a place without context, a world unto itself, a question with no ready answer.

Conner kept his only question to himself: Could he trust Julian Palad? Palad picked up Conner's pistol again and strapped on the holster.

"Are you ready?" he asked.

"Yes, I'm ready," said Conner, "but how about giving me my gun?"

Palad, his political personna as polished as ever, did not hesitate.

"Oh, I'm going to *keep* your gun," he said. "I need it."

"You've already got a gun. You've got the Colt revolver."

"I know, but I need three guns," Palad said. "I look better with three guns. Yours fits me fine and I'm going to keep it."

Conner headed to the back of the house and out the doorway. Some of Palad's men were down by a stream, washing their faces and getting drinks. While they were looking away, Conner grabbed a Browning Automatic Rifle that was propped against a palm tree. En route back to the house he flipped the selector to "automatic."

He approached Palad from behind. And gently pushed the muzzle into the man's back. Palad turned around quickly and raised his hands in the air, then, with a nervous laugh, dropped them.

"What's the matter with you?" Palad said.

"Nothing, I just think you made a mistake about my gun." Palad's expression slid from fun to fear. "Now, you just unbuckle it and you hand it to me," said Conner, "and everything's going to be just dandy."

"I think you'd kill me, wouldn't you?" said Palad.

"No question about it," said Conner. "You're not going anyplace with that gun. That's my protection."

Conner thought Palad might give in, but he underestimated the man.

"You don't need a gun!" he said. "You're going to be with *me*."

"Just unbuckle it and hand it to me," said Conner.

And he did. Conner swung the holster around his waist and tied the leather thong to his leg. He handed the loaded rifle to the man, then turned and walked away.

Palad shook his head in confusion. "Conner," he said, "you're crazy."

Conner stopped and turned around. "How do you figure that?"

"Well, I could kill you right now, and what would it cost me?" he said. "Nobody would stop me."

"You're not going to kill me," said Conner. "If I can't trust the Filipino people, if I can't depend on you for my friends, I'm not going to live through this damn war anyway."

As Conner gathered his stuff, Palad came to him and scoffed at Clay's tattered and sun-bleached clothes. He then rummaged through some of his stuff and handed Conner a fresh blue uniform. "Try this on and see how you like it."

Conner did. A perfect fit. He thanked Palad. And smiled. "I could tell," Conner later wrote, "we were going to be great friends."

TWELVE

Respite

October 1942

Time in the jungle since the Fall of Bataan:
Seven months

FLAUBERT. THOREAU. EMERSON. Stevenson. As Conner's eyes scanned the bookcases in the wealthy man's home, he could not believe his good fortune. Rows and rows of books, the kind of books he had read back at Duke. The complete works of Shakespeare. American novels. Poetry. Following a fifteen-mile trip north with Palad and Frank Gyovai, the barrio of Pio afforded the men a rare touch of heaven in what had been six months of hell.

"This," wrote Conner, "is the place for me. We can stay here until the war is over. I'll just read until I've read them all. And Frank agreed with me. We were hungry for this sort of thing. We'd been a long time without reading material of this kind."

A Filipino who had led them to this house said that the man who lived here had moved to Manila, a common theme for the wealthy. The rich feared being killed by the Huks, who, Conner was learning, weren't only anti-Japanese, but had Communist connections and aspirations of controlling Luzon politically. Happy, as it were, to mix war and revolution. The man also offered to bring food for the Americans since Japanese patrols were intensifying and it wasn't good for the men to be out and about. The setup was ideal. Groups of people took turns bringing Conner and Gyovai food—Palad and his men were elsewhere—each day.

They read day after day, at times by candlelight, the words reminding them of worlds far removed from the jungles of Luzon. They floated on the words, stories, and inspiration of the world's finest authors, any sense of guilt abated by the fact that it was too dangerous to be outside, trying to muster support for a guerrilla army. But in this respite they would prove to be like drowning men being allowed one last gulp of air before going under. The Filipinos ferrying food to them informed Conner and Gyovai that the Japanese had heard they were in Pio. Time to move on.

As much as Conner wanted to go where he pleased, his whereabouts were inextricably linked to those of the Japanese. In reality, he had no more freedom than a dog on a leash. And so he learned to live defensively, going not necessarily where he wanted to—the rich man's house an obvious exception—but where he needed to in order to be safe.

Travel itself had gotten easier. Though he and Palad had cut through the mountains to get to this new area, Conner was surprised at how much less difficult it had been for him. He was healthy again. He had gained some skills, savvy, confidence. He even taught Palad a few things about mountain travel, which only seemed fair since Palad had taught much to Conner about guerrilla tactics in general.

In a barrio just west of Dinalupihan, on something called the Zig-Zag Trail, Palad had taken Conner to the camp of Lieutenant Colonel John "Daniel" Boone, who along with Colonel Claude Thorp, had supposedly been commissioned by MacArthur himself to flee to the jungles before the Fall of Bataan and set up a "spy outpost." Now Thorp was missing, believed to have been captured by the Japanese in late October. But Boone, a Captain Bell, and others seemed to be doing well. They lived in a nice house and had plenty of Filipinos to help them with food. Both men had neatly trimmed beards.

Boone, about five-foot-eight, wore a crew cut to go with athletic good looks and a crisp Vandyke beard. He had played professional golf in

California and had enlisted just before the war broke out. Bell was handsome, too, with blond, wavy hair and a bit taller than Boone, but not as talkative.

The two explained to Conner how their guerrilla organization had come to life, how it worked, where it might be headed. Other such units had sprung up, too, across Luzon. Five miles north, Fassoths' Camp had sprouted behind the efforts of two brothers who'd been in the Philippines before the war, men who'd married Filipinas and had sons. When war broke out, they had burrowed deep into the mountains and created a haven for about five dozen men who had escaped the death march.

Immediately, Conner wanted to check out the camp. Boone discouraged the idea. The timing was bad. The camp was low on supplies and had been raided with regularity by the Japanese. Discord was rampant among the men. Plus, Palad didn't like the idea—and Conner wasn't confident enough to go without him and Boone's men. "I was," Conner wrote, "determined to stay with him."

The men talked of the strong Filipino support for the guerrilla movement, of how Conner could, in essence, be appointed to lead such an outfit. Bell said he and Boone had the military authority to commission Conner with oversight of any area of Bataan or nearby provinces he chose.

Finally, Conner—when alone with Boone and away from Palad—asked about the Huks. The answer was disturbing, to say the least. "He told me that the Huks were a very tricky organization," wrote Conner. "That they were strong, they had managed to collect some 600 to 700 rifles; they had five, six, or seven groups of '101 bands'"—one leader, one hundred men—"and that they were roving through Luzon trying to organize political factions. And he said, 'I'm not sure, I have no definite proof, but I think they're Communist allies.' And I thought, 'That might be possible, but what difference would that make to me?' I didn't think too much about them being Communists, because, after all, the Communists were our allies." Or pretended to be.

Boone told him the Huks could teach him the lay of the land, which was invaluable, but cautioned him. "Above all," he said, "don't trust them, because they will kill you if the opportunity permits. They may show you great admiration one day, but if they've got you cold, they might get rid of you."

The Huks carried identification cards issued by the Japanese, all of them forgeries. A resident Huk in the shop where the cards had been printed ran off a few hundred extra. None of the men had been at home when the Japanese had come around to check the number of occupants per house, so they had escaped official census entirely. Anonymity was encouraged. A Huk engaging an American might introduce himself as "Vespucci" or "Megellan" or "Christopher Columbus." Most were single. Unlike their leaders, few cared about politics. They just wanted to kill Japanese soldiers.

Frankly, Conner wondered if Boone's views had been skewed by some sort of personal grudge. "I didn't think he knew what he was talking about—especially [about] Palad. I trusted him. I figured I had put the test to him a couple of times already."

In the fall of 1942, trust among these fledgling anti-Japanese groups was important in the jungles of Luzon. Without it, you might die. But with it placed in the wrong people, you definitely would die.

AFTER HUNKERING DOWN during a typhoon, Conner and Gyovai moved northeast of Dinalupihan, Pampanga Province, into the lowlands, with Palad and his men. No action, but lots of good contacts, and a chance to improve their language skills and learn the land. But at times, Conner realized, Palad could be cruel to civilians, with whom the Huk leader always had the upper hand. He'd pass a man on a road who was wearing a nice pair of shoes and make him give them to one of his soldiers. Same with other clothing items that he felt his men needed.

Conner objected. "That's the way they go along," countered Palad. "That's the way they expect to be treated." Still, Conner didn't like it. "But," he wrote, "it wasn't my country."

Much of the lowland hiking was done through rice paddies; the water and wear took a toll on the two men's feet. Enough. They discarded their GI boots and started going barefoot. On roads, Conner wore Filipino shoes; Gyovai never put on a pair of shoes again, even if brambles and barbed wire beneath the rice-paddy waters left his feet and ankles an infected mess.

The lowlands offered a semblance of sanity—it was here that Conner had enjoyed the ten-day book-reading experience—that almost made him forget about war. Here that a Filipino woman named Mobitang allowed him, Gyovai, and others to live with her and her elderly mother, feeding them as if they were royal guests. Here that farmers worked their meager crops, storekeepers swept their porches, everywhere men took breaks to gamble on cockfights. Conner started learning the dialect of the Pampangans, their culture, their nuances. Materially, the people had little. But, he wrote, "they seemed to be rather care-free. They were poor people, as most of all those farmers were. But in their poverty they had a happiness. They had a happiness of family, and they seemed to have a security that goes with living close to the soil."

The huts were built on stilts to protect people when the monsoon rains flooded the streams and rivers. Each day, a family member would take a hollowed-out bamboo tube, perhaps six inches in diameter, and fill it with water, then lean it vertically against the grass house; that provided the water they needed for drinking, cooking, and cleaning. Before entering their huts, the Filipinos would use a cup or coconut shell to splash water on their feet to clean them. They washed their clothes—and often the clothes of the Americans—by swishing the items around in the river, rubbing them on a tree, beating them with a stick, then returning them to the river for a rinse.

A town might have hundreds of such thatched-roof huts, a stark contrast to the houses of the area's few wealthy families, which would have a wood frame and tin roof. Nobody drove a car. People walked or rode carabaos, which were often tended to by children.

Conner loved the kids. They taught him Tagalog songs, including *"Paru Paru Bukid."* ("Song About a Butterfly.") Helped him with his

Tagalog. Practiced plays and then performed them. "We sang together. They washed my clothes, fed me what they had, and I attended their parties. I worked in the fields. We talked in the darkness of the night, and I enjoyed their life. And I think they enjoyed having me, too."

If the music of the Filipino poor soothed Conner, a more sinister drumbeat played an edgy backdrop. He was, after all, a man on a mission—not always the case for fled-to-the-jungles Americans, some of whom were more than happy to quietly wait out the war with no deeper purpose; Gyovai described one such man—a colonel—as "a selfish, unfriendly, scared survivalist" waited on completely by a houseboy. For Conner, there was favor to cull. Money to raise. Relationships to build. After a two-week tour of barrios, he returned with about fifty pesos, all in small-denomination bills. The big money had fled to Manila; this movement would have to rise from the peasants.

Day after day, Conner became, as he called it, "a professional beggar" in an attempt to keep his men fed and alive. He would walk fifteen to twenty miles, from barrio to barrio, with a gunny sack, and people would give him chickens, fish, rice, sugar, salt, eggs, bananas, perhaps even some canned American food that they'd stashed away. At farms, he could expect camotes, gondos, eggplant, lima beans—whatever was in season.

"Everyone knew I was coming, and they'd greet me, and be ready for me, having something set aside each day," he wrote. "I'd stop to work with the women in the fields; I'd ride the carabao with the kids; I'd bet with the old men of the barrio who had quit working; I would walk behind the plow with the young men; and I would sit and talk with them. I'd encourage them in their cock fights. I'd bet on one or the other. I'd help the [loser] eat his chicken."

IN SIX MONTHS, Luzon had become a melting pot of disparate political and military positioning: a peasant citizenry being bullied by Japanese soldiers. A ragtag collection of American soldiers—pistols strapped to

PURPOSE   117

their hips—who had eluded, or escaped from, the death march and who were now trying, without much success, to mount a guerrilla force. Filipinos bent on supporting such soldiers. "Fifth Column" spies, Filipinos who, in the eyes of Conner and his men, were doing the devil's work—conspiring with the Japanese. And, finally, the Huks, who, at this point, nobody could quite figure out but everybody increasingly feared.

In a word, Luzon was chaos, the handful of different languages—Tagalog, Pampango, English, Negrito—the least of Conner's and his men's problems.

"There was no law in Luzon except force," Sergeant Alfred Bruce later said. "Who had the most guns was the most powerful."

That reality didn't bode well for those without guns. "The poor citizens were constantly being looted and robbed," said Bruce, "not only by bandits but by the Japanese and Filipino Constabulary who entered the barrio on foraging parties and took everything in sight. They accused all the people as guerrillas and beat them if they made any resistance or complaint."

Occasionally, Conner would bump into other Americans; in the barrio of Delores, it was Bob Leyrer, a pilot who had been part of the 27th Bombardment Group, and a fellow named Raymond Herbert, from Louisiana. At such encounters, the questions were always the same: *Who's dead? Who's alive? Where have you been? How did you get here? Where are you going? Who's helping? Who's not? Who do you trust? Who do you not?* After a while, Conner realized the most consistent theme he'd heard concerned Palad and the Huks. The men didn't trust him or his outfit. The Huks may have been anti-Japanese, but many U.S. guerrillas had started to believe they were also anti-American.

Conner didn't want to believe that. Palad's brashness impressed him, in part, because it reminded him of someone he knew: himself. Or the self that he was subconsciously creating: Part door-to-door salesman. Part Duke fraternity boy. Part Rocky Gause with a touch of Hollywood western hero thrown in for good measure. Still, he couldn't slough off "the common reoccurrance [sic] of coldness on the part of the Americans who seemed to know more about the Huks than I did." So he compromised. The next time Palad and his men moved on, Conner told him he was staying, but would later rejoin him and his men. Not a split for good, just a postponement of traveling together. Palad was good with that. "We parted friendly," wrote Conner.

If Conner had found a certain contentment amid his Filipino exile, so had the other American boys. They had plenty of food. They had the luxury of Mobitang cooking for them. They had access to medicine that was helping make infections and diseases better. "The boys," wrote Conner, "were happy."

At night, they'd sit around and talk of home. Gyovai, the coal miner's son, raved about his mother's cooking and lamented how the mines would swallow men up and spit them out dead. Herbert talked of boxing his way across the Louisiana bayou and winning a scholarship to Louisiana State. Leyrer spoke of his home in Wisconsin, how he'd always dreamed of flying since he was a little boy. And a soldier named Johnny Johns talked of all the girls he'd left behind.

Johns and Herbert fought like me-first siblings. Johns would threaten to punch out Herbert, who would always remind him, "Well, you haven't done it yet." With the boys in good moods, the bickering came across not so much as bad for morale but as good theater. "Ray was five-foot-five and tough as nails," wrote Conner, "and Johnny was tall and slim. They were like Mutt and Jeff."

One night, when Conner was trying to round up some money to help compensate Mobitang, he found himself doing something he hadn't done in a while: whistling. A moon hung high in the Filipino sky. It was dead quiet. He was on a road outside the barrio. "I was thinking," he wrote, "only of the freedom of the night."

The crack of a rifle split the silence. He scrambled into a ditch and lay quiet for what seemed like agonizingly long minutes, heart pounding as if he'd been jolted by a car battery. Eventually, he got up and began walking again, this time swiveling his head slowly back and forth with newfound caution. He wasn't whistling. Still, he wondered if it had just been some errant shot, a gun-cleaning "whoops" in a country where guns nearly outnumbered mosquitoes.

Zing. A second bullet chiseled the rocky road at his feet. Again, Conner scurried to safety. He had his answer. Someone was trying to kill him.

THIRTEEN

A New Enemy

November 1942

Time in the jungle since the Fall of Bataan:
Eight months

Winder, Georgia
November 7, 1942

Dear Mr. Hampton,

Clay and I were very good friends. We went to the Philippines together, danced in the Manila Hotel the night before the Japs entered the city. I did duty with Clay all during the battle of Bataan. Clay was alive when Bataan fell. I'm confident he was taken prisoner there and is now in a prison camp north of Manila on Luzon. Try to contact him through the Red Cross.

Sincerely yours,
Damon J. Gause,
Captain, AC, U.S. Army

CLAY CONNER JR. tried to find a lesson in everything. And, after meeting up with Bruce, the lesson on this trip was how devoted the Filipinos were to the Americans. Bruce had been with the 31st Infantry Regiment and, like Conner, had headed for the jungle instead of surrendering. Now he and Conner were sitting in the front room of a Filipino home eating chicken, rice, and camotes when Bruce suggested Conner take a look at what the neighbors were having for dinner. He pulled aside a cloth curtain and looked inside. Dead rats boiled in a pot.

"How can you not help doing all you can for a people who will put up with sacrifices like that?" wrote Conner. Here were the Americans, who'd failed to defend these people's country, eating like kings. Meanwhile, the Filipinos were eating rat. Conner dug into his pockets and gave the family every dime he had, which wasn't much but reflected his sentiments.

Later, in Delores, Conner gathered his men. Too many Americans were congregating in one place. And the Japanese, he'd heard from Filipinos, were specifically targeting him. A group of Americans, washing clothes at the river, had been surprised by a Japanese tank rumbling down a road and had barely escaped. It was time to move on.

Conner—along with Gyovai, Herbert, and Johns—headed east, toward cone-shaped Mount Arayat, which shadowed central Luzon. But if he had learned anything in his year in the Philippines, it was that their plans had the shelf life of a sun-baked banana. En route, Johns suggested a side trip to a town called Bacolor, where there lived a nurse who had helped him after he'd escaped from the death march. "Maybe she could help us get some money," he told Conner.

Filipinos told them some twenty Japanese soldiers were in the town, but Bacolor was large and the enemy group relatively small. Conner liked the odds. He would go to Bacolor with Johns; Gyovai and Herbert would wait for the pair at a barrio called Pulong Santol—or move on if the two weren't back within five or six days.

Conner and Johns arrived in Bacolor at Clay's favorite time of day, sundown. "I always liked to watch the sun go down in the Philippines," he wrote. "The warmth of the little lights, and the fires of bamboo underneath the pots, cooking rice. To me it represented a simple life of people who were happy. And the children's voices always seemed to be more audible at night. They were always cheerful and you could always hear the song 'Maria Ellaine' no matter where you went."

With help from Filipinos, who whispered "*delicato*"—dangerous—if they knew Japanese patrols were prowling, Conner and Johns made it from the west side of town to the east, where the nurse lived. She worked in Manila, forty miles to the south, and would travel there for days at a time. She said she would seek money from rich men she knew in the city. But when, two days later, she returned, she had no money. The men thought she was a Japanese plant and figured if they gave her money, they would be killed. It was a reminder of how, amid the Japanese occupation, people's decisions were increasingly driven by one thing: fear.

WHEN CONNER SAW the Bacolor Parish Church rising beyond the marketplace like a capital "I" in a lower-case village, he was mesmerized. The Catholic church was a huge gothic structure as beautiful and seemingly out of place as the shelves of books back in Pio. It was more than a century old. Conner couldn't resist. His New Testament reading had spawned all sorts of questions about God that wouldn't go away; finally, he had found a place for answers.

"Let's go in the church," he said to Johns. "How about it? I haven't been in church in a long time."

"Suits me fine," said Johns.

An iron fence, spiked at the top, surrounded the church. Conner rattled the gate. No response. Again. No response. Again. Finally, a Filipino priest approached and immediately whipped a single finger to his lips. Conner whispered that they would like to come inside. "We want to pray," he said. The priest shook his head. No. No. No. Impossible. "Very *delicato*," he said. "*Japons, Japons.*"

"No, listen, we want to go in the church," said Conner. "Get the key. We're going to pray."

The priest gave in, got the key, and reluctantly took the men across a courtyard to the church and let them inside. The floor was slate, the ceiling high, the decor ornate, at least given the bamboo-and-banana-leaf surroundings. All was quiet. Conner walked down the aisle, unmindful of where Johns or the priest or anyone else in the structure might be. He knelt to pray.

Suddenly, noise shuddered from on high: Bats in the rafters burst forth in wing-flapping fury. The three men looked up, then at one another, then, as quiet returned, Conner folded his hands together and bowed his head. "I thanked God for having watched over me," he wrote. "I prayed for my friends, prayed for home and family. I prayed that the war would end. I prayed for the Filipinos. And I felt real good."

He wanted to ask the priest about some of the things he had read in his New Testament, but the man was anxious for the pair to leave. Conner persisted. "He thought it was strange that I was so interested in these things," wrote Conner. The priest ushered them to the anteroom of the parish house and quickly closed the windows. A few Filipinos joined them as if a Sunday school class had organically formed out of nowhere. But the priest, Conner realized, was just going through the motions. As if his mind were elsewhere. His eyes shifted from Clay to the windows to the door—the door that suddenly swung open. *What the—"* Two Japanese soldiers. Two rifles pointed.

Conner whipped his hand to his holster and fired. One soldier fell backward against the door, hit, and the other jumped through the window. Conner and the others scattered like shrapnel. He raced across the courtyard. He saw Johns power through a bamboo hedge and followed suit, only to hit barbed wire and be flung back as if a rock in a slingshot, flat on his back. Shots rang out from windows above, tattering around him. Conner returned the fire, then ran and scrambled over a picket fence and through a graveyard as bullets jackhammered headstones beside him. He shielded himself behind one of the headstones, panting. Obviously, he and Johns had been followed; while they prayed, the Japanese had set up an ambush. But where in the hell was Johnny?

By now, machine-gun fire had zeroed in on Conner, though the tracer bullets in the darkness at least gave him an idea where it was coming from. He fired back, but soon realized this wasn't a fair fight. He had to flee—and did so, first slogging across a muddy canal, then into a rice field, and finally across a bamboo footbridge that spanned a canal. When he was midway across, more gunfire lit up the night. "I could feel and hear my heart," he wrote, "and it sounded like someone striking a big piece of iron with a metal hammer in the middle of a hollow building. . . . I was sure they could hear it."

IF CONNER HAD survived the close call at Bacolor—as had Johns, he soon learned—it was less a victory than a premonition. In the months to come, the Japanese in the area thickened like flies on corpses. And for the first time, Conner learned that a price had been placed on his head: 300 pesos, or around $150. Meanwhile, an increasing reluctance to help Americans rose among fearful Filipino families; caught in the middle of a war between two countries, they were the living embodiment of the political adage that "when the elephants dance it is unsafe for the chickens." Too many of their loved ones were being terrorized by bayonets through the floors. "Again and again they would thrust until everybody on the floor above was still, and only the blood dripping through," wrote Conner. "Then, to dramatize the deed and teach others the meaning of fear, they would burn down the house. Sleep became a thing of terror."

The Japanese also used torture to control civilians believed to be consorting with the enemy. Such brutality cut against the Japanese's "Asia for the Asiatics" propaganda campaign, the main thrust of which was the idea that the small, dark-skinned Filipinos should align themselves with their brothers, the Japanese, rather than the ugly Americans. But the Japanese mistake with the Philippines was assuming the Filipinos craved being part of a Japan-led Asia; no, they craved the freedom to run their own country. And they had found the "velvet glove" approach not particularly inviting when the hand inside that glove was choking them. Some Filipino men responded by carrying shards of glass in their mouth or hiding razor blades somewhere in their pockets so that, if captured, they might strike for an enemy's eyes. It was a reminder that the men were not simply chickens waiting to be stepped on, but human beings.

As 1942 wound to an end in the Luzon jungles, the line between man and beast was blurring considerably.

FOURTEEN

Trust and Deceit

November 10, 1942, to December 23, 1942

Time in the jungle since the Fall of Bataan:
Eight to nine months

AS 1942 NEARED its end, it did so with an increasing sense of regret and a decreasing sense of hope among Conner and his men. The guerrilla movement he had been so passionate about only four months before when meeting with the men in Samal was now like an overloaded bomber trying to get airborne, a good-faith effort weighed down by tons of painful realities. Numbers. Weapons. Organization. Political power. The Japanese soldiers had virtually every possible advantage, among them a lack of unified purpose among the Americans. Some wanted to organize and keep fighting the Japanese. Others were content to hunker down and wait for an American army to rescue them. A few scarred souls retreated not only deep into the jungle, but deep into minds warped by war, not sure whose side they were on. And at least one—who would become known as Tibuc-Tibuc—was an American soldier taken prisoner, Conner had heard, and set free by the Japanese contingent upon him serving as a spy for them. A traitor.

"We were a scattered, disorganized lot," wrote Conner, "and we were hunted more as rats than as American soldiers." Meanwhile, the hope that the Pacific fleet would arrive, drop anchor, and send thousands of men to their rescue had become nothing more than wishful thinking, a crumbling hope to keep alive whatever resolve a man could muster.

The only solace Conner clung to was that, unlike many others, he was still alive. Based on what he had heard over the months, perhaps three hundred American soldiers had either eluded capture back in April or escaped from the death march that followed. He figured maybe half were still alive. Disease killed dozens. The Japanese killed more. And a hopeless few did the job themselves, not that many others, including Conner, hadn't considered that option or wouldn't consider it in the future.

At the base of such hopelessness was the difficulty of knowing, as a U.S. soldier, who was on your side and who wasn't. This was not like the traditional wars Conner and his men knew of: battles fought with clear-cut fronts. At Duke, Conner had been in physical education classes where you simply split the class in two. One half wore blue smocks, the other wore their white T-shirts. If the game were dodge ball, the blues fired on the whites in one direction and the whites did the same in the opposite direction. Alas, on Luzon, nobody knew who was on what team, what the actual goal was, and whether the guy next to him—if even wearing the same color—could be trusted. Confusion, it's been said, is the first weed to sprout in war. On Luzon, it grew with the speed of bamboo.

Politically and militarily, Pampanga and nearby provinces were as rough and tangled as the Luzon jungle itself. Nationalists favored a continuation of the existing government, their hopes pinned to the eventual U.S.-promised independence for the Philippines. Socialists, branded with a strong Communist element, wanted revolution: abolishment of the landlord system, wide distribution of land, relief for peasants, and immediate independence from the United States.

When the Japanese had moved in, the Nationalists held the political power and thus were marked men. Leaders of towns and barrios were allowed to stay in their positions to preserve law and order, but, in essence, they did so as marionettes of the Japanese puppet masters—and, fair or not, they were seen by the public at large as collaborationists. The Socialists exploited the chasm, the Communist-leaning Hukbalahap rising up to wield their power at gunpoint.

The group emerged as equal-opportunity rebels, collecting weapons from both Japanese and American forces. By the time of the April 1942 surrender, there was hardly a Filipino of fighting age who didn't have a weapon and a cause, whatever it might be. The problem for Conner and other American soldiers now was figuring out whether such men, going back to his simpler days at Duke, wore blue shirts or white shirts. And, in time, figuring out the same for a few of the Americans among them.

Confounding the already-tangled military landscape were differences between the Huks and the USAFFE, both supposedly fighting the same Japanese enemy. Or were they? Tactically, the two were on different pages. What little critical mass of guerrillas Colonel Thorp had mustered up north was done so with a long-range plan of destroying important Japanese installations, communication networks, and highways. The Huks, on the other hand, favored small raids, which might have little effect on the Japanese occupation but which looked good to impressionable Filipinos, who might be considering the idea of joining the Huk movement.

Another difference deepened the discord between two groups that were ostensibly fighting the same enemy. As guerrillas, the Americans were starting from scratch; they needed to not only organize fighting units that had scattered during the April surrender, but also organize Filipinos willing to support them, hide them, and feed them. Without the support of the people, no guerrilla band can exist.

Meanwhile, the Huks, were, in essence, "of the people" and thus had no such problem. The solution might have seemed obvious, to merge forces—USAFFE and Huks. The Huks would get the military skills of the American soldiers, and the Americans would get the Huks' knowledge of the countryside and support of the people. But Colonel Thorp—and not everybody agreed with him on this—believed that politics and war were a bad mix; guerrilla units, to be effective, had to be military organizations bent on one cause—victory—and not a political party with weapons. The Huks loved their weapons, but their leaders weren't about to give up their political ties, even if they kept such ties under wraps when engaging the Americans. Thus, an impasse. Said Conner, "In the barrios, you were either pro-Huk or you weren't alive."

What further confused an already-foggy landscape—beyond numerous dialects—was the Japanese Fifth Column, or "Ganaps," Filipinos of Japanese descent sympathetic to the "East-for-Easterners" line of thought and to hell with the rest. They were mainly in the business of information—or misinformation, though hardly alone in that pursuit. Amid the confusion, dozens of frustrated political leaders, ambitious men, and plain old bandits positioned themselves for personal gain; in essence, independent contractors using the country's chaos to their advantage. Rounding out this dubious demographic mix were fence sitters whose only commitment was to whichever side seemed to be winning this shadow war.

All such factions considered, a guerrilla band might be composed of USAFFE, Huks, Ganaps, and bandits, all spying on one another and otherwise working at cross-purposes, flanked by a few seemingly powerless fence sitters whose loose lips could tip the scales of power. A white man was, most probably, an American fighting for his country. But he also could be a German commissioned by his Japanese allies to impersonate an American. Or he could be Tibuc-Tibuc, the traitor.

"It was," wrote Conner, "a mess." And the problem wasn't just beyond the ranks of U.S. soldiers, but within those ranks.

WHEN VISITING FASSOTHS' Camp, ten miles to the north, Conner had been impressed with the elderly brothers who ran it, Bill and Martin. More than seventy men had been staying there at one point, the Fassoths' many connections keeping a steady supply of food and medicine rolling in. But, over time, dissension had eaten away at the camp like a malaria parasite. At its root, determined Conner, was plain old fear.

"Most of the men were suffering from cases of nerves brought on by the frightful scenes through which they had passed, and the fact that Japs were prowling around within a few miles did nothing to calm them," he wrote. What's more, many were sick with disease. And the food, though better than most places, wasn't easy on the stomach, even if men were able to avoid the cockroaches, bat, and rat that Conner had tried.

"Frightened, hungry, and feverish, the men were in no mood to put up with even minor irritations," he wrote. "And a serious irritant was the matter of rank." Officers and enlisted men clashed with regularity; when you don't have much—and the guerrillas didn't—then you hold all the tighter to whatever you do have.

Communication, or lack thereof, didn't help matters. In late August, Colonel Thorp had broken into a rage when getting a letter—hand-delivered, of course, by a Filipino runner—from Colonel Gyles Merrill, suggesting that he, not Thorp, was running the guerrilla show on Luzon. Later, Thorp calmed down after Merrill backed off, having learned that Thorp had orders from MacArthur himself.

If, amid such messiness, a man were concerned only about survival, obscurity would be the wiser choice of valor, though that was nearly impossible to maintain as a guerrilla leader, a lesson Thorp had just learned the hard way. Word arrived that he had been betrayed, possibly by a Ganap who'd infiltrated the USAFFE under the guise of being a pro-American Filipino, and taken prisoner. Merrill became Luzon's guerrilla leader.

A Captain Ralph McGuire had escaped the raid that claimed Thorp. An explosives expert, he spent the next four months doing serious damage to bridges, convoys, and radio installations used by the Japanese. But, ultimately, he, too, was betrayed by an insider and taken prisoner. And lest those American guerrillas who remained did not understand the danger of their continued opposition to the enemy, the Japanese offered a warning. It was on display in a town hard to the South China Sea, Botolan, hanging from a tree in the marketplace.

Captain McGuire's head.

THE RAIDS CAME nightly now. Conner and his men—Gyovai, Johns, and Herbert—decided to head far north, to Balete Pass, inland from the Lingayen Gulf. Perhaps the natives would be friendly, Conner thought. And the map showed terrain crumpled with mountains, ravines, cliffs, and the like, the kind of obstacles that would dissuade Japanese pursuit.

On the fifth day, they arrived in the area of Mabalacat, about halfway between Manila and the Lingayen Gulf, and flanking Fort Stotsenburg, which naturally was crawling with Japanese—estimated by some as up to twenty thousand. It was here that Conner reunited with Pablo Aquino, Jimmy Espino's uncle and the man at whose house that first guerrilla meeting had taken place in Samal. Before the war, Aquino had dabbled in Filipino politics. His brother, Benigno, was the representative to the Japanese Empire and, in fact, was now in Japan as an emissary. But Pablo was interested in guerrilla warfare, and even if his brother had ties to the enemy, he was heading up one of the Huk battalions.

Aquino took care of Conner and his men. Fed them. And warned them that continuing north would spell doom for them; the Japanese soldiers in the Canabatuan area would pounce on them, he said.

When Conner asked about Julian Palad's whereabouts, Pablo was surprised Conner did not know.

"Dead," Pablo said. Killed by the Huks' own "board of examiners." Palad had apparently turned traitor and sold out to the Japanese. Conner couldn't believe it. He liked to think his instincts about people were good. Palad may have been an ego-driven swashbuckler who, Conner believed, lacked respect for Filipinos not serving with him, but a traitor? The news shook him. Who else might he have misjudged?

"Come with us," Pablo Aquino said.

The Huks were heading fifteen miles southeast, to the Canaba Swamp area, for a meeting of the organization's military committee. They guaranteed Conner and his men safe passage, good food, and a grand view of Mount Arayat. The travel would be across swamplands, and thus easy, he said. Conner and his men huddled. OK, they agreed.

The trip proved not to be the paradise they'd been promised. The food was bad, the travel difficult, and the Filipinos along the way strangely reserved. "The people," wrote Conner, "were under fear. We could tell and sense that they were taking orders from the Hukbalahap, and although we could see that they wanted to be friendly with us, most had little to say and little to do with us."

At the small town south of Magalang, Conner and his men—Gyovai, Herbert, and Johns—were brought to a shed where they were told they could sleep. In the distance, across a field, Conner saw a farmhouse with guards in front of it. He and his men set up their mosquito nets and blankets, and talked for a bit. Conner expected an interrogation; wasn't the Huks' interest in the men because of what they knew about Japanese operations in the area? Nobody came to them with questions.

Conner's suspicion deepened; indeed, the already-wide playing field of deceit was about to stretch even wider, brushing the edge of absurdity. He slipped across the field to the farmhouse and demanded to talk to Aquino. Inside, fifty men were packed into the house, sitting on the floor, each with a weapon at the ready. Conner's eyes swept the room, looking for intentions in the faces of others.

"Are you a friend of Ramsey's?" a man asked him.

"You mean Lieutenant Ramsey, of the 26th Cavalry?" Conner hadn't met Ed Ramsey, but his reputation was as a guy who bled red, white, and blue, even if his ego could get the best of him.

"That is the name he goes by"—Conner's brow furrowed—"but he is not really an American," said the Huk. "He only poses as one. He is truly a German, an ally of the Japanese. He came to the Philippines to pose as an American, and he has gathered a lot of information regarding the guerrilla operation, and has reported it all to the Japanese."

"What is the basis for your accusation?" Conner asked.

"We have it on good authority," said the Huk. "We uncovered his true identity, and we know him to be a traitor."

This was absurd. "You've made a mistake," Conner said. "Ramsey is not a German spy."

This angered the man and, sensed Conner, those around him.

"If you believe that," the Huk said, "if you defend him like this, then you, *too*, must be a member of the German underground!"

The words felt like daggers in Conner's back. He'd been warned about the Huks from Thorp and others. Now, for the first time, Conner sensed he might be wearing white and the Huks blue. But, surrounded by fifty men, now was not the time to raise the possibility. And the Canaba Swamps were surrounded by Japanese; Conner and his guys were dead men if they dared go it alone. It was another ugly irony of guerrilla warfare: Sometimes you needed the protection of the very men you opposed.

The next day, in outriggers, Conner and his men went with the Huks to a barren island where the guerrilla outfit had set up a retreat of sorts, bamboo barracks where they sometimes came for rest. The four men were told to bivouac here. They were given no food until the next morning, when a soldier tossed them some raw fish. The following day, a few well-dressed, obviously well-educated Filipino men arrived on the banks and approached the foursome.

Conner had always gone out of his way to be friendly to the Huks; this was, after all, their country, and the two groups, he reasoned, shared the bond of not wanting the Japanese to control it. Now he had already made the call for himself: Either he was leaving or they were going to have to kill him.

The well-dressed men, he soon realized, were—like the man the other night—suspicious of him. They talked of all the support the Huks had given Conner. How if Clay knew Ramsey so well he, too, must be a traitor. How fond Conner had been of Julian Palad, who, they'd come to find, was working for the Japanese. What did this all add up to?

"If anybody is a traitor in this group, it's not me, it's not Ramsey, it's not Palad," said Conner. "So it must be you."

"We're not trying to cause you any trouble," the man said. "We're only trying to find out who you are."

"You know who I am as well as I do. And there's only one thing we want from you: transportation out of this place."

Impossible, he told Conner. The next day, with about one hundred Huks now gathered, the military committee convened for a daylong session in which they laid out what they said was a cut-and-dried case that all four Americans were working for the enemy. What's more, they said, Conner and his men had failed miserably in organizing any sort of guerrilla outfit. And why? Because they couldn't even organize themselves. The Americans were guerrilla laughingstocks. Throw a handful of Americans together, and in a week, they'd be quibbling about rank or who was doing all the work and who was sloughing.

But there's a way out of this mess, the foursome was told.

Join us. They would all be made colonels. And be part of a guerrilla organization that had a semblance of purpose.

Enough. That night, as the moon rose and a guard snored, Conner led Gyovai, Herbert, and Johns down the bank to the waters. The silhouette of a man appeared. It was a Philippine Scout who had seen what was going on and, like Conner, knew their only hope was escape. In the moonlight, the scout paddled the foursome away, through an area known as the Fish Ponds and down a river. At each bridge crossing, the scout would have them lie facedown on the bottom of the boat to avoid being seen by the Japanese guards. Johns was frightened; he jumped ashore and hurried away into the darkness. At one dock, Filipinos warned that the Japanese were everywhere; they mustn't stop. But they still handed the Americans cigarettes, bananas, even a can of pork and beans.

At dawn, they arrived in a town called Minalan a few miles to the north. Houses jutted out over the banks of the narrow stream they were traveling. In the quiet of the morning, Conner looked to see dozens of Filipinos welcoming them. How, he wondered, had they gotten word so fast that the Americans were coming? The Filipinos waved, smiled, and, when the *banca* arrived, handed each man his own woven basket of food.

The sun was rising. The spirit strong. The people had heard on KGEI in San Francisco talk of the Americans returning to the Philippines. "We were encouraged," wrote Conner. "Even though we were tired, without sleep all night; even though we were discouraged because we had not been able to go north, we felt better. These Filipinos had re-established my faith in people."

A faith that had only begun to be tested.

FIFTEEN

Hope and Betrayal

December 24, 1942, to February 8, 1943

Time in the jungle since the Fall of Bataan:
Nine to ten months

Jan. 1, 1943

Captain Damon J. Gause
Winder, Georgia

Dear Captain Gause,

Through Leroy Cowart's mother and a Mr. Dewey Hampton we learned that you knew our son Clay Conner Jr. very well. Since you had already written them concerning him I decided not to make any more demands on your time as I know the public undoubtedly has swamped you with requests for information concerning their relatives in the Philippines. However, as time goes on and the mystery of the fate of our men over there seems to become more complicated I find myself instinctively turning to you, since you are the only one in this country so far as we know who was with him over there, for some personal word as to his actual condition, both mental and physical, at least when you saw him last.

If you knew him well you most likely know too as we do that confinement and inactivity would be about the hardest thing possible for him to endure so therefore I am greatly concerned as to what imprisonment may do to him mentally more than physically. All the stories told by those who have returned from there have been heart rendering as the cruelty and inhumanity of the Japs seems to be equaled by no other race so the general opinion back home seems to be that death is preferable to being their prisoner. If that is true naturally we hope for the most merciful way out for Clay Jr. It is so easy for people who have no one over there to say "If he is a prisoner he will be alright." That is just idle talk and only aggravates anyone who has relatives in such a position.

The only consolation we have is that naturally Clay Jr. is cheerful, has plenty of grit and is adaptable to most any situation and so those qualities may carry him through to endure most anything to regain his freedom. He will be hard to beat we know.

We are very glad you were lucky enough to get back home and you certainly deserve the best America has to offer. Good luck. Thank you in advance for an answer if you have time to do so.

Sincerely,
Mrs. Clay Conner Sr.

The Filipinos in the barrio of San Basilio did their best to give Conner, Gyovai, and Herbert a nice Christmas. They built a makeshift place in a rice field for the men to hide out, and on Christmas Eve, they brought gifts of food like the men had rarely seen: chicken, rice, pork, and all sorts of sugar-rich concoctions.

On Christmas Day, the villagers assigned guards to the men so the soldiers could watch the festivities: children's plays, singing, dancing. At one point, Conner and Gyovai—fast becoming close friends—serenaded the village with their rendition of a Tagalog song, *"Paru Paru Bukid."* *More! More!* The people loved it. So did Conner and Gyovai.

"We had a wonderful time," wrote Conner. "And we forgot the Japs even existed. We'd forgotten the war was on."

With the new year, however, he couldn't afford to forget that for long. He resolved to travel more, in hopes of finding an area where the Japanese and the Huks would quit hounding him long enough so he could establish a guerrilla unit. "The day after Christmas," he wrote, "marked the end of my aimless wandering."

Instead, Conner had his eyes on an ambitious trek west through the Zambales Mountains to the town of Morong, near the South China Sea, in an attempt to muster support in a place that might not be crawling with Japanese soldiers. Conner had hated the mountains since the day he'd struggled down that shale wall with Private Ernest Kelly only weeks into the jungle experience; but he also realized that the Japanese did, too, which is why he'd find less resistance trying to organize there than in the lowlands.

Before leaving, Conner stopped in Tala. Francisco showed him where he had buried Conner's journal, inside waterproof bamboo tubing, and Clay—as he had months before—reminded him he would be back at war's end to claim it. Much had changed in the barrio. Francisco and Maria's little boy with the mental paralysis had died. Agado, Francisco's brother, had returned to the lowlands to farm. And Japanese patrols had increased, blowing through the area like unexpected wind gusts to search, threaten, torture, and kill. The Americans who'd been staying here—guys Conner knew well—had decided to burrow deeper into the jungle: Schletterer, Lawrence, Keith, and Boyd.

The catch-22 of guerrilla development was twofold: Leaders needed clusters of men to carry on their mission, but the larger the cluster the more food that was required—and, thus, the less to go around for each man. What's more, the larger the cluster the more attention they'd get from the Japanese patrols and, thus, the edgier a Filipino barrio might be about harboring the men. And so it was that while the Americans were glad to see Conner and Gyovai, frankly they weren't keen on them staying.

Gyovai, much to Clay's dismay, wanted to stay, even if nobody had

Clay Conner, age three.
CONNER FAMILY COLLECTION

Conner, second from the left, as a Duke cheerleader.
DUKE UNIVERSITY ARCHIVES

EVERYTHING UNDER CONTROL LOVE TO MIMI AND YOU ANSWER=
CLAY CONNER.

CLASS OF SERVICE				1201	SYMBOLS
This is a full-rate Telegram or Cablegram unless its deferred character is indicated by a suitable symbol above or preceding the address.					DL=Day Letter
					NT=Overnight Telegram
				(19)	LC=Deferred Cable
					NLT=Cable Night Letter
	A. N. WILLIAMS PRESIDENT	NEWCOMB CARLTON CHAIRMAN OF THE BOARD	J. C. WILLEVER FIRST VICE-PRESIDENT		Ship Radiogram

The filing time shown in the date line on telegrams and day letters is STANDARD TIME at point of origin. Time of receipt is STANDARD TIME at point of destination

NAJ99 VIA RCA=F CEBU 15 16/NFT

1942 MAR 16 AM 9 19

LC H C CONNER=

174 N GROVE ST EASTORANGENJ=

EVERYTHING UNDER CONTROL LOVE=

CLAY JR.

Three weeks before the Fall of Bataan, Conner was his usual upbeat self when a friend sent this telegram home for him from the island of Cebu. CONNER FAMILY COLLECTION

Only about one in 300 U.S. soldiers chose to head for the jungles instead of surrender. Those who didn't, like these men, were forced onto what became known as the Bataan Death March.
NATIONAL ARCHIVES

Soon after the Fall of Bataan, a Filipino fighting organization known as the Hukbalahap formed as the "People's Army Against the Japanese." The Huks, as they were known, would vex Conner and his men more than once. INDIANA HISTORICAL SOCIETY

In Pampanga Province, Conner and his men lived in huts as crude, though larger, than this Negrito-built dwelling. MANILA DEPARTMENT OF THE INTERIOR

IT'S NO NAME I WOULD CALL IT HIDDEN VALLEY.
SURROUNDED BY MTS AND PEAKS—ONE WAY IN.
OUR LARGEST, CLAY HOGAN
AND GUNNER
LIVED HERE WITH US
SIZE 14' X 20'
BOHO SLAT SIDES
NOV 1944

RAISED
CHICKENS
PIGS

BROOK

FG

OVER

Frank Gyovai's sketch, done in November 1944, of the flag-accented final hut in which he and the others lived: "Hidden Valley." At 280 square feet, it was the largest of their five "permanent" locations. INDIANA STATE HISTORICAL SOCIETY

On January 30, 1945, in Concepcion, Lt. Gen. Oswald Griswold accepted the tattered flag from Conner, up front in light shirt, and the others. MALCOLM DECKER COLLECTION

An upbeat group of eight survivors at Concepcion, January 30, 1945: Kneeling, left to right: Clay Conner Jr., Charlie Stotts, Robert Allen Campbell, and Bob Mailheau. Standing, left to right: Frank Gyovai, William Bressler, Doyle Decker, and Albert Bruce.

INDIANA HISTORICAL SOCIETY

LEFT TO RIGHT: Frank Gyovai, Russ Lindersmith, Bob Mailheau, and Doyle Decker, soon after Conner and his men emerged from the jungles in January 1945. Lindersmith, who'd known Mailheau before the surrender and whose ship was in port, was stunned to see his pal still alive. MALCOLM DECKER COLLECTION

LEFT: Conner and his father, soon after he returned safely from the Philippines.
CONNER FAMILY COLLECTION

RIGHT: Conner with Gyovai's mother, Ethel, when he came to West Virginia in August 1945 for a celebration in honor of Frank's safe return. When Gyovai dreamed of home, Conner said, it was usually about his mother's cooking. INDIANA HISTORICAL SOCIETY

Clay and Elizabeth on their wedding day, June 25, 1946, flanked by Clay Sr. and Marguerite Conner to the left and Jack Thomson and Esther Thomson to the right. CONNER FAMILY COLLECTION

Clay Conner Jr.'s four sons in the early years of the pony farm that their father developed in honor of his father's Kentucky roots: back, left to right, Clay III and Jack, front, left to right, Jim and Tom.
CONNER FAMILY COLLECTION

Conner's headstone at Crown Hill Cemetery in Indianapolis included a reference to the same Romans verse that had meant so much to him on Luzon four decades before. **PHOTO BY BOB WELCH**

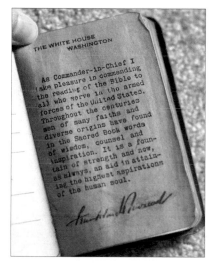

The New Testament that he'd once initially refused remained one of his prized possessions as he grew older. **CONNER FAMILY COLLECTION**

Conner brought home the same Colt .45 that had saved his life numerous times. **CONNER FAMILY COLLECTION**

LEFT: Conner in his mid-fifties.   CONNER FAMILY COLLECTION

RIGHT: Conner shortly before his death in 1983.   CONNER FAMILY COLLECTION

Clay Conner Jr.'s four sons today, left to right: Tom, Clay III, Jack and Jim.
CONNER FAMILY COLLECTION

exactly thrown down the welcome mat. So it would be just Conner and Ray Herbert heading to Morong. "I was disappointed," wrote Conner, "but I didn't make anything of it. We were all on our own. It was up to each of us to make our decisions and so we shook hands, and Ray and I left."

THE PAIR'S GUIDE was a Negrito, from the same tribe as the man who had concocted the potion that had seemingly saved Conner from malaria in Tala: small, deep brown, barefoot, and wearing only a loincloth. Black, kinky hair. Piercing eyes. Fingers worn smooth, apparently from digging. A bow and quiver of arrows on his back. And an infectious cheerfulness. He was, Conner learned, part of a tribe that, centuries ago, had ruled Bataan but been pushed deeper into the forest, which seemed to be just fine with them as they showed little interest in joining even the most simplistic Filipino culture.

The man would dart into the dense foliage and return with a handful of berries. He would be only feet away from Conner and Herbert but be almost impossible to see, his dark skin giving him an almost magical camouflaging with the jungle. He would disappear and then, just as Conner and Herbert got concerned, yelp from a limb above them. Conner was intrigued by him—and by the Negritos in general. "I was totally fascinated by them," he wrote. "I wanted to know everything about them."

That night, the guide led them to a small Negrito settlement on the west side of Mount Natib and Conner found himself less fearful than intrigued. "The people made their living by stripping *wauki*," he wrote. "It was a long, round vine that grew on the surface, and under the surface of the ground, about as thick as your index finger. It would be in strips of maybe fifty yards by thirty yards. And they would strip off the tributary vines, making it one clean, long vine, then, with a sharp knife, split it." They then used the strips to make bamboo chairs or tables that they could trade for camotes or rice from Filipinos on the edge of the mountains. "It was amazing to watch them," said Conner. The Negritos gave

Conner a crack at the craft and laughed as he bumbled along in utter failure, his only consolation that he hadn't severed a finger in the process.

The primitive people wore hardly anything—even the women. Ate leaves and roots. Built shelters of banana leaves thrown over a few pieces of bamboo to form a teepee of sorts. And slept around the fire. After a spirited swim in the river, Conner and Herbert joined them.

"They go to bed rather early, and in the middle of the night, stir the fires [to] keep away mosquitoes and what-not in the jungle," he wrote. "They sit about warming their hands and feet, and then talk again for about an hour before they sleep again. And we got up and joined them. I thought that was the best part of the night. It was quiet, almost like another world. They were happy, laughing. . . . We joined the Negritos about the campfire and talked to them about different things, trying to find out their way of life—what they were interested in, their religion, their beliefs."

As with seeing "Bataan" in the clouds over Mount Mariveles, Conner sensed another premonition as he spent time with the Negritos. "I knew at the outset that [the Negritos] had killed other white men who tried to violate their sanctuary," he wrote, "but I knew in my heart and mind that one day I would become one of them, and they would look to me as their brother."

Though Conner and Herbert left the next morning, Clay sensed an odd attachment to a group of people who couldn't have been any more different from the song-and-dance fraternity boy than if they'd arrived from a distant planet. "The little children," he wrote, "were sorry, I think, to see us go."

Strangely, so was Conner.

BY EARLY 1943, occasional rumors of MacArthur's return washed across Luzon like frothy ocean waves, sudden splashes of hope amid the doldrums of day-to-day existence. Not that Conner thought it would happen immediately—or even at all—but hope itself, whether built on anything substantial or not, was better than no hope at all.

Still, as he stared out at Subic Bay from a town called Olongapo, his impatience needled him. The ocean looked inviting. No Japanese. No Huks. No disease and rotted bodies and political jungles to negotiate. He thought of China. Australia. Why not? A "Hail Mary" escape by boat, the sort of semi-crazed thing a guy like his old pal Rocky Gause might attempt.

The idea had sparked to life after Conner met a boat builder in the seaside town near Morong, his initial destination. True, the Filipino's style leaned toward the primitive side, "best described like a Robinson Crusoe operation," Conner wrote. Still, it was *something*. And, as a solution, seemingly so much simpler than the complex grind of the jungle, where disease, terrain, and foliage were hardships enough, much less when you added the tangled layers of social, political, and military sausage. Just two guys and a boat riding the winds of freedom. "I thought we might get us a boat and sail out into the South China Sea," he wrote. "Maybe we could even hit China. It seemed like a wild idea, but anything was better than what we had been putting up with."

Later, Conner and Herbert were invited into a Filipino home that overlooked Olongapo Bay, nothing fancy, but a wood-frame structure complete with beds, and wicker furniture on the deck, two rocking chairs that Conner and Herbert soon retreated to, cold drinks in hand. Given the way they'd been living for the past nine months, the two might as well have been at some Florida Keys beach club. They listened to the surf roll ashore beyond the sway of coconut palms. Looked to the bay and the sea beyond. "It was a beautiful sight, a wonderful spot," wrote Conner. "And Ray and I kind of let down. We just talked about all the things we had on our hearts." What they'd been through. Where they were. And where they might be going.

Nearing his one-year anniversary in the jungle, had Conner made the right decision—to go it on his own instead of surrendering? Only about one in three hundred men had taken this chance—roughly half were already dead by now—though Conner remembered Captain Mason predicting even lower survival rates. "One in a million" would make it, he'd said. The way things had gone, figured Conner, the captain was proving wiser by the day.

"The life of a guerrilla fighter is exhausting—physically, mentally and nervously—lonely, perilous, hard in every way," wrote "Yank" Levy in *Guerrilla Warfare*. "The guerrilla must sometimes work in isolation, must lurk in the shadows. And take terrifying risks in broad daylight."

Deep down, Conner knew the boat idea was wishful thinking, a trading of one set of problems for another: They would have little food and water, little idea what course to set, and little energy to row. Beyond that, machine-gunners on passing Japanese ships would arm-wrestle each other for the fun of bagging two American fish in a saltwater barrel.

Oh, well. The sun slipped into the South China Sea. Conner watched the horizon grow dim, almost as if he'd forgotten what lay beyond.

CONNER AND HERBERT began holding meetings to organize guerrilla forces. Each night, men from the area reported about 7 P.M. as the setting sun washed the sand, huts, and jungle beyond in hues of pale orange. "Every night," wrote Conner, "[Filipino leaders] brought new men to be indoctrinated. We swore them in, gave them their orders, told them what their duties would be, sent them into Bataan to find weapons if they didn't have any, and taught them how to use them and where to hide them. And then we gathered information from them as they performed their duties daily. Some of them were working for the Japanese in the towns, in their camps. And little by little, we gathered information concerning [the Japanese] operations."

Finally, his guerrilla operation was getting some traction. Soon, Conner knew much about the Japanese: How many trucks, rifles, and men they had. Where their reserves were located. How they traveled and when. "We assigned men on demolition work for bridges, railroads, and men who were to cut off the retreat of the Japanese at the time Americans landed," Conner wrote.

Meanwhile, nearly every day, a Filipino runner would arrive with news about guerrilla operations from other places on the peninsula. One day the message involved Lieutenant Ramsey, the guy the Huks were sure was a German; he was arriving soon. The next day he did.

Ramsey was full of news, including reports that the American forces, indeed, were on their way back. Conner remained doubtful. He hadn't seen an American plane in the sky for almost a year. If they were truly returning, wouldn't some bombing already have begun? "But whether or not it was true," Conner wrote, "it was good to hear news like this."

Conner shared his experiences of the Huks claiming Ramsey was a German spy—and accusing Clay of the same. Ramsey hadn't heard about Conner's run-in with the Huks, but he told Conner he'd already been captured once by the outfit and was certain they were planning to kill him before he had escaped. Conner was curious how the Huk movement had, like a chameleon, seemingly changed its camouflage. Once pro-American, it now seemed like something else.

Ramsey explained how the Huks—in particular Luis Taruc, mayor of a lowland town—had, in essence, used the Americans to gain power. When the Japanese arrived in December 1941, Taruc had pledged his loyalty to Colonel Thorp. He did so ostensibly as a means of channeling Filipino anger against the Japanese. But, in reality, said Ramsey, Taruc did so because sticking a "pro-American/anti-Japanese" label on the force would attract young Filipino men—and provide great impetus to have mayors and police chiefs release those men from the census roles.

It worked. But then the lizard started changing its colors. Its leaders suggested that the Filipino force change its name to Hukbalahap, or the Huks, because it was a Filipino name and more attractive than a jumble of initials, USAFFE, that meant nothing to the locals. In truth, said Ramsey, the Huks emerged as the foundation of the Communist Party.

Everything Ramsey said checked out with Conner, who had begun to realize it wasn't coincidental that he and his men were almost always raided by the Japanese within a day or two of Huk contact. At the same time, the two-faced Huks were adroit at posing to the Filipinos as the most ardent of nationalists. Conner left the exchange with Ramsey reminded that as his time on Luzon deepened, it was only getting harder telling the good guys from the bad.

THE MIDDLE-OF-THE-NIGHT NOISE seemed to be coming from down on the beach. Conner bolted up from his sleep. He threw on his clothes, slapped on his pistol, and ran toward the commotion. Ramsey had already left for Boone's camp; Herbert was still fast asleep. A group of men in an outrigger had just beached. Conner stayed hidden until he could determine whether this was friend or foe. Soon, Conner determined, despite the muffled voices, that one of the men in the group was an American who, with the help of Filipinos, had apparently just escaped from the Japanese.

"I walked forward and met them on the beach, and he looked at me—and he was afraid," wrote Conner. "I shook his hand and introduced myself."

The man—olive-skinned, jet-black hair, piercing eyes—acted like a hunted animal. Shivering. Spent. Nervous. He mumbled that his name was Fred and glanced back and forth along the beach, apparently still worried about pursuers. "He was shaking and very ill at ease, like a man who had been beaten and trapped and then escaped," wrote Conner. "He didn't trust me, I could see that. He looked at me as if I were not his friend. That puzzled me."

Conner took him to a thatched hut. Seeing Clay's pistol, the man asked if he had another. Conner said no.

"Can I buy it from you?"

The Filipino men who'd accompanied him in the boat neared. Seeing them, the man scurried away to the other side of a shack. Conner wondered if he was sick, perhaps mentally unstable. Later, the man calmed down and told Conner his story. He was, indeed, an American soldier.

Had some Mexican blood. Came from Newark, New Jersey—Conner's neck of the woods—and had come to the Philippines with an army air corps pursuit group. He'd escaped from the death march and been captured, beaten, and taken to Abucay Prison Camp near Manila Bay. He'd escaped while driving a truck.

Conner asked him about other Americans at the camp, and he talked of many, some of whom Conner knew as well. Some, the man said, had died in the camp, others en route. Back at the house, Conner gave the man a room to sleep in. Meanwhile, Herbert, who'd missed the action, awakened.

Conner wondered aloud if Fred could be a German whom the Japanese were using as a spy. "But," he wrote, "it was a sure thing that Fred was an American. He knew the American cities, and he particularly knew the Newark area. And I discharged all suspicion and knew he was truly an escapee."

In the days to come, the newcomer relaxed, laughed, became fun to have around for Conner and Herbert. He spoke Spanish. Told a good joke. And loved to box; he and Herbert sparred here and there in light-hearted matches.

By now, Conner and the others had survived for ten months. But on the night of February 10, a Filipino guerrilla—one of Conner's men—awakened him. "Sir, you must leave immediately," he said. "The Japanese are on their way." The trio scrambled east into the night jungle, tripping, falling, reeling from leaves and branches that slapped back from the man in front. Behind them the three heard gunshots and saw the smoke from the barrio rising in the sky.

In a moment to catch his breath, Conner realized the just-hatched guerrilla setup in Olongapo had saved their lives. Had it not been in place, the three likely would have died in their sleep or been captured and tortured. But the smoke and gunfire they left behind suggested that the Filipino men in his outfit weren't as lucky. And that Conner and the two others would suffer the same fate if they didn't hustle their way east.

THE TRIO PRESSED on. Eventually, they found the Zig-Zag Trail, the only east-west pathway through the Zambales in this region, and were heading east, back to Banaba. Conner and Herbert were doing fine, but by midday Fred began stumbling. He pitched forward and fell down. By now, Conner had seen enough men do the same thing that he immediately assumed it was some sort of jungle fever biting deep. They were in Negrito country. Conner found a pair willing to help. The man couldn't walk, so it was decided the Negritos would take him in while Conner and Herbert outran the Japanese. Later, they'd send back help.

Soon, the pair arrived at one of Colonel Boone's outposts. Conner sent word to Boone's headquarters about the man who needed help. The next day, Boone and Ramsey arrived. They asked if Conner was certain the man's name was Fred—"Yes"—and then asked Clay to describe him. "Five-eleven-and-a-half. One seventy-five. Jet-black, curly hair and deep piercing eyes. Rawboned and tense. Olive-colored skin. And tough."

Ramsey and Boone looked at each other. "Tibuc-Tibuc," said Ramsey.

Conner's brow furrowed. "You mean, the American that sold out to the Japanese?"

"Yeah," said Boone, "one of the guys the Japs released from prison camps to report on American activities."

Conner seethed.

The Negritos, when the trio arrived, said the man had left—and, of course, they hadn't tried to stop him. He was, after all, an American, right? Ramsey told Conner that Tibuc-Tibuc's deception had cost the lives of a number of American soldiers after they'd been ratted out by the traitor.

"The more I heard, the madder I got," wrote Conner. Many of the men he'd organized and trained back in Olongapo were probably killed in the raid he had escaped, the Japanese having obviously followed "Fred" to the American's guerrilla hideout.

You can escape from one enemy, Conner realized, and yet not shake free from another: the conscience. "I told [Ramsey and Boone] I would take up vigilance on the Zig-Zag Trail, and that probably 'Tibuc-Tibuc' would be coming through in a truck with his friends, the Japs, and I would wait there until I got them all," wrote Conner. "I would get my vengeance."

Conner waited a full week for Tibuc-Tibuc. The man never appeared. Conner slunk back to Boone's camp like a man with blood on his hands, the blood of the Filipino soldiers who had been found—and killed, he assumed—by Clay's own ignorance. Conner hated failure, especially his own.

AT CAMP O'DONNELL, on the plains to the north, nearly twice as many Americans had died at the prison camp as had perished on the hundred-mile journey to it. The camp was a cesspool of disease, torture, and hopelessness. But good fortune smiled on Sergeant Bato. From August 1942 to January 1943, the Japanese paroled all Filipino prisoners at O'Donnell who were still alive—roughly half the fifty thousand. Their releases were contingent upon their signing a sworn oath never to violate the laws of the Japanese government. Sergeant Bato was among those who signed, though his true allegiance lay elsewhere.

He returned to his home in Sapang Bato, where malaria and dysentery had ravaged the people like a typhoon. Soon, Bato was among those wracked by disease. He teetered on the edge of death. Days became weeks, weeks became months. His wife tended to him the best she could, slowly nursing him back to health. When he was well, he asked about the much-coveted item he had brought back from the battle at Morong. She took him to the family chest and reached her hand inside the pillowcase.

The flag was still there.

SIXTEEN

The Hunted

February 1943 to March 1943

Time in the jungle since the Fall of Bataan:
Ten to eleven months

WHEN CONNER MET Bob Mailheau, the man had a pistol to his head. Conner knew this to be true because he was the one holding it.

Conner had returned to the lowlands to shuffle the deck and see what new hand to play. Not that any of the others had been particularly impressive, especially his time in Olongapo, which had begun with promise, escalated to relative bliss—significant guerrilla organization and dazzling China Sea sunsets—but ended badly.

Herbert decided to team up with Corporal Boone and a Lieutenant William Gardner and head elsewhere. And who could blame him? It wasn't as if Conner had proven to be good luck. Still, Johnny Johns, a live wire whom Clay enjoyed, rejoined Conner and stayed with him, night and day, as Clay went through yet another sweat-and-chill malaria attack.

Soon, Boone and Ramsey arrived. In a few days, Alfred Bruce, whom Conner had run across earlier, straggled in with a fellow named Tommy Musgrove—and with an estimate that Japanese garrisons had increased in the area from twenty to seventy men. On February 22, some five hundred Japanese soldiers flushed guerrillas out of lowland areas north of Dinalupihan. Conner and his men barely escaped after their hut was torched. Boone's camp was hit. At Fassoths' Camp, a dozen Americans were captured and were heading for POW camps, where many would die.

Meanwhile, if only 100 to 150 American guerrillas were still alive at this point, many were in the lowlands. Too many in one place for safety's sake, Conner thought. It was time to split up. Time for new configurations of who was traveling with whom. Conner and Ramsey decided to team up. Conner wanted Johns to join them, but Johns and Ramsey didn't get along, so Johnny passed on the offer. In Conner's eyes, Ramsey could be a bit full of himself—he reminded him of somebody he used to know back when he had mirrors to look into—but he was tough, smart, and a worthy travel partner. The two headed north and farther east than Conner had even been. They were just outside the barrio of Natividad, in the the Lingayen Gulf province of Pangasinan, when a Filipino man appeared from the darkness.

"Have you seen Bob?" he asked in broken English.

"Bob who?" said Conner.

"The American who lives in the barrio with us."

Whoever this "Bob" was, he was apparently missing. The man beckoned the two to follow as he checked out the place where the man he called Bob had been hiding. They did so, but with pistols drawn. The man scampered up a ladder and into a grass hut, then motioned for the men to follow. Cautiously, Conner headed up. Ramsey stayed below. In the moonlight, Conner realized the room was empty. Was this a trap? Could "Bob" be Tibuc-Tibuc? The man nodded to another room. Eyes still on the Filipino, Conner backed slowly that way, peered sideways into the room, and saw a man lying on the floor. He knelt over him, pistol aimed, cocked it, and then issued a staccato warning: "Don't move or I'll kill you."

The man shook to life in a panic. "Don't shoot!" he said. "I'm an American!" A handsome, athletic-looking soldier extended his hand in friendship. "Hello," he said, "my name is Bob Mailheau."

Conner hesitated a moment, then stuck out his hand. "Hello," he said. "My name is Sam White."

PERHAPS THE ALIAS was a devious nod to his traitor, "Fred," whom Conner surmised could still be tracking him down. Perhaps it was simply to dust his tracks from the Japanese in response to the rumor that the Japanese believed Conner to have been recently dropped on the island by a submarine in advance of a planned American return; hundreds of Japanese soldiers were supposedly trying to hunt him down with hopes of interrogating him. Or perhaps, as Mailheau would one day tell an interviewer, it sprang from Conner's long afternoons in the Jersey movie theaters. "Maybe he did fashion this 'Sam White' personality simply because of what he had seen on the big screen while growing up," he said.

At any rate, Conner concocted an alias that, from this point on, he used on occasion, including that of his meeting Mailheau. Conner later said it was for protection, and was derived from "Uncle *Sam* the *white* man." How often he trotted out the name isn't clear, but as trust became more of an issue, Conner began doing whatever was required to keep that trust, even if it meant using an assumed name.

Meanwhile, he quickly came to trust his new acquaintance, Bob Mailheau; in fact, Clay was infatuated with Mailheau when he learned Bob had grown up in Hollywood, just a few blocks from stars such as Mickey Rooney. Conner fired movie star–related questions at him, the kind of questions his mother would have asked, too. *Had he met Rooney? What was he like? What other stars had he seen?*

Mailheau, Conner came to learn, had been part of the 24th Pursuit Group out of Clark Field. The back of his skull had mostly healed from being slammed with the butt of a rifle before he'd escaped the Bataan death march. He'd been taken prisoner at Mariveles and, about a week into the forced march, slunk into the jungle while on a rare rest stop just southwest of Guagua. Like most of the prisoners, he was in sad shape, but he managed to get to San Fernando, where Catholic sisters helped him recover. Because San Fernando was on the death-march route, Japanese soldiers frequently stopped to look for escapees, but they never found Mailheau. The sisters hid him in the attic, not that there was much to hide. He weighed seventy-two pounds, less than half his normal weight.

Mailheau's father was a captain of detectives for the Los Angeles Police Department. Bob had been a track star at Hollywood High School and won a scholarship to the University of Southern California. He liked a good time. In fact, he had enlisted with an eye toward serving in the Pacific because the action was in Europe and he didn't want any part of it. "He didn't fit well in the war," Conner wrote. "He didn't want to be [here]." But as long as he was, he was tired of just sitting around in this hideout. Could he join Conner and Ramsey?

Conner liked the idea. Ramsey didn't, but he agreed to let Mailheau go with them at least for a while. Mailheau then told the two about another American, Joe Donahey, who had built himself a hideout in a dried-up drainage ditch. Conner went to see him.

"I'm Joe Donahey," he said, extending a hand, "from East Jalopy, Iowa." He was short, maybe five-foot-seven; skinny, perhaps 120 pounds, and ragged, his hair having not been cut in months. His clothes hung on him like swamp moss. No gun, but a hat like no other Conner had seen. "It hung all over his head, down around his face, and it was cut in many places so the brim dangled, and he'd kind of look out between the sliced places. He figured this would keep the people who saw him from recognizing that he was a white man." He had a split personality. Sarcasm dripped from him like a leaky faucet—"Aren't things wonderful today!"— but he never seemed completely relaxed, always sensing a Japanese soldier behind this mango tree or that hut.

Donahey had escaped from the death march, too, a bold move that belied the belief of some fellow guerrillas that he was "scared of his shadow." At any rate, he joined the trio. They headed for Banaba, a barrio of Pampanga Province where a large family, the Hardins, were known to offer five-star service to American soldiers. En route, it became clear that Conner and Ramsey had their differences. Conner liked Bob and

Joe. "I got a kick out of both of them," he wrote. Ramsey thought they were extra baggage. "Ramsey figured they were just somebody else to eat the food," wrote Conner. "He wanted to dump them."

Conner was intrigued by people, idiosyncrasies and all. Ramsey, in Conner's estimation, was not. Rather than engage Bob or Joe in conversation, Ramsey would "busy himself with the Filipinos, always [taking] the important attitude that he was the leader, he was on a very important mission, and so on."

BANABA WAS SUSTENANCE to American soldiers starved for more than just food. Here, Conner and the men met two families—the Hardins and the Lumanlans—who, as the weeks unfolded, treated them like kin.

Mrs. Hardin was about sixty-five years old, had thirteen children, and hated the Japanese. She was a little larger than the average Filipino, about five-foot-two-inches, and plump. "She had a good smile," wrote Conner. "She was warm. Her face was round. She had no teeth at all in her mouth. She was always barefooted. And you would never see her when she wasn't smoking a cigarette. She called us her boys, and there was no doubt about it that she loved us just as much as if we were really her own children."

Meanwhile, the Lumanlans, if a tad more guarded, also treated the men well. Godofred Lumanlan was the defacto barrio mayor and, as such, was bound to be under the scrutiny of patrolling Japanese soldiers who might suspect him of helping the enemy. He went to the woods each day to cut down trees. But if he made money off the Japanese, who bought his logs, he invested in the well-being of the Americans. Like many Filipinos, he realized that their freedom lay in the hands of the Americans being able to somehow turn this defeat into victory—and that they would need help from the natives to do so. And he realized, too, that Japanese propaganda extorting their virtues as leaders of the Filipinos was hollow hypocrisy, based on the Japanese soldiers' murder, torture, and rape of the people whose country they'd taken.

Lumanlan had sons, one of whom, seventeen-year-old Democrito, emerged as almost an extension of the American guerrillas. When the Conner unit pushed north, it was with deep gratitude to the two families—and without Donahey, who didn't like slogging through rice paddies and going to unfamiliar places where the Japanese might be hiding. He stayed in Banaba.

Meanwhile, Conner, Ramsey, and Mailheau continued on, with plans to get to the lowlands north of Fort Stotsenburg because that's where the food was. The fort area would be the most dangerous place any of them had ever traveled through; thousands of Japanese were stationed at what had once been an American installation. Getting past it would be akin to someone trying to get across the Duke campus while steering clear of students. But two Americans, Sergeant Wilbur Jellison and Lieutenant Charles Naylor, had a hideout to the west of the fort and could offer advice on getting through. So the threesome found them in their cliff-side hideout, a spot well hidden by trees and undergrowth.

The guests offered a rare treat: sake. Conner passed, believing, he said, that drinking, weapons, and enemies were a dangerous combination. Ramsey gladly drank his sake—and Clay's. Soon, he started mouthing off, in particular questioning Conner about his relationship with the Huks. If he hadn't been friendly with them, they would never have permitted him to escape, Ramsey said.

That's odd, said Conner, because Ramsey escaped from them, too. Had he been too friendly, too? Conner's comeback lit a spark in Ramsey that whooshed into a forest fire. Finally, Conner said he'd had enough.

"If you've had all you wanted," slurred Ramsey, "then why don't you do something about it?"

Conner wanted to. He thought about reaching for his pistol. But that was crazy. Jellison, probably tougher than them both, came to the rescue. "You guys have had too much to drink," he said. "Go to bed."

Conner hardly slept. Above all, he valued allegiance to the righteous cause at hand; Ramsey had questioned his allegiance. In essence, he had called him a traitor. In the morning, Ramsey apologized, even asked Clay to forgive him. Conner nodded his acceptance, but if his head forgave his heart still burned with anger and a dash of hurt. Ramsey changed his mind and decided to go south to Manila; Conner wanted to go north in an attempt to get beyond both the Japanese and the Huks in northern Luzon. At a stream to wash up, Conner ran into Mailheau. He told Bob he was leaving—without Ramsey. Bob said he was leaving, too—with Clay.

The Ramsey-Conner feud probably stemmed from the two of them being so much alike: swashbucklers who dreamed big and took great pride in being in charge. Though few arguments got as intense as the Conner-Ramsey scuffle, the guerrillas bickered almost as much as they smoked.

"There was a lot of irritation between people in a group," wrote Private Leon Beck, who had escaped the death march. "By being forced into this close association with others, their habits grated on everyone's nerves." "Consequently, there was grumbling about everything. They grumbled if they had to get up and go the bathroom at night and disturbed someone else—even to the way they smoked or the way they ate."

Days got stiflingly hot. Nights, however, could be so cool that the men would strip leaves off trees and burrow down in them to stay warm. To start fires they would use a flint rock and steel, and punk from trees. But the rains, in particular the typhoons, made that nearly impossible. "There's nothing you can do about a storm," said Beck. "You're in the dark and there's no way to even light a fire. All in all, it was pretty miserable. . . ."

Meanwhile, the jungle darkness at night deepened the loneliness and wore on their nerves. Technically speaking, a year would offer only twelve nights of complete darkness, but to Beck and his men, a sliver of moon did little to lighten the inky black. "There were times when I was [obsessed] with the desire to see light," he said. "I was so sick and tired of dark being dark. . . . It was just lonesomeness."

The challenge was also trying to adjust to doing without so much of what they'd once had. "We had no toothbrushes, we had no toothpaste, we had no toilet paper, we had no cooking facilities, no heating or cooling apparatus," Beck wrote.

Over time, it squeezed the men like a vise: the doing without, the stress of knowing the enemy lurked in the jungle, the uncertainty of the Americans returning, the diseases that triggered weeks of fevers and chills, and the assortment of jungle rot: fungus infections, athlete's foot, butt blisters. Amid it all, the unspoken challenge was: adapt or die. Adapt to the culture, the elements, the terrain and foliage and everything else. Or, ultimately, be victim to it all.

Once, a group of men was helping move a Filipino family that had supported them for months. While crossing a mountain, a soldier named Cahill refused to carry a few of the small children.

"You son of a bitch," said Beck. "You were good enough to eat the rice that this lady got up and pounded the same day she gave birth. You're going to [carry] those kids or I'm going to leave you here on the trail." The man sat down on the trail and melted into sobs.

Ultimately, the problem took care of itself. On the east side of the mountains, Beck and the man got into an argument over mosquito netting. That did it. Cahill talked a buddy into joining him. Together, the two walked to nearby Floridablanca and did something that, a year into their jungle experience, suggested how challenging some men found it.

They raised their arms and surrendered to the Japanese.

COMMUNICATION IN THE jungle was an inexact science. With the "bamboo telegraph"—Filipinos racing through the jungle with written or spoken messages—senders seldom could be sure if their missive got through. Now, in March 1943, the bamboo telegraph again clacked with news. A Filipino runner told Conner and Mailheau that two Americans were up ahead. Part of Pablo Aquino's Huks outfit, one a tall fellow, the other a *real* tall fellow. Sounded like Frank Gyovai and six-foot-five Eddie Keith, two men whom Conner hadn't seen since New Year's Day. Conner sent the runner back to inquire of the shorter man's name. Half an hour later, back he came with paper on which was scrawled the signature "Frank Gyovai."

This was needle-in-a-haystack stuff, Conner finding the guy whom he admired more than any man with whom he'd served. He was thrilled to see Frank, and Gyovai was no less thrilled to see Clay. Gyovai and Keith had found nothing but trouble since the group split up ten weeks ago. Japanese patrols. Fifth Columnists. And, of course, death. A guy named Mann had been captured and killed; same with Kelly, the private who'd briefly hung back with Conner in his first days in the jungle. "It kind of made me sick," wrote Conner of hearing the news.

Gyovai and Keith had similar aspirations to go north. When Aquino—the same Filipino leader who had met with Conner and Gyovai on that September 1942 night in Samal—heard of Conner's plans, he scoffed. He wanted the men to go south and meet with the Huks' military committee in the swamps, something about promotions. Conner had already experienced the Huks' swamp "promotions"; they were headed north. Aquino, ostensibly an ally of Conner's when he'd tried to launch a guerrilla unit in Samal, now sounded to Clay like a salesman with a tired pitch.

"You'll never get through," said Aquino.

There will be no Huks for guides, he pointed out, with visible concern for the well-being of Conner and his men. The Filipinos in the area around Canabatuan in Nueva Ecija Province were mostly pro-Japanese—and the price on the men's heads had risen, giving added impetus to those seeking to capture or kill them. "It's impossible to go north through that area unless you've got a tight network of men who are working for you," Aquino said. "Come with us to the south."

Fool me once, shame on you. Fool me twice, shame on me. Conner, Gyovai, Mailheau, and Keith loaded up and headed out.

North.

CONNER WAS SICK again. He was like a malaria-stricken cat with nine lives; on Luzon, guys joked that he should have been dead months ago.

Now, along the road to Lara as darkness settled in for the night, Gyovai bent over to pick him up.

"I got ya, Clay," he said in his usual blustery tone.

"No, no."

"Gotta keep moving," said Gyovai. "Dark's when we make our good time."

Gyovai carried Conner on his back all night. Quite a difference from Clay's first day in the jungle, when he had been all but abandoned. You met all kinds on this island. Some who saved your life. Others who wanted to take it. And a few who didn't care one way or the other.

They arrived in Lara—the farthest north they'd ever ventured—and were allowed to sleep on the floor with a family of Filipinos. It was almost dawn when Conner and the others awoke to find four well-dressed Filipino men sitting on a bench, staring at them. The family was gone.

"Are you mayor of the town?" Conner rasped.

"Yes. How did you know?"

"By the way you dress."

Conner looked around. Something wasn't right—and it wasn't just his health. Through the window, he realized not much was stirring outside, which was odd, even if it was a Sunday.

He went on the offense. "We're not surrendering," Conner said. "You're wasting your time."

The four men looked surprised. Conner was a step ahead of them. The mayor talked of the good treatment prisoners could expect, mentioning Colonel Thorp, Captain Barker, Captain McGuire, and Lieutenant Ramsey. The guy clearly hadn't done his homework, Conner realized. McGuire's head, last Clay had heard, was on display in Botolan. And he informed the mayor that he'd been with Ramsey just days before.

The mayor begged to differ. "I have been informed by the Japanese that Ramsey had been taken."

Conner didn't like the sound of the statement. *Informed by the Japanese.* Sounded a lot like a guy who had a working relationship with the enemy. Usually, the Japanese only did their informing of Filipinos at the tip of a bayonet. When the men left, Conner whispered to the three others, "We need to get out of here." There was a large price on their heads—and a certain Filipino mayor seemed anxious to cash in on it.

Though early, the day was heating up. So was the situation. Outside, the villagers stood still, as if they knew something. The men climbed down the ladder and spread out at the bottom to take a look around. A Filipino man pointed for the men to head south, his face creased with worry.

"Japon! Japon! Japon!" Gyovai's cry sent the four scurrying vaguely southward.

Shots rang out. Bursts of machine-gun fire dotted the dirt. Conner and the others scattered like the random darts and dashes of a fireworks shell gone wrong. Less than a quarter mile from the barrio, they ran into the teeth of a fifty-man Japanese patrol. Feverish and frantic, Conner still registered, in an instant, betrayal. *Tricked. The Filipinos sent us right into the trap.*

When the men turned to head the other way, however, what Conner saw ahead changed his thinking entirely. The size of the Japanese force to the north was far greater than what the foursome had faced to the south. *The Filipinos outside sent us in the direction of least resistance; they truly tried to help us. But as for the mayor who betrayed us: Someday I will return to Lara and kill him.*

For now, Conner needed to turn his attention to eluding the Japanese. He jettisoned his musette bag, including Junko, in a bamboo thicket to lighten his load. Now it was a matter of endurance. A test of wills. A question of resolve. He saw a clearing and began running through the chest-high cogon grass with the panicked zeal of a hunted animal.

IN THE MOIST, tropical heat, Conner awoke in the most discombobulated state he'd ever known—and that included a few morning-afters clouded by too many bottles of San Miguel at Manila's Jai Alai Club. His body felt as if entombed. Stiff. Covered in mud. Parched. Mosquitoes jockeyed for whatever morsel of flesh they could find of him, which wasn't much given his earthy coating.

Where was he? What had happened? Had he been buried alive? No, he realized as the fog started to clear: He had buried *himself* alive. Now he remembered. To hide from the Japanese patrols that had been tailing him for days after the ambush, he had dug himself into the mud and breathed through the reed. It was either that or put his last remaining bullet through his skull, which he had briefly considered.

He must have lost consciousness or fallen asleep, perhaps both. Then, somehow, amid his delirium, Conner had wriggled free from his mud hole and slid down to a creek's edge. Now someone was tugging on his arm, trying to help him into a *banca* (boat)—to either get him to safety or, with a reward in mind and the body as proof, to kill him.

PART FOUR

PERSEVERANCE

SEVENTEEN

Growing Numb

May 1943

Time in the jungle since the Fall of Bataan:
Thirteen months

May 7, 1943

Dear Mr. Conner:

The records of the War Department show your son, Second Lieutenant Henry C. Conner Jr., 0-429,144, Air Corps, missing in action in the Philippine Islands since May 7, 1942.

I fully appreciate your concern and deep interest. You will, without further request on your part, receive immediate notification of any change in your son's status. That the far-flung operations of the present war, the ebb and flow of combat over great distances in isolated areas, and the characteristics of our enemies have imposed upon some of us the heavy burden of uncertainty with respect to the safety of our loved ones is deeply regretted.

Very truly yours,
J. A. Ulio
Major General
The Adjutant General

The young Filipino's eyes darted left and right as if to make sure nobody was watching. Once he had gotten Conner into the *banca*, he slipped his hand into a bag. Conner didn't have the strength to reach for his own pistol. What an inglorious way to die after all he'd been through: helpless to defend himself against a mere kid—and from people whom he'd thought were his friends. Betrayal.

"*Tubig?*" said the young man, handing Clay a canteen he'd fished from the bag.

Conner's eyes squinted and his head tilted slightly in surprise. He took a cautious swig of the water. "My name," the Filipino said earnestly, "is Marco Polo." Conner didn't know whether to laugh or cry; didn't know whether the man was Huk or not. He only knew that he seemed to be on Clay's side. In fact, may have saved his life.

The Filipino took Conner a few miles down the river, to a safe area—"no *Japon*"—and said good-bye to him. Conner shook his hand. "Thank you, Mr., uh, Polo."

Conner needed to try and connect with the three others—Gyovai, Keith, and Mailheau, that is, assuming they'd made it past the Japanese gauntlet. The last thing he'd heard from any of them was Frank's scream of "I'm hit, I'm hit." Using the North Star, Conner walked at night toward where he thought the three others might have wound up had they survived the attack. Midway, a Filipino offered him a course correction, saying Clay had about two miles to go.

As peaceful as the night was, the thing about being a guerrilla was you could never totally relax. You were always looking over your shoulder. You were always the fugitive. And to be caught was, in essence, to be killed. "To be a prisoner of the Japanese was like being caught in a twentieth-century version of Black Plague, a Yellow Death," wrote Gavan Daws in *Prisoners of the Japanese: POWs of World War II in the Pacific.* That's because the Japanese paid little or no regard to the Geneva Convention rules of war that they'd signed but never ratified. In German prison camps, the POW death rate was only four percent; in Japanese camps, twenty-seven.

The American guerrillas, of course, had heard the stories, but as Conner made his way to a hoped-for rendezvous with Gyovai, he was reminded—as he was when he'd read through the Bible time and again in Tala—that fear no longer grated on him.

"It was lonely," Conner wrote, "especially after the experience of that day. However, I wasn't particularly worried now. I wasn't afraid either. After so much pain, and so much sickness, you kind of [lose] consciousness. You kind of get numb to being afraid. You build up within yourself a resistance, and a challenge, and you kind of wait for trouble. You wait to meet it head-on."

When he heard the voices in a barrio, Conner found cover beneath the leaves of a banana tree, lest the moonlight give him away. In a few minutes, a certain voice sounded familiar: an American talking far too loudly in a place crawling with the Japanese. It was, unquestionably, his pal Frank Gyovai.

When he saw Conner, Gyovai threw his arms around his friend. "He just kept beating me on the back, and on my shoulder, and grabbing my arm," wrote Conner. "I'd never seen him so glad before—so happy. I knew I had a friend for life." Frank, it turned out, had only *thought* he'd been wounded during the ambush; the pain, it turned out, was from something else, a sharp piece of flying bamboo or ricocheted rock.

Neither had heard from Mailheau or Keith. But within a couple of weeks, they stumbled across Mailheau, who was fine and said Keith had made it, too. By bamboo telegraph, Mailheau had heard Keith was hiding out near Concepcion to the northeast. Conner and Gyovai also bumped into Sergeant Alfred Bruce and Private Tommy Musgrove, who joined them as they continued the journey north. One night, a Filipino family invited them for dinner; the meat was sizzling on a spit over an open fire, a rare sight and smell in these parts. Conner and Bruce loved it, Gyovai not so much. He went outside and vomited—soon after Bruce had told him he had just eaten a dog.

IN THE MONTHS to come, Conner and his men survived a similar ambush to the one at Lara. Conner got through another malaria attack. He heard that the families of a Filipino family who'd helped them near Concepcion—even the children—had been killed by the Japanese. And he nearly lost Gyovai as a partner. Frank wanted to team up with Keith, whom they'd reconnected with. Conner was heading back for Banaba. When Clay went to say good-bye to Gyovai, Frank didn't seem particularly upbeat about the new setup.

"Why don't you come with us?" said Conner.

"Bob and I don't get along," he said. "I don't think he wants me along."

"It doesn't make any difference to me what or who Bob likes," Conner said. "I have nothing but respect for you, Frank, and as far as I'm concerned, I'd rather be with you than any man I've met in the war."

Gyovai paused a moment, then reached out his hand. "All right, then," he said, "we'll stick together until this thing's over."

So Conner, Mailheau, and Gyovai headed for Banaba. On September 3, 1943, the group arrived at day's end at the hideout of a Lieutenant James Hart, who'd been holed up in the same spot behind the town of Bamban the entire war. At nightfall, Bruce and Musgrove showed up, too.

Hart, of Watsonville, California, was dark-haired, handsome, and—thought Conner—brilliant. He was among the few, like Conner, who had headed for the hills rather than surrender. With the help of a Filipino connection to the lowlands, he had acquired a vast library of books, maps, and charts. People would bring him newspapers from Manila, and, based on the maps, he charted the twists and turns of the war. For whatever reason, the Filipinos told Conner, the Japanese had never discovered his hideout.

Conner was fascinated by the setup. Along with the wealthy man's bookish house in Pio and the house perched above Olongapo Bay, this was the kind of place where Conner could blissfully ride out the war. But that night, after everyone else went to sleep, Conner felt a rare sense of unease, almost as if the jungle had eyes.

His life had become such a constant mantra of movement that even bedding down for the night carried with it a sense of vulnerability. Enough. Conner went to the Filipinos and asked if they could lead him and the others deeper into the jungle, away from Hart's camp. The Filipinos were puzzled. The Japanese had never bothered this area, and jungle travel at night was difficult and dangerous.

"Clay, let's stay for the night," said Gyovai, who was worn out.

"No, we're *not* staying for the night," Conner said. "You can stay if you want to, but I'm going on." The Filipinos agreed to lead the party into the darkness. Gyovai and Bruce reluctantly fell in line, but Musgrove stayed behind.

By morning, as the trio awakened in their new locale, Lieutenant James Hart and Musgrove were dead, the Filipinos burned to death, the books smoldering. An American and two Filipinos were captured in the raid. Hart had fired away with his .45, but when he realized how outnumbered he was, he took a trick from the Japanese. He put a bullet through his own head.

LATER, AFTER THE trio had barely digested that news, they were met near Banaba by Democrito, the son of the town's mayor, who shared another chilling incident. It involved Lawrence, the Louisiana guy whom Clay had sparred with. Democrito had seen some of it and had heard about the rest. Lawrence was wading through a flooded rice paddy when a volley of rifle and machine-gun fire burst from a road. The soldiers surrounded Lawrence in a half circle, then slowly began wading toward him, rifles poised. Lawrence raised his hands in surrender.

They beat him. Kicked him. A half dozen took their shot at him. He was taken to the local Japanese headquarters, where a Captain Tanaka was in charge. Lawrence was questioned. Tanaka apparently didn't like the response. Lawrence was fastened to a bar and suspended by his ankles. Water was pumped into him until his stomach was distended. At Tanaka's command, Lawrence was beaten across his bloated belly with hardwood rods about the size of broom handles. Under this beating everything broke loose inside him, and water was forced from every outlet of his body. He continued to defy Tanaka. Enough. The captain whipped out his sword and, in a powerful burst of anger, all but cut the man in half.

The Japanese soldiers did not kill Raymond Herbert, Conner's partner on the trip to Olongapo, the buddy with whom he'd briefly shared the idea of floating to China, weeks of Subic Bay sunsets, and at least one heart-on-their-sleeves conversation about life. No, the Huks killed Raymond Herbert, Conner heard. They took him into custody in northern Tarlac, tried him for the catch-all charge against most Americans—treason—and shot him.

Hart, Musgrove, Lawrence, Herbert—guys Conner knew were falling left and right. So, too, were Filipinos by the handful, people who were literally giving their lives to protect the Americans. Meanwhile, Naylor had a bullet in his arm; he and Jellison—the guys who'd helped Conner's group get past Fort Stotsenburg—had been flushed out by a Japanese raid.

Conner not only used his "Sam White" alias more often, but he and his men stopped telling anyone where, specifically, they had been or were going. "There was a big reward for us," wrote Gyovai. "They were going to get us, regardless of the cost. People would ask us where we were going, and we'd say we were going to Japan; where did we come from? We came from America."

Meanwhile, they realized they needed to quit wandering and hunker down until things with the Japanese cooled. They needed rest. And security. They needed Banaba. Mrs. Hardin. Democrito. People who cared about them, not people trying to kill them. That was the irony in the jungle. "We knew our only hope for freedom rested in the hands of our American allies," Democrito said. And the Americans knew their surviving rested in the hands of the Filipinos.

MRS. HARDIN NOT only fed the Americans, but infused them with hope. Her favorite line when she saw Conner was *"Pa ca tops ng guerr,"* ("After the war things will get better.") For now, despite the price on the heads of Conner and his band of merry men having risen to twenty-five thousand pesos—thousands of dollars—he was safe with her and her family. To make sure, she and Democrito's family recommended the men settle behind the barrio, in a place the natives called "Combing Corral," which had been used for cattle herders. Now that the Japanese had taken all the cattle for slaughter, the soldiers never went to the spot. If Conner and his men would live there, she would bring food from the marketplace in the lowlands once a week. This would be the first of five places Conner and his men would live in the Banaba area.

Now a year since beginning their "one in a million" quest to survive the Luzon jungle, Conner and his men settled west of Banaba, in Zambales Province. Here, Conner's mood lightened. He occasionally broke into song-and-dance, doing a bit of Tarzan meets Fred Astaire. Meanwhile, the first home-like setting in a long time turned Conner's thoughts to his mother and father and New Jersey, images that got fuzzier with each passing month. He turned his thoughts to how much he had taken his parents for granted—parents whose heart problems always concerned him.

"I want you to know that I am deeply grateful for all the sacrifices you made to make me happy," he wrote in a letter that would, like others, be buried in the ground until war's end. "My only regret now is that I didn't show you more consideration. Very few, if any, young people were as fortunate as me in having such thoughtful, unselfish, reliable parents, but being a 'know it all' I never told you personally how much you meant to me. Well you know now; and my first aim is to show you some day your efforts were not in vain."

Conner promised—even handwrote IOUs—that when the war was over, the Hardins and others who were helping the Americans would be reimbursed. Meanwhile, the men did what they could to help, be it lugging water, tending the gardens, or fixing things around the house. When a Filipino became sick with what some thought was beri-beri, Gyovai concocted an antidote similar to the stuff the Negritos had made for Conner: dust from palay mixed with water and a little salt, and baked on a skillet as if it were cornbread. Several weeks later, Conner learned the man was back on his feet, doing well. The Filipinos promised Gyovai they would take him to a gold mine up a creek to repay him, but Gyovai declined. "What," he said, "would I do with a gold mine?"

Mrs. Hardin, meanwhile, emerged as a do-it-all servant, not out of compulsion, Conner noted, but out of compassion. She got food and medicine for the men. Cooked for them. She even suggested that Joe Donahey give up his backwoods retreat in Banaba and join the Combing Corral enclave, which he did. "His ways were unusual," wrote Conner, "and, actually, he was very funny."

"Funny" was a rare commodity in these times and places, as Jellison would attest after joining the group, along with Naylor, for a few days. He had been wounded when taking a bullet after fleeing the Japanese raid triggered by a Filipino who had snitched on him and Naylor. He had his arm in a sling and revenge on his mind.

When the rainy season blew in, Mrs. Hardin could not manage the trips to the lowlands and back. Democrito Lumanlan, though only seventeen years old, volunteered to take her place. "Son," his father had told him, "I don't think the Americans are coming back. If you want to help these people, you go ahead. I won't stop you. But it is dangerous." Democrito became the men's new connection to food and medicine.

Conner called him "Crito" for short; Crito called Conner "Mr. Clay." They soon were like brothers, the Duke-educated officer and the Filipino schoolboy, a kid, who, Conner soon realized, had the courage of a seasoned warrior. To avoid suspicion from Japanese patrols and make his resupply trips to the lowlands, Crito posed as a student en route to and from school. He tucked messages inside a rolled-up pant leg to avoid detection. He used a ten-year-old Negrito boy, Tacio, to walk ahead and alert him if Japanese were in an area. He endured exposure to the ugliness of war, be it a beheading or an American colonel forced to be a Japanese sergeant's driver.

The Japanese would offer Filipinos money—$250 was the going rate—to "sell" or turn Americans in to them. Though that sometimes happened, it was the exception to what was generally a pro-American rule. "When the sergeant being driven around by the colonel wasn't looking," Crito later recalled, "people in the market would put cigarettes, money, and sugar in the pocket of the colonel."

Anti-American propaganda was foisted on the Filipinos with regularity. Recalled Crito: "They'd say, 'Don't help Americans. They are no good. Americans are very tall, very white. Weak. The Japanese very small, very strong.'" Crito's incentive to help Conner and his men lay in what had happened to his brother, who'd been fighting for the Americans. "The Japs put a grenade in my brother's belly," he said.

Beyond the fact that Crito was the Americans' lone link to civilization, he spoke good English. Conner liked his father, Godofred, too, but the two were different. Whereas Crito zipped to the lowlands and back seemingly without fear, his father grew increasingly worried about helping the Americans. Ultimately, he told Conner his family must stop their support. Conner was disappointed but understood; the man's family had to come first, ahead of strangers from another country. And the man had already lost one son to this war.

Crito melted into tears. "He wanted to stay with us, but of course, he couldn't leave his family," Conner wrote. "He was only a young boy." Conner and Gyovai decided they would head south, back to Bataan, thinking perhaps the Japanese situation had cooled down there. "As much as I hated the mountains," wrote Conner, "I knew that was the only place we could survive."

They left with Crito in step with them; he wanted to walk with them to Banaba before saying good-bye. When they arrived in the barrio, Mr. Lumanlan approached his son. "I have made a mistake," he said, then turned to Conner. "If you move deeper into the jungle, you will be safe and we will be safe. But we can still help you."

Conner was touched by the compromise, something seldom seen in the hardscrabble world of war, where each day brought home the harsh realities of life in the jungle. The most recent incident involved Jellison, who caught wind of who his Filipino betrayer was. Jellison pretended to befriend the man. Then, wrote Conner, he discreetly pulled out a switch-blade and "jammed the blade into the man's spine, ripped him wide open . . . and left him on the trail bleeding to death."

TO FIND A suitable place for the men to hide, Crito enlisted the help of two Negritos who had occasionally visited the men, Maurio and Humbo, nephews of one tribe's chief. Just as back in the States, jungle real estate with Japanese soldiers roaming around was all about location, location, location. Humbo nodded when hearing the request. He pointed west into the mountains and told of a place on an old, never-used trail with much overgrowth. Perched above a canyon, next to a stream that cascaded hundreds of feet into the basin. "No one find you there for million years," he said.

It took about an hour from Banaba to reach the place. Humbo had been right. So thick was the jungle foliage that someone could not even notice the canyon itself, much less the hideaway tucked onto a well-foliaged shelf.

Gyovai, gun and a grenade hanging from his belt as usual, went to work with his bolo knife, cutting bamboo, gathering banana leaves, framing the hut. The challenge invigorated him. Maurio and Humbo helped. Crito brought food. Soon a dwelling sprung from the jungle floor, though barely big enough for Conner, Mailheau, and Gyovai. Ten feet wide at the front, eight feet high, maybe fifteen feet deep. Banana-leaf roof. Thatched siding. And open in the front. When the rains came days later, it kept the trio dry. They called this camp, the group's second in the Banaba area, "Lost Canyon." It was the closest to the enemy—to Clark Field and Fort Stotsenburg—they would set down roots: seven miles. But that's not why Frank Gyovai would later call it the "worst" of the five dwellings they would build near Banaba.

The reasons would emerge soon enough.

EIGHTEEN

Blind Faith

June 1943 to September 1943

Time in the jungle since the Fall of Bataan:
Fourteen to eighteen months

All these new experiences in the last nineteen months have made me take on a more serious outlook on my life without (I hope) destroying my sense of humor. I realize there is something for me to do in this world and I want with all my might to do it. All my life I have had the best, thanks to you, and now I want to do my part and "give." I also realize that one does not need wealth in order to give, but only love, and that I am trying to do.

However, my blood is still running fast in my veins and I want so much to again be free so that I can spread my love throughout the world. Then when my time comes I will meet it with open arms. I am not looking for fame. I am looking for solitude and peace within my heart.

My spirit is young and commands me to conquer the world, yet here I am, a fugitive.

—Clay Conner,
the last portion of letter to parents dated June 1, 1943

ON JUNE 1, 1943, from the Lost Canyon hut above Banaba, Conner began a lengthy letter home. He wrote it over eight days and prefaced it by saying, "I have carefully explained to Democrito that he should bury this in the ground until such time as the American Forces again return to the Philippines and then carefully mail it to you."

He began at the surrender of Bataan, writing, "Defeat is hell." He wrote of his physical demons: exposure, hunger, exhaustion, malaria, yellow jaundice, and diarrhea. "God was my healer." He talked of Porter and Dunlap dying, and asked that his folks notify the boys' parents that their sons were buried with honorable markers on their graves, their names chiseled into wood. He said that what he'd learned in his readings of the Bible was "far greater than a four-year college education." He spoke of close calls and adventure. "The Lord looks after fools, they say. I can truthfully say that I have experienced as much if not more than Stevenson's David Balfour, Hugo's Jean Valjean, and Stevenson's Jim Hawkins. Alan Brecht, the famous Scotch Revolutionist, underwent many of the same experiences that we are meeting day by day. Frank Buck sought fame and fortune bartering with pygmy tribes of Dark Africa. We not only barter with them for their food, giving only promises, we live with them in the jungles without Mr. Buck's modern expeditionary equipment. Wild, exciting, death-defying experiences . . . we have had them all."

He mentioned losing Junko, "my life long monkey companion," in the raid at Lara. He talked of his contempt for the Japanese, who have "beat, maltreated and cold-bloodedly murdered many young boys in an attempt to prove to us [their] superiority and great strength"; and of his respect for Filipinos who helped Americans—and his desire to make sure they get compensated after the war.

Finally, he thanked his parents for all they had done for him. "Not a day goes by that I don't spend hours thinking about you two." And, as always, he ended with "Everything under control."

HIS LETTER WAS cheerier than his life actually was in the weeks to come. In a separate journal, Conner wrote that he "was disgusted by the whole war." It was August 9, 1943, and across Luzon the guerrilla movement was at low ebb, little getting done as rains pelted the island with vexing consistency. Conner's foursome counted thirty-five straight days of it in one stretch. Rain that made fires nearly impossible. Rain that soaked through the thatched roof of a hut so small a fourth man couldn't sleep in it. Rain that droned on through endless days soaked in boredom, every card game by now seemingly old. Food was running low; their daily menu was rice, salt, and their rice-based excuse for coffee, a concoction made from dried field corn that was placed in a hot skillet until it turned black, whereupon it was pounded and boiled. Mailheau called the time "depressing."

Gyovai was no cheerier. "Cold, damp, and miserable," he wrote.

With the rains came leaches—segmented worms that would glom on to the men as they walked through the saturated bushes, forcing them to stop and scrape them off before their blood-sucking got too intense.

At night, they tied their shoes to the beam of the roof so rats wouldn't chew the leather, though that didn't always stop the nocturnal attacks. Other ground-level enemies lurked. Once, when Gyovai reached for a tin plate, a snake slid across his arm. He spun around, threw it on the ground, picked up a machete, and sliced it in two.

But the more consistent problem, at least from June to November, was rain. "[It was] hard to get firewood, to get our food cooked," said Gyovai. "We had many problems. The stream would be high. We couldn't even get out of the house, and were confined to small quarters. And occasionally we would get on one another's nerves and we'd have minor spats."

A typhoon blew through, knocking down trees. Streams rampaged to dangerously high levels, making it impossible for Crito to get food to the men. The three were eating only twice a day, measuring rice carefully to make sure everyone got an equal amount. The Negritos hauled a dead cow up for the men, but it was crawling with worms. Though Conner still had the Bulova watch his parents had given him, he had earlier hocked his Duke ring to get money for food. When they'd be out of cigarettes, the men would find already-smoked butts, gather them together, and sift out enough tobacco to roll new ones.

"The past is gone and well spent, I feel, as I did everything I could to justify my existence," wrote Conner in a contemplative journal entry. "I might add that many of those moments were very happy ones."

It was as if Conner were trying to convince himself that all was well; such was his optimistic nature rooted in a childhood of making the best of an often-gone father. But just as he would reach the summit of this motivational mountain, he would slip back down. "The present is unprofitable namely because of our confinement," he wrote, "but nevertheless, as true-blooded Americans we are making the most of it." Then again, he lost his footing. "The future remains to be seen and although every cloud has a silver lining I cannot for the life of me see any silver in view."

One day, Conner called the two others together. He had a plan that had the potential to help them all, a plan that might seem far-fetched but could, in the end, work. He was going to surrender to the Japanese.

THE OTHERS WERE disbelieving. But Conner was dead serious, and when he set himself to a task, there was little that could stop him. He talked of the prices on their heads. The constant running from the Japanese. The lack of food. By now, jungle rumors had it that the Japanese would treat Americans who voluntarily surrendered with—Mailheau remembered his exact words—"the utmost respect, guarantee[ing] safety, food, medicine, and the opportunity to rejoin comrades in the comfort of humane prisoner of war camps."

Mailheau rolled his eyes, but let Conner continue. "Clay said he felt he should be the one to initiate the move to surrender," Mailheau later said, "and if the Japs lived up to their claim he would get word to us and then let us decide for ourselves. A very noble move on his part, but I knew those SOBs would never live up to their word since they had us."

The others agreed it was a bad idea. Ultimately, Conner changed his mind, though not without a fight. "I was totally convinced," said Mailheau, "that Clay would have done what he suggested just to see if life would be a little better for us all."

AS THE WEEKS wore on, the deep jungle foliage became too much. Gyovai was feverish, though still able to do some work. Conner tired of the middle-of-the-day darkness. Mailheau wanted a change.

"Frank needed to be occupied cutting timbers or doing something of a manual-labor nature," wrote Conner. "Bob needed amusement. Neither were available." So, Conner decided to throw a new challenge out, at least to appease Frank: find a place to build a new shelter. The others were easy sells on the idea.

In August, they relocated to a similar place but one offering more daylight. Giant trees covered with vines reached out over the canyon like angled flags, splashing the lush green with tufts of orchids. A stream nearby emptied into a small pool just big enough for baths, then, similar to the old place, cascaded wildly over the cliff and into a canyon hundreds of feet below. From the cliff the men could see Fort Stotsenburg in the lowlands. Predictably, Gyovai got his bojo bolo and started hacking down green bamboo for another house. Soon after the move, his disposition improved, even if he showed signs of malaria. After the dreariness of their former place, the men proudly named the new hideout—their third near Banaba—"Shangri-La."

Gyovai's house was L-shaped and bigger than the previous one. The beds were built up off the floor, giving the men "higher, clearer, cleaner sleeping." An indoor fire pit helped keep away mosquitoes at night. Thanks to Crito, Shangri-La even had a mascot, a chicken named "Pegleg" that had gotten tangled up with a snake and had its leg broken. Gyovai, master of all things mechanical in a way Conner was not, had built a wooden splint for the little guy.

Everything was perfect. That is, until early the morning of August

29, when Conner heard the usual sound of Gyovai brewing coffee. On a typical morning, they'd get up, poke the fire back to life, drink coffee, and have a smoke. Only this morning was different.

Conner's eyes would not open.

PANICKED, CONNER CALLED for Gyovai to help get him up. "Frank," he said, "take me to the stream." A foreign matter had, in the night, crusted over his eyes like sand on glue. He tried to rub it away, but to no avail.

Conner bent over and splashed water in his face. Gyovai returned to the hut, perhaps not sensing the magnitude of the situation. But he did when he heard the cry.

"I'm blind!" Conner yelled. "I'm blind!"

Mailheau joined Gyovai in a run to the stream. They helped Conner back to the hut, feeling helpless. "As I sat there," Conner later wrote, "I was determined to see. I was determined that this wasn't going to change anything."

Not change anything? It was hard enough with 20/20 vision to dodge bullets and bayonets; hard enough to get through foliage so thick it could swallow a downed plane like quicksand; hard enough to get up at night and take a pee without spraining an ankle or falling into a ravine. Conner was fooling himself, his bravado getting ahead of his brain. And he knew it. "I was afraid," he wrote. "I needed help."

He asked Gyovai to get to the lowlands and have Crito find, and bring him, a doctor. Two days later they returned. No doctor. The fear of the Japanese and the Huks was too great. Crito tried to hold back tears of failure. Conner was touched when hearing the sniffles and, two days later, when Crito brought extra supplies—and books—to celebrate "Mr. Clay's" twenty-fifth birthday.

Conner reached out and touched Crito. "From now on," he said to the boy, "you'll be my eyes."

Crito led Conner from place to place. Mailheau read to him. Conner tried not to change his habits. He still wore his pistol, though that almost proved costly when he heard something or someone stirring and fired shots that direction.

"Clay, it's me, Frank!" yelled Gyovai. "Don't shoot! Don't shoot!"

Conner rationalized his blindness with the thought that it was only temporary—and tossed in some humor to lighten the mood. He joked about how dangerous it was if a blind man with a gun had to ask his assailant, "Who is it? Who's there?" But day after day, as he lived in almost total darkness, the reality grated on him: His sight might never come back. Hell, he'd be no better off than a peg-legged rooster.

On September 15—two weeks since the blindness hit—he awoke to light. Objects were still fuzzy, particularly straight ahead, but it was progress. "I was encouraged," he wrote. "Terribly happy." Within days, he could distinguish the figure of another person or the shadow of a wooden pole holding up the house. By October 1, his sight was a long way from perfect; he could see fine peripherally, but little straight ahead. Still, he could see well enough to protect himself with a pistol. And that's what really mattered.

THE TRIO VISITED three other Americans living, they learned, about two miles away on the same cliff: Doyle Decker, Bob Campbell, and Donahey, the latter who bounced from one group of guerrillas to another like a jungle pinball. Decker, twenty-five, was a rough-hewn farm kid from central Missouri who'd dropped out of high school to help his father work the fields. After enlisting in 1941, he'd met Campbell in the same 200th Coast Artillery Regiment. At thirty-four, Campbell was by far the oldest of the bunch, having spent a stint in the marines before joining the 200th. He and Decker had both escaped the death march, though not together, and had met up at Fassoths' Camp, leaving two days before a raid.

The trio's camp was clearly a better setup than Conner's clan—and the men were getting a decent supply of food and medicine support from lowland Filipinos. Whatever this ragamuffin band of American guerrillas was becoming, the two were invited to join their fledgling guerrilla outfit, and did so, even if they continued to live separately.

Mailheau soon found reason to be thankful for the merger. He developed tonsillitis, a malady easily fixed back home but potentially deadly in a jungle thick with disease. But Decker, though suffering from dysentery himself, braved a rainstorm to get iodine in nearby Banaba that not only cleared up the problem but likely saved Mailheau's life.

Meanwhile, Donahey rejoined Conner and his men. Normally, his quirkiness might have raised spirits; he occasionally tossed in jokes like they were grenades—as if just to remind folks he was still around. But, lately, his normal aloofness had slid into an all-out funk. Gyovai remained somber; normally, seeing a first-class hut like Decker's would have inspired him to do more with their own, but it didn't. He'd lost his snap during a bout of malaria and turned strangely inward; it'd been a long time since anyone had heard his Tarzan cry. Frankly, Conner was worried about him. Sometimes, Frank would sit and stare at nothing, Conner wondering where his mind was.

Mailheau's body, meanwhile, was nicked with bullets from skirmishes long gone, had nearly died from tonsillitis, and had dropped to about 125 pounds. He could justify a certain grumpiness. But his cutting remarks were grinding on Gyovai worse than ever. "Bob and Frank were despondent," Conner wrote. "They argued a lot, and once in awhile they'd fight. I would have to separate them."

What's more, the scarcity of food continued to wear on them; desperate for sustenance, Gyovai killed Pegleg and served the rooster for all, though not without regret. To an outsider, it may have seemed like a minor loss, but the men's desperation—particularly Gyovai's—magnified the pain.

Based on maps he'd seen in the Japanese-language *Manila Tribune*, Conner tracked troop movement and calculated latitudes and longitudes to figure out that the soonest MacArthur might return would be June 1945, nearly two years away. "This seemed to discourage Bob and Frank, but it only meant one thing to me," Conner wrote. "We must prepare for the future. We had to build ourselves security, and this meant a force— a guerrilla force—which could not only defend us, but stimulate the Filipino people in a pro-American way."

At times, Conner and Gyovai would talk deep into the night, and Clay would see Frank staring off to somewhere far away, and sure enough, he'd drift back to his mom's home cooking in West Virginia. But Conner's mind was elsewhere. On the Negritos and an alliance with them.

The Negritos, descendants of the earliest settlers of the Philippines, had more contempt for the Filipino/Malayans, who, in their eyes, had pushed their people deep into the jungles from the ocean-fronted lowlands. Conner likened the Negritos to American Indians, a peaceful people but also a proud, turf-oriented people who, when pushed, pushed back—at times with all the subtlety of their pig traps: bamboo spears attached to a bent, spring-loaded tree, their power unleashed when someone dared to intrude on Negrito territory and tripped the trigger. Now, as World War II deepened, thousands of Japanese and a few hundred American soldiers were doing exactly that. Pushing.

If not rulers of the jungle that stretched beyond their home on the lower stretches of Mount Pinatubo, the Negritos were a force to be reckoned with. Dark-skinned and small, they blended into the palm-leaved jungle as if part of the trees and plants themselves. Negrito tribes to the north were called Pugots, which, in that region's dialect, meant "goblin" or "forest spirit." They understood the nuances of the jungle. They took advantage of its resources like nobody else. And, at times, they defended it with a bravado that meant bloodshed. It was the Negritos who had wounded Lieutenant William Gardner; perhaps because of his dark skin—he was a full-blooded Indian—he may have been mistaken for a Japanese soldier.

The men owned little beyond spears, blow guns, and bows and arrows, but they could pierce a hand-sized bird—or, for that matter, a soldier's eye—from twenty feet away. "Their arrows," wrote Britisher H. Wilfrid Walker, who had lived among them in the Zambales Province a few decades earlier, "were often works of art, very fine and neat patterns being burnt on the bamboo shafts. The feathers on the heads were large, and the steel points were very neatly bound on with rattan. These steel points were often cruel-looking things, having many fishhook-like barbs set at different angles, so that if they once entered a man's body it would be impossible to extract them again." The women fashioned enormous baskets that they carried on their backs, and "raincoats" made of palm leaves that spread, like fans, around the body. "Whenever I met them they were always smiling," wrote Walker.

They had only nominal connection to any culture beyond their own and, though they occasionally danced and sang and celebrated, they mainly busied their lives trying to kill and cook birds, animals, and reptiles for food. Not that they were dullards. "The countenance of the average Negrito [is] not dull and passive . . . but is fairly bright and keen, more so than the average Malayan countenance," wrote ethnologist William Allan Reed in 1904.

The Negritos' world was small and as simple as their dress: Men seldom wore more than bright-colored loincloths, women sometimes less. They had no comprehension of the Pacific Ocean, which began a week's walk to the east and stretched to grand worlds beyond. They were not interested in the Japanese winning this thing called World War II. Not interested in American forces returning to reclaim the island of Luzon; had no idea, in fact, where the Americans had come from and why they were here. Not interested in much, frankly, other than living the primitive lives their people had lived for centuries—and perhaps in the gold rings that glistened from the fingers of a few of these strange newcomers. Noted one early observer: "They pay tribute to no one."

Once, a Negrito, Pan Dalangita, was discovered to have a compass, not a typical accessory for this live-by-the-sun-and-moon tribe. Turns out that while he was camping near Mount Pinatubo about "twelve moons" before, an American soldier had threatened him. Dalangita put an arrow through the soldier's heart—and, just like that, he had a compass and more.

Such stories would have deterred some from the idea of building bridges to the Negritos. Instead, it challenged Conner as he, Gyovai, Mailheau, and Donahey wiled away the days at Shangri-La. The hideout, which they considered the guerrilla unit's first official "headquarters," sat on the eastern flank of Mount Pinatubo and about ten miles west—and slightly south—of the Clark Field/Fort Stotsenburg sites and some twenty thousand Japanese soldiers. Conner saw the Negritos as more mysterious than dangerous. After all, hadn't a Negrito saved his life back in Tala? Perhaps the Negritos could help Conner and his men—and they could help the Negritos.

By now, a year and a half since eluding surrender to the Japanese, Conner's resolve to live had taken on a certain "devil may care" tone. As he'd written after the night walk following his rescue by "Marco Polo": "After so much pain, and so much sickness, you . . . kind of get numb to being afraid."

Conner was impressed with how smart Maurio and his brother Humbo were—and told them so. "They seemed surprised," he wrote. "Back in their own tribe they were not regarded as particularly brainy. They assured me that if I could talk to their leaders, I would find some *really* smart men. I saw then that I had made the mistake so many white men make in talking to the natives—jumping to the conclusion that because they do not understand English they are dumb. With the help of Maurio and Humbo I started to build up my Negrito vocabulary."

Conner had been smitten with the Negritos from the first time a young boy guided him and Ray Herbert to Olongapo. And he hungered to learn more about them. Admired their warrior skills. And respected them as warriors. "I call them 'brother,'" he wrote.

CONNER FOUND IT odd that prior to setting foot in the Philippines, the U. S. Army Air Corps had done practically nothing to teach the men about the various cultures of people they might be encountering. At the same time, the troops were hammered constantly with information on venereal disease. "But," he later wrote, "nothing about [the natives'] philosophies or thoughts or loves, nothing about economics or religion."

Learning about, teaching about, and respecting native cultures had never been a strong suit of the U.S. armed forces. This, after all, was a military that, in the 1940s, was willfully discriminating against its own men—by federal law. Black soldiers and white soldiers could not march together in a parade, eat together in a canteen, or serve together on a front line; in fact, only a handful of black units were allowed to engage in combat against the enemy. Most blacks drove trucks, mopped floors, and did other work far from battle zones. And in 1944, *Yank* magazine printed a letter from a black U.S. soldier who wondered why blacks like him had to eat at the outside back door of a Texas luncheonette while white German prisoners of war were happily served inside.

Meanwhile, in the Philippines, the United States' treatment of Filipinos was stained by half a century of bigotry hiding beneath the more austere label of "imperialism." At the turn of the twentieth century, as America wrested control of the Philippines from Spain, it did so under the leadership of presidents William McKinley and Teddy Roosevelt, the latter of whom wrote of blacks as "a perfectly stupid race."

Filipinos became, in the eyes of many Americans, "Pacific Negroes." Wrote H. L. Wells in the *New York Evening Post*: "There is no question that our men do 'shoot niggers' somewhat in the sporting spirit." Anyone doubting the credibility of a far-removed newspaper editor could read the post-massacre words of a soldier who was there, and under the command of General Loyd Wheaton: "Orders were received from General Wheaton to burn the town and kill every native in sight . . . about 1,000 men, women, and children were reported killed. I am probably growing hard-hearted, for I am in my glory when I can sight my gun on some dark skin and pull the trigger."

A lowball projection suggests the United States killed three hundred thousand Filipino civilians around the turn of the century, according to James Bradley in *The Imperial Cruise*. Filipinos were flogged, waterboarded, and hung from trees. "No cruelty is too severe for these brainless monkeys," wrote an army private from Utah. Major Edwin Glenn had forty-seven prisoners kneel before him to "repent of their sins"; he then had them bayoneted to death.

Such a depiction of Filipinos was not limited to war. In 1904, at the St. Louis World's Fair, President Roosevelt made sure the largest part of the fairgrounds was used to create what amounted to a make-believe Philippines. More than a thousand Filipinos were shipped to St. Louis, where—with no voice in the matter—they were depicted as "monkey-men" and, in the words of one fairgoer who wrote his wife, "the lowest type of civilization I ever saw," according to *Gateway*, the magazine of the Missouri History Museum. Visitors saw Filipinos dressed in military garb, twirling their rifles and obeying the commands of a white American officer.

If, by the 1940s, the American-to-Filipino bias in the Philippines had faded, a remnant of it persisted like jungle heat. Prior to the Japanese attack on Luzon, officers lived like aristocrats, whose drinks were mixed, polo horses saddled, and golf cubs cleaned by Filipinos.

Americans on the island tended to see the natives as one-dimensional servants, hardly the equal of those whom they served. "They would clap their hands loudly and yell, 'Boy?'" wrote Lieutenant William Gardner regarding the pre-attack days on Luzon. The average American's "insulation from the people gave him no understanding of them, and what knowledge he did gain was largely limited to his servants, the bar boys, and the whores."

CONNER, ON THE other hand, was interested in, educated by, and engaged with Filipinos and Negritos. By now, Crito, had become like a "brother" to him. Clay had written love letters for the young man to give to Crito's special girl, inspired, Conner wrote by "my grand and glorious days at Duke under the Carolina moon. But it didn't matter in the end. She ran off with the ice man." And his interest in the Negritos was obvious. "I was totally captivated by [them] from the first moment I met them," he wrote. And, in essence, wanted to join the tribe.

Still, against the backdrop of subtle bigotry that had settled comfortably into the U.S. military psyche, Conner's idea to merge with a band of Negritos cut against every social taboo the U.S. armed forces had ever tried to reinforce.

As Conner pondered the Negritos, however, he considered more deeply how the tribe might be able to help the Americans' cause—and vice versa. Being so close to Fort Stotsenburg, Conner and his men were well positioned to report to higher command information on the movement of thousands of Japanese once the American forces returned and the war became a fair fight again. The Negritos were only a few miles away, in a village called Magcabayo, which sat on the flanks of Mount Pinatubo. "And once I had the Negritos organized, no one could break it up," Conner wrote. His trump card? "No spies [for the Japanese] could pose as Negritos."

Over the days to come, the idea thundered through Conner with the energy of the stream that flanked their hut and cascaded gloriously into the gorge below. The more he considered it, the more he liked it. After all, wasn't one of the strengths of a guerrilla army improvisation? The ability to take whatever raw ingredients were available and make something of them to use to your advantage? After all, who knew the ins and outs of this jungle better than the Negritos?

And so, on the morning of October 2, 1943, as Mailheau tried to breathe life into a fire in their hut, Conner broke the boredom with a recommendation.

"I was just thinking," he said, "that if we could organize the Aetas to follow us, our troubles would be over."

Donahey, back on his bunk, acted as if he hadn't heard Conner. Mailheau blew through a bamboo tube to try to spark a fire that was as lifeless as the men's moods. "To hell with this damn fire," he muttered. "I don't care if it ever starts."

Gyovai, shivering from another bout of malaria, looked up from his crouched position by the pit. "Why can't you relax, Bob?" he asked. "I've heard your yaps and steam blowing for eighteen months. I don't want much more of it."

Mailheau's Irish temper ignited. "If you don't like it, what the hell you going to do about it?"

Gyovai unfolded his disease-racked body with the slow determination of an arthritic man three times his age. He went face-to-face with Mail-heau, which did nothing to stop Bob's needling.

"You got a lot of room to talk, Gyovai," he said. "You moan and groan about your malaria enough."

Gyovai eyed him for anxious seconds, then walked to the door and left. Mailheau returned to poking the fire. Donahey fumbled around for a cigarette.

"What a brainstorm that is," Mailheau said. " 'Clay Conner, junior commander of the pygmies.' Boy, you must be out of your mind."

"You damn fool, you know how sick Frank is," said Conner, pointing an accusing finger at Mailheau. "He may blow up any minute."

Mailheau shrugged. Conner banged out the bamboo door, then down a path that cut into the twisted jungle, toward the river. Regarding Gyovai, he'd caught what the others had missed. He knew Gyovai inside and out. Knew how easily Frank hurt. How he was just a small-town boy from West Virginia who missed his mom and her cooking. And though tougher than horsehide outside, he had lost his way in a place far deeper than this jungle.

CONNER FOUND GYOVAI standing in the shallows of the river that plummeted hundreds of feet over the cliff as a waterfall. Frank was close enough to the edge that he could almost see into the canyon a few hundred feet below. Conner froze. Stared. Then, careful not to panic, splashed into the shallows of the stream. Mist from the plummeting falls below hung in the air, shrouding the scene in eerie uncertainty.

Gyovai, head turned away, was squatting in the knee-deep shallows; to Conner, it looked physically impossible that the river's current wasn't dragging him over the edge.

"Frank," he said, his words calmer than his heart, and his voice raised almost to a shout to overcome the roar of the waterfall. "Frank, hold on."

Gyovai whirled around like a guilty man caught in the act. He was drenched. And one stumble away from being swept over the falls, whether he wanted to be or not.

"Frank, what will I tell your family when I return home?"

No response.

"Things aren't all that bad," said Conner. "Honest, I've just hit on an idea that will change everything."

The words bounced off Gyovai like bullets against a battleship. He dropped his head, staring back to the edge of the falls. For Gyovai, life had become meaningless. What was the use?

Conner felt like a man walking across a minefield. He stepped closer to Gyovai but not too close. One false step and he could spook Gyovai to jump—or fall in himself.

"What we lack," said Conner, "is any power. If—if we could organize the Aeta tribes, we would have plenty of support. Damn it, Frank, we could live like kings. We could even the score with the Japs. You don't want to die without doing that, do you?"

Looking down at the water, Gyovai stayed as still as a heron stalking a fish.

"What do you think?" said Conner.

Next to him, thousands of tons of water cascaded off the ledge. Gyovai tried to speak, but his voice broke. Finally, he said, "What's the use, Clay?"

"Frank, you've got to snap out of it, old man. We may have had a few tough breaks lately, but it's going to be different now."

Conner went on about his plan to organize the Negritos. About how it was their only hope to survive this war and get home to their families.

"But here's the thing, I can't do this alone."

For the first time, Gyovai looked up.

"Frank, I need your help."

Gyovai's head turned slowly toward Conner. For just a moment, the two men's eyes met, and something important was exchanged in the silence.

"I don't know if I can get back out of here," he said.

"Go slow," said Conner. "One step at a time."

Gyovai, unsteady, pivoted. He stumbled on a rock and started to fall. He swayed backward, then forward, and finally balanced himself. Against the knee-deep current, he started making his way toward the bank with a Frankenstein-like gait. Conner edged out deeper. He extended a hand. Gyovai shook his head sideways.

"Take it, Frank," he said.

Gyovai stopped, looked at Conner, then reached out his hand. Conner grabbed it and helped him to shore. Gyovai wiped his eyes. He nodded slightly at Conner, lips pursed, then headed back toward the hut.

Conner walked behind him. He would tell nobody back at camp what had happened. Ever.

NEW RESOLVE. THAT'S what they needed, Conner realized. And forming an alliance with the Negritos in an attempt to vex the Japanese was exactly that. Any return of American troops, he figured, would be at least a year away. Meanwhile, it wasn't enough to simply stay alive; they needed purpose, adventure, chance—all the stuff that he'd felt so keenly back on that night in Samal as Pablo Aquino first rallied the guerrillas—before tipping his hand to his Communist bent. Gyovai, in particular, needed physical tasks; needed to be building things. Mailheau needed new interests. Conner needed to dream and scheme and write. And Donahey—he just needed to be left alone.

The Negritos, Conner realized, had needs, too—needs that perhaps the Americans could help them meet. If they would allow Conner and his men to link with them and share their food, the Americans would get sustenance and security. The Aetas, as Conner so often called them, had rattan, bananas, crops, salt, and wild boar, though much of it was obtained through raids on neighboring tribes. It was often a blood-for-food economy. In return for support from the Aetas, the Americans could help the Negritos get medicines they needed from the lowlands, get beyond their penchant for violence, come to understand the value of compromise. If the tribes could unite, Conner reasoned, they could demand to be bargained with by the Filipinos in the lowlands and get what they needed without bloodshed.

It was, Conner realized, idealism flowing as wildly as the Shangri-La waterfall. But risk had its rewards, didn't it? After all, the Americans on Bataan who hadn't risked—who had surrendered, chosen *not* to risk— look where it had gotten them. Word had it that Cabanatuan Prison Camp wasn't exactly the Manila Hotel. Eighteen months later, how many of those who'd marched there at the prod of a bayonet tip were even still alive? If nothing else, the four of them were that: *alive*.

At dinner that night, Conner again raised his idea. The others deflected it, not with the barbed defiance of earlier in the day but with humor, which Clay took as a sign of progress.

"Frankly, Conner, I'd rather be a pool shark back in East Jalopy," said Donahey.

Conner wanted to fling back an angry response, but he calmed himself.

"I haven't seen any square balloons blowing toward East Jalopy lately, Joe," he said.

Donahey laughed at the nonsensical line. "That reminds me of the time the Filipino boy asked you why you didn't call up MacArthur down in Australia and tell him to send you a submarine," Donahey said. "And you said: 'Hell, what am I going to call him on, a megaphone?'"

Even Gyovai laughed at that. Still, Conner's idea was taking flight with all the grandeur of his squadron's "air force" back in Manila.

For a few months now, Maurio and his brother Humbo had been stopping to visit the white strangers on occasion. At times, they'd bring vegetables and crops from their farms. Maurio was learning a little English and teaching Conner a little Negrito and more Tagalog, which a few of the Negritos spoke.

On the morning after Conner's failure to get any traction with his idea of organizing the Negritos, Maurio and Humbo showed up for breakfast. After small talk, Conner hit them up: Would they take him to Magcabayo so he could meet their uncle, the chief, a man named Kodiaro Laxamana?

Both recoiled. No, no, no, they said. Conner gently pushed. "You be killed," Humbo said. Conner pushed a tad harder. Reluctantly, the two agreed, but not today, as Conner wanted; instead, he could go the following day.

Mailheau and Donahey didn't like the idea of Conner leaving, even if Bob himself had, long before, suggested that linking to the Negritos might work. Actually doing it, however, was another matter for him. "You're nuts, man, to go back there," Mailheau said. One way or the other, Conner was bound to wind up on the end of a spear or arrow. Oddly, Gyovai, though hardly upbeat, was not resistant. "Do what you have to do, Clay," he said.

That he would, even going so far as promoting himself from lieutenant to major to impress the Negritos. "I thought they were marvelous," he said later of the Negritos. "I was crazy about them."

Or just plain crazy.

NINETEEN

Building Bridges

October 1943
Time in the jungle since the Fall of Bataan:
Eighteen months

THE SOUNDS OF *tambulies* echoed through the jungle and across the gorges the next day. The native carabao horns caught Conner by surprise as he, Maurio, and Humbo headed toward Magcabayo. Gossip, it seemed, spread as effectively through the dense forests of the Philippines as it did through Manhattan elevators. In a place where little ever changed, Maurio and Humbo hadn't been able to resist trumpeting the news of Conner's meeting with the chieftain, Kodiaro Laxamana; it gave them a touch of status among their tribe.

Magcabayo lay in shallow valley on Mount Pinatubo's northeast slope. Steam hovered on the jungle floor as morning broke. The setting inspired Conner. In the midst of war, he felt as if he'd stumbled across a Shangri-La a bit more expansive than the one he'd just left. But his arrival in the village itself dampened his spirits. More than one hundred pygmies awaited, most with arms folded across their chests. Conner believed that he was the first "intruder" to try to make peace with them like this. Kodiaro (Kuh-JEHR-O) had cautioned the tribe the previous day; indeed,

Maurio and Humbo had earlier relayed to Conner what the leader had told his people:

> As you have heard, a white man, Major Conner, is coming here with my two nephews, Maurio and Humbo. We are not sure of his purpose, but it is definite that a white man would not make so difficult a trip for nothing. Maybe he is a spy. I knew many white men before the war, and they were very good to me, but now these men are prisoners.
>
> Major Conner is a stranger to us. It has been said by the Filipinos that many of these white men are friendly with the enemy. They call themselves Germans. It may be that he is seeking personal information of our lands and holdings. You must hide all your personal possessions and stolen carabaos. Let him see nothing.

The crowd of men, Maurio and Humbo reported, had roared approval. Some began jumping up and down. A few pulled on the strings of their bows. Now Conner was seeing—feeling—the resistance firsthand. Though eager to forge a bond, he wasn't naive. With the Negritos, "either you're a brother or you're dead," he later said. The people were solemn; as he neared, none came forward to greet him. The men had scarred the skin on their chests and arms with self-inflicted burns and cuts, signs of strength and courage. He discreetly slipped off his watch and slid it into his pocket.

He scanned the group inching toward him. Their skin was the color of dark chocolate and smudged with dirt; their hair was long and kinky. The men were dressed in only loincloths, mostly bright red or blue. Most were squatting on their haunches, bows and arrows slung over their shoulders. They smoked hand-rolled native cigars made from dried tobacco leaves. The women had rags tied to their waists like skirts, large knives tethered to the cloth, nothing covering their breasts. Two of them hacked away at a log with such knives. Others crouched in a circle, peeling camotes. A few did nothing. Some looked sickly, particularly a baby that had a skin disease called "boney." His skin was scaly, like a fish's.

Soon he appeared: Kodiaro, the chieftain of this particular tribe. Like the others, he was small, maybe five feet tall—if on tiptoes. But he had the feel of importance—he had three wives—and did nothing to hide it. He wore an American campaign cap, an army shirt, a pair of short pants, and no shoes. A .45-caliber pistol was strapped to a belt around his thin waist. In some ways, Conner thought, the man looked almost comical, like a child playing dress-up. But Clay wasn't about to smirk. He needed the respect of this man and his people. It was, he believed, the Americans' only hope of survival. Without a new network of support, without some renewed sense of meaning, their days in the jungle were numbered: Either they were going to trip up and be killed by Japanese soldiers, or they were going to find themselves atop some cliff, like Gyovai, and end the futility on their own.

THE NEGRITOS HAD only a few hundred words in their vocabulary, Conner had learned, but did much of their communicating with emphasis on particular words, with hands, and with eyes. Conner knew Kodiaro and some of the others spoke a bit of Tagalog. So in whatever he could muster from his language lessons with Maurio and Humbo, he greeted the chieftain.

"*Magandang hapon. Kumusta ka?*"

A glint of surprise warmed Kodiaro's face ever so slightly. A white stranger saying good afternoon and how are you?

"*Mabuti naman,*" Kodiaro replied.

"*Ako si* Clay Conner."

Kodiaro smiled ever so slightly. "*Ako si* Kodiaro."

Kodiaro looked around at his people. They were all surprised that the white man had spoken a language some of them knew. Conner kept making small talk in Tagalog, at one point mentioning that he had run out of tobacco. Kodiaro barked a staccato command. A little boy, perhaps ten years old, stepped out from the circle of people and presented Conner with a tobacco leaf. Conner smiled.

"*Maraming salamat,*" he said.

Conner turned to Kodiaro, who knew a little English, and asked if he might say a few words to the people. Kodiaro nodded yes. From a pocket, Conner pulled out a couple of tattered sheets of paper with a short speech that Maurio and Humbo had helped him write in Tagalog.

"I know the enemy destroyed some of your people," he said, mentioning specific names and incidents that had been told to him by Maurio and Humbo. Among them: a time when a Negrito had been blown to bits by a Japanese soldier who, when surrounded, detonated a suicide grenade rather than surrender. "They have tried to destroy me and my men, too. It is time we join forces and be strong together." He clasped his hands together in a bond. "Together, we are one."

He told them he and his men could help them get supplies from the lowlands, salt and meat. Could show them how to trade goods with other tribes instead of killing one another. Could give medicine to them that would help heal their wounds.

It was not the first time a representative of America had made promises to those in the Philippines, beginning a generation before with the Spanish-American War, in which the United States had come under the guise of protecting and wound up plundering. Conner's affection for the Negritos, however, had not been conveniently invented, but nurtured over months of getting to know—and genuinely respect—these people. A Negrito had given him a concoction that had rid him of malaria. A Negrito had led him and Herbert to Olongapo on Subic Bay. Two Negritos—Maurio and Humbo—had become helpmates to him and his men at Shangri-La.

Undoubtedly, he had been the beneficiary, not the benefactor, in these relationships. And, clearly, he was trying to build this new bridge for reasons of self-preservation. Still, Conner believed the Americans had much to offer the Negritos, including a knowledge of Occidental medicines that could save lives, understanding of a judicial system that could prevent eye-for-an-eye bloodshed, and perspective on the Japanese Army, of which they had little.

The Negritos had never heard a white man speak Tagalog, let alone one who talked about friendship. Still, Conner sensed hesitancy, which didn't surprise him. He knew these people tended to believe only what they could see. So when he noticed a little girl, perhaps ten years old, with a deep sore on her leg, he gestured to her mother as if seeking permission to help. She nodded.

He bent down on a knee. He took three sulphathiazole tablets that he kept in the watch pocket of his pants, cut one in half, and powdered it into a rag. Gently, he cleaned the wound. The eyes of the little girl locked on him as if he were either miracle man or magician; it's doubtful she'd ever seen a white man before, much less had one touching her. Conner knew he had only two and a half tablets left and that they were the only thing standing between him and infection. But he gave them to Kodiaro.

"Tell her I will check her leg in a week, and if it's not better," he said, "I will give her more of the medicine."

As the day stretched on, Conner stayed among the people. When offered camotes, he ignored how dirty the sweet potatoes were and how badly they smelled; instead, he ate them with gusto, even tried to like them. He talked crops with the men, held the "boney" baby, and sang songs with the children. Made eye contact with a few of the prettier young women, one of whom was Kodiaro's daughter. When the people retired for the night, each family's feet pointed toward the fire, like spokes on a wheel. Conner lay down and stretched out on the bare ground like them.

He felt the warmth of the flames on his feet. Looked to the night sky splashed with stars and the "Carolina moon." Prayed his usual prayer. And thought, with a sense of whimsy, how strange that has life had come to this: the Duke grad bedded down with a hundred-plus Negritos in a far-off jungle. People with no calendars because time was all but meaningless to them beyond counting the moons until harvest.

But Conner knew time. Knew it had been eighteen months since he had seen that Bataan-shaped cloud in the sky and taken to the jungle.

Now he had no idea when, or if, American troops would take back the island of Luzon. But he had no control over that, no control over much of anything, for that matter, least of all whether hundreds of pygmy Negritos were going to warm to his gesture of friendship or kill him. It was, he realized, one of those either-or propositions: either a tragic ending to what had already been a painful story or a slightly crazed beginning to what might be an epic tale. As an occasional spark from the fire popped, he turned to his side and fell asleep.

IN THE MORNING, Kodiaro granted Conner permission to read to the people an official proclamation from the Japanese that they had foisted on barrios across the island. An interpreter translated the message. "The Japanese high command," Conner began, "has requisitioned the services of several hundred thousand Filipino women between the ages of sixteen and forty-five, as temporary consorts, for the estimated one million Japanese soldiers in Luzon. . . . This measure will serve to accomplish a number of desirable objectives." If the Japanese had grossly overstated the numbers, Conner wanted the Negritos to understand what the Japanese were really all about. Understand what was being asked of Filipino women, whether they were Negritos or not. He continued:

> First, it will give the Filipino race the benefit of wholesale infusion of superior Japanese blood. Thus raising the Filipino race as a whole, and promoting closer understanding and ties between the Japanese and Filipino people. In answer to objections on moral grounds, the Japanese point out that all women of Japanese men married or single are required to produce children for the Empire.
>
> Second, the arrangement will promote the happiness and contentment of the Japanese soldiers who are stationed here for the defense of the Philippines and Greater Asia. In fact, they point out that the Filipino people are under a burden of undying obligation to these

gallant, daring [heroes], who may soon be called upon to spill their blood for the safety of the Philippines. They ask, "What better means of showing their gratitude have the Filipino people?"

As a further guarantee against effective opposition it is intended to inflict the death penalty on all who publicly or privately oppose the program. The Filipino people must be improved.

Kodiaro apparently understood. He looked down in disgust. Conner picked up a stick and tried to sketch a rough map of the world to explain the war situation. He explained the failure of American relief to arrive. "America far away," he said. "Would take seven hundred days walking, twenty-three moons, to get from United States to Luzon. On water. Not easy."

Kodiaro seemed more interested in the pistol on Conner's hip, a much finer one than the gun he had. Conner sensed it was time to leave.

"*Maraming salamat*," he said, shaking Kodiaro's hand. "*Paalum*."And then he left.

CONNER RETURNED TO Shangri-La. Gyovai, Mailheau, and Donahey weren't impressed with whatever progress he thought he'd made. Or had he made any progress at all? Conner found it hard to read Kodiaro and the Negritos, not surprising given the gaping chasm of differences between the two cultures.

For the four Americans, the routine continued: Morning baths in the cold stream. Breakfasts of rice and camotes. Well-worn bull sessions on the war. A few walks. Another bath. Dinner. And smokes around the open fire.

Gyovai and Mailheau were getting along better; Bob had apologized to Frank for being rough on him. Donahey was his usual withdrawn self, there but not really there. By now, he was so addicted to cigarettes that his yellowed fingers looked as if he were holding one even when he wasn't. On Saturday—not easy for the men to remember days of the week—Crito arrived with newspapers from Manila, as usual, and a few books and food, though not much. Taking information from the paper, Conner updated on his map where Japanese troops were likely now. Later that afternoon, he started thumbing through one of the books Crito had brought, a history of the Philippines.

"Listen to this," he said to the others. "It's about the early history of the Aetas. It says here that they once were the only people on the island, and were driven from the rich lowland areas into the mountains by the Malayans. Because of their isolation and suppression they have remained backward and feel themselves inferior to the Filipinos."

"I don't get it," said Donahey.

"It's simple," said Conner, his enthusiasm ratcheting up a notch. "Instead of appealing to the Aetas with intent to organize against the enemy, why not play on their feeling of inferiority? Why not prove to them they're wonderful in their own right, which they are? Why not organize them with the idea of seeking equality in trade relationships?"

The men weren't tracking, as if Conner were on one train and they on another. Outside, the sound of footsteps shuddered the conversation. Conner unholstered his pistol. The others grabbed knives. The footsteps grew closer.

"*Magandang hapon*," said a male voice outside. "*Kumusta ka?*"

Conner frowned. It was Kodiaro, but this was no social call. He meant business—and it had nothing to do with a Conner-Negrito merger. He opened the bamboo door. In broken English, he told Conner he wanted to make a trade: Conner's .45 automatic for his.

Conner looked at Kodiaro, then at the group of warriors behind the chieftain. He knew the right answer.

"No," he said instead.

Clay was familiar with his pistol. It had been with him since Savannah Army Air Base. It was his livelihood, his life. "And, besides," he said, "it is bad luck to change. If you are good with one, you may not be good with the other."

Kodiaro's eyes squinted slightly, his head tilted a touch.

"Then I will duel with you," the chief said. "If you outshoot me, I will give you my gun. If I outshoot you, you will give me your gun."

Conner did not like the proposition. His vision was still severely blurred from his temporary blindness. He had practiced little. He knew that to lose his pistol was to become more vulnerable to whatever enemy wanted to kill him—Japanese, Huk, or, heaven forbid, disgruntled Negrito. But he couldn't back down.

The two stood forty feet from a spindly banana tree that Kodiaro designated as the target. Kodiaro checked his gun, aimed, and fired. The bullet dusted the dirt in front of the tree, missing the target completely.

Before Kodiaro's gun was back in its holster, Conner drew and fired. Bark from the palm tree splintered. He put the pistol back in its holster, flipped the flap shut, and waited, feeling less smug than fortunate that the position of the sun had silhouetted the tree so nicely for him.

Kodiaro looked his gun over carefully. He pursed his lips and nodded his head slightly, then held it out. A deal was a deal.

Conner took the gun, looked at it, then handed it back. "I don't want your gun, Kodiaro," he said. "I want your friendship."

TWENTY

Liberty and Justice

November 1943 to December 1943

Time in the jungle since the Fall of Bataan:
Nineteen to twenty months

WHEN DAYS LATER, Conner next ventured to Magcabayo, Kodiaro reached into his pocket—he preferred Western pants to a loincloth—and handed Clay a compass. He told Conner it had come off a U.S. soldier his tribe had killed. Was this a threat or a gift of bonding? Conner assumed the latter, a symbolic gesture that, even if Kodiaro had not intended as much, suggested to Clay that he was pointed in the right direction with the Negritos.

But if Conner had great respect for Kodiaro—"he was sharp, kind, intelligent, aggressive"—and if Kodiaro was welcoming him, Clay wasn't so sure about the hundreds of his people. Soon, he heard of an incident in which he thought he could help. A Negrito boy had been killed, apparently by a Filipino, on Mount Cutuno a few miles southeast of Magcabayo. As Conner arrived at a Negrito enclave on Mount Delijap, Kodiaro and his men were preparing to head to the lowlands for *tabla*, meaning, essentially, "one of yours for one of ours." Eye-for-an-eye justice. The law of the jungle. The Negritos believed it was their salvation. To achieve eternal life, the boy's death had to be avenged by the killing of whatever Filipino had killed the Negrito boy.

This, Conner realized, was his chance. "Let me prove to you and your people that we have ideas that can help you," Conner told the chieftain, as if emulating the Fuller Brush salesman he once was. "Hold a trial just as they do in my country. Find the guilty person, and let the guilty person pay for his own crime. Why kill an innocent party?" Kodiaro found the idea odd, but was intrigued enough to not stand in the way.

Conner and the Negritos would gather, he decided, on the trail to Banaba, not far from Shangri-La, and then go to the lowlands together, picking up Mailheau and Gyovai along the way. When the trio showed up at the designated place and time, the Negritos were already there: four hundred of them.

Conner stood before them and presented his plan. They would split into three groups, Conner leading one, Gyovai one, and Mailheau one. They would approach Banaba from the east, the south, and the north, each of the three Americans leading nearly 150 Negritos. "We would surround the area, pull in all the [Filipinos] out of the fields, establish guards, and hold a trial," Conner wrote. "We would take the guilty man and send him into the mountains for *tabla* with the family who had been offended."

That the people had come encouraged Conner. But as he talked, such encouragement evaporated fast. The Negritos squatted on their haunches, listening but not reacting. One of their self-appointed lieutenants stood and said they did not like the idea of going to the lowlands; if they got cut off or were trapped, their families would be left alone. If they were to fight, let the Negritos fight in the mountains, on their own turf. Better to return home and send out a small party to exact their revenge. In other words, they favored business as usual.

Conner's emotions exploded, part of it frustration, part of it Hollywood: "I'd always heard the Negritos—the Aeta—were a proud people!" he shouted in cobbled Tagalog—and with more passion than in any football cheer he ever led. "A brave people! A people who accepted a challenge! But at this moment, frankly, I am ashamed of you! Because you are acting out of fear!"

It was a high-risk ploy, to touch the pride of a people who thought nothing of skewering a man with a spear for stealing a pig, much less a man who'd dared question their integrity. But Conner wasn't through. "I am ashamed of you," he said, "because you are afraid to stand up for what you know is right. If you want to go home, go home, because that is what cowards do. That is why the Filipinos do not fear you. That is why you've never had a break. That is why you've had to beg and kill for salt. Because you are cowards."

Kodiaro leapt to his feet. "This is not true!" he shouted. In the pause that followed, what hung in the humid tropical air was the possibility that Conner had pushed too far. And that the Negritos were now primed to push back.

"We want to do the right thing!" Kodiaro said.

Now Conner wasn't sure which way the wind was blowing. He scanned the faces for clues, then looked back to Kodiaro.

"We will go to the lowlands!" Kodiaro shouted. "Every. Last. One of us!"

Kodiaro's words whipped the Negritos into a shout-and-hoot frenzy. "The blood-curdling yells that they let out were obvious," wrote Conner. "They were going for blood. They were going down to fight and kill!"

Conner mentally recoiled. What had he done? Whatever energy he'd stirred in the Negritos had become like a runaway boulder tumbling down Mount Pinatubo. The Negritos filed down the trail, half-running, with their bows and arrows clutched in their hands. Conner knew he couldn't stop them now. Only one thing could do that. Siesta time, as it turned out. Before entering the barrio, the Negritos suddenly bridled their warrior energy and lay down to rest. Conner huddled with Gyovai and Mailheau during the reprieve. The Americans' only hope was to act as a buffer between the two groups and communicate to them a better idea than settling this with blood.

WHEN THE NEGRITOS approached the barrio from three sides, the sight of them churned the Filipinos into near hysteria. "They had never seen anything like this before," wrote Conner, "and they thought they would all be killed."

Conner stood on a wooden bench and, with whatever Tagalog he could muster, quieted both sides. "We are here," he told them, "for one purpose. Not to attack, but to hold a trial. Yes, we could get the guilty man and send him into the mountains for *tabla*. But we want to know the facts. We want to know the truth."

With that, he, Mailheau, and Gyovai placed a chair up front. Conner told people this was the "witness stand." Negritos. Filipinos—both watched in puzzlement. As Conner began asking questions of the Filipinos, the story came out: A Filipino man had gone to the mountains to cut banana leaves, a man who now stepped out of the crowd. The war had cut the production and supply of paper in the area, so banana leaves had become the replacement; when heated, they were pliable and could be used for wrapping meat and fish instead. There was money to be made at market with the leaves.

But when the Filipino spotted a Negrito on a trail, he feared the man would kill him. So the Filipino had killed the Negrito instead. At that, a roar rose among the Negritos. They demanded *tabla*. Conner, Mailheau, and Gyovai thought perhaps the Filipino had killed the man in self-defense, but there was no such evidence. Conner decided to take a chance, to see if bringing these two groups of people together could lead them to find a solution on their own. So he agreed that the man should be turned over to the Negritos for *tabla*.

The eyes of the man on trial flared like the eyes of a horse spooked by a snake. His family began screaming, pleading that he not be taken to the mountains. Then, noted Conner, something amazing happened. "The Negritos," he wrote, "were affected by the emotions of this family. They could see that this man was not a malicious man, but one who had acted on impulse."

As the roar of the Negritos ebbed, the Filipinos saw an opportunity. They began to bargain for their friend's life. They offered vast supplies of salt, rice, carabaos, and such. They told the Negritos that they would be willing to work with them, cooperate with them. The Negritos told the Filipinos that there were other items they could use—banana leaves, rattan, and wild bananas.

In time, an agreement was reached. The man was returned to his family. The Negritos abandoned their desire for *tabla*. Conner's idea had worked. And in weeks to come, it began paying dividends far beyond what he'd imagined. It won him and his men favor with the Negritos. It had spared a man's life. And it started a poor man's trade agreement between the Filipinos and Negritos. If that wasn't enough, it also led to something of a three-way agreement: the Filipinos would bring Conner and his men information on the Japanese if the Negritos would protect the Filipinos when they ventured into the mountains.

All three parties would benefit from the information-for-security plan. Many Filipinos worked for the Japanese at Clark Field, which gave them access to knowledge about such things as artillery installations, airfields, and tunnels. Negritos knew little about the Japanese, but everything about the mountains, and thus could help keep the Filipino lowlanders safe when they needed to travel through the high country.

With the Negritos now trusting him, Conner used the momentum to propose a uniting of all their tribes. "All the tribes would pledge allegiance to one commander and follow his decisions implicitly," he told Kodiaro. "If the Filipinos caused trouble, the whole of the Aeta organization would go to the lowlands and demand justice. As it is now, the Aetas of one tribe care nothing of the other tribes' troubles, and will not bother themselves to help one another. 'United we stand and divided we fall.'"

In a sense, unification. The Negritos—at least Kodiaro's tribe—approved of the merger. A new relationship, a new rhythm, a new resolve. "The Negritos were terrific when it came to helping us," Gyovai later said. "We owed our lives to them on a couple of occasions. Clay did most of the arranging, but I did most of the legwork. I had these little fellows carrying supplies up into the mountains. And we had safaris going back and forth."

Meanwhile, Conner hit "the campaign trail" to talk to the dozen other Negrito tribes, including one headed by a man known as "King Tomas." Kodiaro warned him to steer clear of those who practiced head-hunting, and Clay was only too happy to oblige his new friend's sugges-tion. Despite a couple of misunderstandings—one man thought Conner was going to steal his daughter—he returned to Shangri-La encouraged. "I felt I had won a moral victory over the natives."

It was further solidified when Conner and his men rallied the Negri-tos to explore an incident he'd heard about in which Filipino *ladrones* (robbers) had apparently attacked Banaba and were looting the people, taking livestock, having their way with the young women. When Con-ner's men arrived, shots rang out. These weren't Filipinos, but Japanese. Dozens and dozens of them. When the last shot was fired and the last arrow zinged, thirty-six Japanese soldiers lay dead.

The Negritos—moved by Conner's charisma and convinced the two groups had, in the Japanese, a common enemy—emerged as enthusiastic supporters of him and his men. And the Filipinos, too, were grabbing guns and becoming part of the guerrilla unit. At last, Conner and his men had enough momentum to not only call themselves "guerrillas" in name, but win the approval of Colonel Merrill.

The 155th Provisional Guerrilla Battalion was officially organized on December 2, 1943, and based in the Pampanga Mountains. It consisted of Conner, Gyovai, Mailheau, Decker, and Campbell and "two companies of Negritos and one company of Philippine Scouts, ranging from fifty to 100 men," wrote Conner. It was named the 155th in honor of the 155mm "long tom" howitzers, among the finest pieces of artillery around.

"Overnight, we had branched out into a big unit," Conner wrote. It was as if Conner, since that night at Pablo Aquino's house in Samal, had spent fifteen months blowing on the embers of this guerrilla idea and it had finally burst into flames. As if his and his men's "aimless wandering" had come together for a grand purpose. As if, in some small way, the 155th were honoring the very spirit of those Americans and Filipinos whose sacrifices Conner had written about the previous spring in a poem called "The Lost Legions of Bataan," which read in part:

Hardships and cruelty no mercy to seek,
The enemy stabbed all the wounded and weak,
Their bodies are beat but their spirits not meek.
Honor the Lost Legions of Bataan
All of those now who remain on the roll.
Wait patiently to return to the fold
Fight they will do till their bodies are cold
Honor the Lost Legions of Bataan!
Honor the men who shed blood in the siege
Honor the nurses, their glorious deeds,
Honor their code, their tradition, their creed,
Honor the Lost Legions of Bataan

TWENTY-ONE

Desperate Measures

January 1944 to February 1944

Time in the jungle since the Fall of Bataan:
Twenty-one months

GIVEN THE UNCERTAINTY of the Pacific fleet returning for them, Conner seriously mused about the possibility of never leaving the island of Luzon—and, at times, not so much with a sense of fatalism as with a sense of fascination. "Frank couldn't wait to get out," Conner would later say. "Frank was going back to the coal mines, and yet he couldn't wait to get out. I was going back to a fairly affluent society around New York and I wanted to stay. I was tempted to stay."

Decades later and thousands of miles away from the men's jungle existence, such thinking might seem outlandish for the outsider. At the time, however, Conner and his men were essentially jungle orphans who, for reasons they didn't know, had been left to fend for themselves—indefinitely. For those thrown into such situations, adapting to the new environment may, at first, seem difficult and awkward and even wrong, but, seasoned with time, it becomes the new normal. Certainly they held out hope that one day they would hear a buzz overhead and see American planes in the sky, but at this point—approaching two years in the jungle—

nothing but rumors suggested the United States was returning anytime soon.

Like author Daniel Defoe's Robinson Crusoe, whose weeks became months and months became years and years stretched to twenty-eight, at some point the shipwrecked man must stop pining for rescue and realize this is his new reality. He must build himself a life in the context of not what he left behind or what he hopes to return to, but what he has now. And, meanwhile, do whatever necessary to stay alive.

Far removed from the desperate circumstances, the outsider may cringe when hearing of starving, shipwrecked sailors who, say, consider cannibalism. But the will to survive is strong. And "the fog of war"—the absolute chaos into which armies and civilians are thrown when killing becomes a daily way of life—only further blurs the lines of the hard-and-fast rules back home.

"You don't train a person in the jungle to live like an American," said Conner. "You convert an American in the jungle to live like a Negrito."

Said Mailheau with postwar hindsight: "It's important to understand that in 1943, the American forces were bogged down in the Solomons and New Guinea, and it appeared to us that we may have to hold out for up to ten years before expecting any relief from our troops."

Conner himself later chided those who failed to put themselves in the time, place, and circumstances of soldiers left on Luzon, while simultaneously questioning the men's decisions. "Anytime you make a judgment after a war like this and you say, 'If I had been in that circumstance, I wouldn't have done that. . . . You don't know what the hell you'd do to save your life. You don't. You make that decision while you've eaten steak and hot potatoes and hot bread or biscuits. You've lived in the American style. [On Luzon], you don't make those decisions with that kind of chemistry. You make the decisions after months of hardship, isolation. You're cut off from your own family and your country."

By now, Conner realized that the few Americans still alive in these jungles were breathing because of an alliance they had with Filipinos; he knew of too many men who had tried to go it alone and died or were captured because of it. The Negritos' pig-trap protection, meanwhile, was proving amazingly effective. In the previous six months, the daily stress of being on the run from the Japanese and the Huks had been replaced by a semblance of normalcy.

But the law of the jungle was a capricious law. One minute a soldier could feel completely safe, and the next minute be impaled by a Japanese bayonet. Larry Lawrence, in that flooded rice paddy, might have felt blissfully at ease in the moments before being surrounded by that Japanese patrol, but he was soon silenced forever with the sweep of a sword. His mistake was going it alone, which made him vulnerable to the birds of prey.

A capricious law, indeed. Though Conner and his men now found themselves in the good graces of the Negritos, who knew what might happen if something rubbed Kodiaro the wrong way and his favor was lost? If Conner or one of his men somehow angered a member of the tribe who was closely aligned with Kodiaro? Or if a neighboring Negrito tribe did harm to Kodiaro's tribe because of their unhappiness with the Kodiaro-Conner pact? Too much was riding on this one relationship. The Americans needed to either diversify their relationships so they were less dependent on the Negritos, figured Conner, or strengthen their bond with the Negritos so nothing could sever it.

It was now February 1944, just short of the men's two-year anniversary of jungle survival, and Conner had come to believe that seeking help elsewhere was fruitless. *With whom? Where? How?* Their only option, he figured, was to cinch down their ties with the Negritos. So, one day, Conner went to Gyovai and Mailheau with an idea that he thought would do exactly that. An idea born of the men's desperation and of Conner's imagination.

It was simple, really: To seal their bond with the Negritos, Conner would enter into a tribal union with a daughter of Kodiaro's.

WHEN CONNER UNVEILED his plan to Mailheau and Gyovai, they thought he was kidding. He assured them he wasn't. "Frank and I tried to argue

Clay out of this line of thinking, but he persisted," Mailheau later said. Conner, Mailheau said, wanted to "[create] a bond that would assure us some means of security and a chance to survive and eventually return to our homeland."

Unlike with Conner's idea to surrender, however, this time he wasn't deterred by the disapproval of Gyovai and Mailheau. Conner went to Kodiaro with his bid—ostensibly, a willingness to continue teaching the Negritos about the ways of the Japanese Army, to show them new ways to seek justice, and to offer them new opportunities for political power among the Filipinos. "Kodiaro was thirsty for education, thirsty for knowledge, thirsty for information," said Conner.

The chief heartily approved of the bond. The ensuing union tightened the bond not only between Conner and Kodiaro, but between Conner's men and the tribe at large. "The family," wrote Mailheau, "was delighted. We were definitely 'all in the tribe,' so to speak. . . . I'm convinced Clay had our best interests in mind."

In time, the bond between the tribe and the Americans would be tried and tested in ways nobody might have imagined. For now, Mailheau could only shake his head. "Clay Conner," he said, "was a man unto himself."

IF NOT KING of the jungle, Conner was emerging as a clear leader—to the Negritos, to the Filipino civilians, and to his own men, even if at times a few thought him too big for his now-tattered britches. By now, after so much wheel-spinning in 1942 and '43, dozens of guerrilla outfits like Conner's were emerging across Luzon, often with the same dynamic: once-bickering groups of men now finding a semblance of unity, because of—or despite—the leadership of such "little kings," in the words of one of them, Lieutenant Robert Lapham. (His guerrillas controlled much of Luzon's great Central Plains.)

As 1944 unfolded, the 155th emerged as a bona fide guerrilla unit. The handful of Americans were now leading hundreds of Negrito soldiers.

Lieutenant Felipe Maningo, a Filipino, was leading 150 Philippine Scouts. They were gathering information on the Japanese while working three provinces: Eastern Zambales, Pampanga, and Tarlac, all of it coordinated by Conner at the headquarters near where the three provinces coincided.

Conner had established himself with courage, undying resolve, and a quick draw with his .45 that left Gyovai shaking his head. Nobody kept his holster as slippery as Conner, who moistened it with coconut oil. "I couldn't get my Colt out of my holster before he'd have his out, cocked, and pointed down my throat or anybody's," said Gyovai. To be sure, Conner was hardly the young lieutenant of pre-surrender Bataan, the guy whose men wouldn't have followed him to the latrine, much less into battle.

But what also played into his success was humility—bowing to the knowledge, customs, and power of the natives. Indeed, Conner's willingness to honor the locals was helping keep him and his men alive. And his perseverance to prevail, like a quarterback who somehow "wills" the ball into the end zone, instilled hope in men who needed faith in something to survive.

Meanwhile, Gyovai soared with newfound purpose, too. If Conner was a thinker, Gyovai was a doer. "He had to be busy every minute," Conner wrote. He cut timber, notched logs, and built an aqueduct made from banana tree bark. He packed supplies into the mountains like a mule and did most of the cooking; mended clothes and butchered pythons; a true jungle renaissance man.

Mailheau left to team with Doyle Decker, Bob Campbell, and Donahey in the lowlands; Conner wanted them closer to Banaba, to work as an intelligence-gathering unit. Bob and Frank, though civil to each other, were better off apart. In fact, Gyovai seemed more upbeat than ever. "The Negritos loved him," wrote Conner, "because he did everything they did, and quickly adapted to their way of life." By now, the lanky kid from West Virginia had truly "gone native." He hadn't worn shoes in over a year; in fact, he wasn't wearing much of anything these days. He wore only a loincloth, his head topped with a scraggly straw hat, his ever-present pistol's holster strapped to his bony hip as if surgically affixed. His "Tarzan yell" had regained its power.

"Although he was generally cautious, his whereabouts in the mountains were no secret," wrote Conner. "He could often be heard for miles, chanting the Aeta Negrito's songs as they traveled barefoot through the jungle together."

If there was an almost comical side to Gyovai's adaptations, *The U. S. Army Survival Manual* points out that such embracing of the local culture is actually smart: "Act like the natives. . . . Deal with the recognized headman or chief to get what you want. Show friendliness, courtesy, and patience. Don't show fright; don't display a weapon. Treat natives like human beings. Respect their local customs and manners. Respect personal property, especially their women."

When one of the 155th's Negrito lieutenants died of tuberculosis, Conner and Gyovai went to the funeral three miles east of Mount Dudu. The ceremony fascinated Conner. "His family gathered, the *tambulies* were blowing, and all of the relatives for many miles around were bringing food for the celebration," he later wrote.

When the moon was high, some three hundred people gathered around the man's house, a bamboo lean-to, where he had died. Three witch doctors, or *medicos*, crouched down, their faces lit by a lantern fueled by coconut oil. They placed food on a banana leaf and a sliced-in-half coconut shell filled with water, in front of the light, then began rocking back and forth, chanting, moaning, crying out. Outside, others began doing the same, moaning and chanting in unison.

"You couldn't help but feel its influence," wrote Conner. They were, he later learned, praying to God to show them the face of the man who had died; his face was to appear in the water of the coconut shell, a sign that he was safely in heaven. Once assured, they would commence to feast, which happened momentarily. The *medicos* reached the food to the sky and spilled it on the man's grave to signal the start of eating, laughing, and dancing that lasted until the sun appeared.

If his relationship with the Negritos deepened, Conner's relationship with some of his own men sometimes was strained. Closer to the lowlands, Decker charged that Conner and his men were mistreating the Negritos, which peeved Clay no end. He had, he believed, proven his allegiance to the Negritos—and they theirs to the 155th Squadron. In his mind, the allegation was nothing but a smoke screen for what had really angered Decker: Conner's sudden escalation in rank, lieutenant to major. In the jungle, it was not uncommon for those leading guerrilla units to bump up their rank, in part for their egos but mainly to increase their status with the natives, who remained the Americans' link to survival.

"Come to think of it," suggested Decker, "what proof do we have that you're even an officer in the first place?" Things got heated. Conner bristled. He pulled out his pistol, in fact, but soon had it back in its holster. The two sides talked instead.

"By morning," he wrote, "we'd hashed it all out. It was another one of those tension things. It was a long war. It had been a long time since we'd seen American planes."

TWENTY-TWO

Pledge of Allegiance

March 1944 to May 1944

Time in the jungle since the Fall of Bataan:
Twenty-one to twenty-five months

FROM THE SIDE of Mount Tambo, a few miles south of their previous location, Gyovai began building yet another new house in March 1944. It was always good to keep the Japanese guessing about their whereabouts. From the mountain perch, the men could see Mount Pinatubo and Luzon's lowlands beyond, to the north, and Fort Stotsenburg and adjacent Clark Field to the northeast. "It gave us a feeling of freedom, of release, of belonging," wrote Conner.

While Gyovai cut logs—the dwelling would be a tropical log cabin—Conner continued rallying support for the 155th. He developed a finger-printing system for the Negritos as a means of taking a census because it was, Conner found, impossible to do so with names. Gyovai, mean-while, finished their finest house yet, complete with split-bamboo floor, beds, tables, chairs, and water piped through bamboo from a quarter mile away. It was, Conner wrote, "a masterpiece." And to top it off, Gyovai carved a garden area out of the jungle that was soon planted with corn, lima beans, camotes, and rice. They called this camp, the 155th's fourth, "Mount Tambo," because of its location.

When he was finished, Gyovai-the-workhorse went to the lowlands and, in a driving rainstorm, hauled a roughly one-hundred-pound bag of rice through the jungle for the Negritos, who'd offered him a bundle of fresh tobacco in return. When he arrived at Tambo, Gyovai reached to shake Conner's hand in welcome and promptly collapsed at Clay's feet. Conner was frantic. The two had vowed to finish out this war together; now, Gyovai lay sprawled like a dead man. Unresponsive. Feverish. Pale. Conner gently shook him, massaged him, spoke to him. Nothing.

Alive, but not really alive. Minutes became hours. Hours became days. No change. Conner dispatched Crito to the lowlands for a doctor, but none would come. Finally, the Negritos brought three "hoodoo doctors." All women. The trio kneaded Gyovai like bread dough. Pounded here, pounded there, then showed Conner a hard ball in the center of Frank's stomach where, they said, the sickness had consolidated. They stripped bark off nearby trees and put it on the lump. "Soon his sickness will be gone," they said. In five days, Gyovai sat up and, though weak, began eating.

"He just sat there in the chair in front of the fire with his eyes staring straight ahead," wrote Conner. "He never talked, he never showed any expression, and he was almost like a man in shock." But gradually, Gyovai regained his strength. Conner quietly rejoiced. And, said Gyovai, "kept hovering over me like a mother hen," a far different Conner than the guy at field Hospital #1, before the surrender, who said of the wounded soldiers: "I didn't appreciate the suffering that these men were going through."

More than two years before, Conner and Gyovai had gotten into this mess together. And Conner wanted them to get out of this mess together.

COLONEL GYLES MERRILL was honest, committed to the American cause, and so proud of his boozing that he bragged about his flower beds back at Fort Bliss in Texas being ringed with empty tequila bottles. He was fifty-two years old but looked seventy-five, one of the many officers deemed venerable enough to be given out-to-pasture duty in the Philippines. A relic from World War I, a 26th Cavalry guy who could point to a photo of himself next to a horse-drawn artillery battery during a German mustard-gas attack. So leather-skinned that he claimed mosquitoes never got an ounce of blood out of him. And so stubborn that when the Japanese forced the Americans on the death march, he escaped, among the oldest men to do so.

Naturally, Clay Conner thought the world of a swashbuckler like him.

As the rainy season deepened—Conner's third since arriving on Luzon—Merrill was pressing for more surveillance and better communication. By now—July 1944—a few American submarines had touched shore on the western coast, sneaking in transmitters, receivers, and at least one typewriter that soon sped up Conner's correspondence with Merrill and others. Sailboats were arriving with supplies, including a MacArthur propaganda ploy: books of matches with "I Shall Return" printed on them, which went over better with Filipinos than "it's about time" U.S. soldiers.

For the first time since the Fall of Bataan, a communication line had opened to the southwest Pacific, including Australia. Merrill wanted Conner and his men to start feeding him information about the Japanese, particularly about the heavily populated Fort Stotsenburg area. Negrito and Filipino runners were established to take messages back and forth from Conner's post on the eastern flank of the Zambales Mountains to Merrill's headquarters on the western flank, northeast of San Marcelino, each trip taking about two to three days.

Elsewhere on Luzon, guerrilla units sometimes went on the offensive against Japanese patrols, which was rare in the Zambales-Tarlac-Pampanga provinces that Conner and his men frequented. Part of that was their nearness to Stotsenburg, where thousands of Japanese soldiers could quickly avenge an attack. Part of that was sheer numbers; a basic tenet of guerrilla warfare is to only attack when victory is highly likely. Colonel Russell Volckmann, in northern Luzon, had twenty-two thousand Filipinos under his authority; Ramsey and Lapham, thirteen thousand each; and Anderson, the man Conner had escaped with, seven thousand. Meanwhile, Conner's 155th had—he claimed in a November 23, 1944, letter to Merrill—a few hundred Filipinos and "approximately 3,000 Negritos," though he may have been "rounding up" on that number. Finally, part of that was simply following orders. MacArthur had commanded guerrillas on Luzon to refrain from any major military engagements that might trigger harsh retaliation against the Filipinos. Yes, gather information. Sabotage if possible. Stay alive. But trying to defeat a well-fortified enemy with pistols was never a goal of the guerrillas.

Merrill decided to prepare for MacArthur's expected return by setting four principles for guerrilla units: protect civilians while incoming forces were defeating the Japanese; collect intelligence to send to MacArthur; organize and train guerrilla forces to be ready when the time came; and avoid combat until the Americans returned. Merrill believed the most important thing in forging an effective guerrilla unit was a toughness galvanized by an empathy for the native people's plights. He once wrote:

> Only by having a common political aim of working completely for the people and the country, and of sacrificing one's life and family in return for an ultimate victory, can we make an anti-Japanese guerrilla troop a united and unbreakable force.
>
> The second important point in a political war is to make the masses of the people a strong fortress. If an anti-Japanese guerrilla troop cannot [unite] the masses of the people and uphold their interest . . . such a guerrilla troop [has] no future. In the water alone can a fish live and grow, so with the support of the people alone can a guerrilla troop exist and grow. Once a fish is out of the water it will die, so once a guerrilla troop loses the support of the people it would have no means for existence.

Such thinking—that the Americans needed the Filipinos as much as the Filipinos needed the Americans—was a far cry from the United States' approach to the Philippines at the turn of the century. Indeed, in the jungles of Luzon, a fresh tropical breeze was blowing.

THE STORY WAS told around a campfire one May night by a Philippine Scout, Agapito Macasual, a former 26th Cavalry trooper. Conner wasn't there, but Mailheau and Decker were mesmerized by it. The scout told about Sergeant Gaetano Bato and the 26th Cavalry's American flag: How he had taken the flag from a dead comrade during the Battle of Bataan and vowed it would one day fly over Luzon.

"He lived in Sapang Bato," said Macasual, "though I do not know if he is still alive."

The flames of the fire flickered as Decker and Mailheau wondered where this was going. "But I am willing to go find out. Willing to see if Bato would like his flag to fly once again—above those of us of the 155th."

With the blessing of Mailheau and Decker, Macasual left in the morning for Sapang Bato. He returned three days later. Bato was, indeed, alive. What's more, he was not only interested but anxious to turn over the flag to the 155th as a way to complete his self-imposed mission. In the dark of night, to avoid detection from the Japanese, Bato presented a neatly folded but tattered flag to Mailheau, Decker, and Macasual. In the moonlight, they could not help but see tears in the man's eyes, which triggered a rare dampness in their own. But it had been a long war with little to touch their hearts, and this had done so.

Conner was thrilled to hear of the flag. He was only too happy to have the 155th take this "baton" and finish the relay. The men of the 155th made an unwritten resolution "that the flag henceforth be flown every day in defiance of the invaders from the north, and as a symbol of freedom, democracy, and eventually, victory," wrote Mailheau.

Fort Stotsenburg was less than fifteen miles away and thick with Japanese soldiers, but nobody was about to let technicalities get in the way. Gyovai hastily prepared a bamboo pole, and in minutes the flag was flying. "It sent chills up and down our spines," Conner later wrote, "to see an American flag flying over Luzon again."

The Negritos were less spine-chilled than curious. "We tried our best to teach them, all at once, how to salute, how to raise and lower it, and that it shouldn't touch the ground," wrote Conner. "The Negritos liked the discipline, and I could see that they would make good soldiers."

He also saw just the man to lead them: Bato. He asked Bato if he remembered how the American officers organized, taught, and trained the Philippine Scouts before the war. Then Conner told him about his idea to train the Negritos in a similar fashion. Teach them not only to salute the flag as it was raised and lowered each day, but to work together to take on the enemy. To be soldiers.

"How about it, Sergeant?" Conner said. "Would you like to do that?"

Bato embraced the job with an enthusiasm Conner found rare in these times. With permission, Bato had his wife and children moved to the area; three of his men built houses for themselves and for the Bato family. In a few short months, the Negritos mastered the rudiments of basic army training. "Sergeant Bato performed a miracle," wrote Conner. He, Gyovai, and Donahey went to Mount Dudu for an inspection of the troops.

"It was like the old Saturday morning inspection back in cadet school," wrote Conner. The Negritos were armed with 1903 Springfield rifles, which they cleaned and used to present arms. A color guard advanced and posted the colors. The Negritos placed hands over hearts and, in English, repeated part of the Pledge of Allegiance.

Each day, the flag flew over their decidedly primitive "headquarters" on Mount Tambo. From Mailheau's perspective, the addition of the flag and the involvement of the Negritos and Filipinos had solidified the men in a common purpose. "We were a symbol of hope for them, a rallying point," he later said. "Keeping that light of freedom alive. They looked to us much as we looked to that flag."

Conner watched the tattered flag waft in a light breeze. It was like some mangy dog that nobody wanted—unless they understood the story behind it. Where it had come from, what it had cost, and what, on a deeper level, it meant. "I made a solemn oath," wrote Conner, "that this old glory of the 26th would once again wave over Fort Stotsenburg."

TWENTY-THREE

The Showdown

June 1944 to September 1944

Time in the jungle since the Fall of Bataan:
Twenty-six to twenty-eight months

We'll Be Missing You Son—This Xmas.
When Christmas comes, dear son you know
That we'll be missing you.
Remembering with all our hearts,
Through everything we do.
Hoping that you're safe and well, and sending out
a prayer,
That He whose birth we celebrate, May keep you
in his care.

**—CARD BOUGHT BY CLAY CONNER JR.'S MOTHER
IN ATLANTIC CITY IN HONOR OF HER SON, 1944**

Dec. 19, 1944

Dear Colonel Herbert,

I seem to have reached rock bottom now as to my endurance to this terrible suspense and silence concerning the fate of our son Lieutenant Henry Clay Conner Jr. Living for 31 months fighting the daily battle of fear within yourself and yet managing to hold to your faith that somehow your boy has survived all that Hell just does something to you in spite of yourself that words cannot express. I have concentrated on occupying my mind with war work and USO and just returned from a short vacation but wherever I go or whatever I do nothing relieves the tension, only definite word either from or about him will do that.

Since quite a few men seem to have returned now who were either prisoners . . . or had been in the hills, surely someone knows something about Clay Jr. I have written to quite a few in the past who returned but none of them could tell us anything so sometimes I wonder if they are under government restrictions regarding missing men. If you could refer us to any such men who might be able to give us just any personal information about him it would help us to carry on. I believe you realize if anyone does, what a strain we are under. . . .

With kindest regards,

Sincerely,
Mrs. H. C. Conner

27 December 1944

Mrs. Marguerite Conner,
174 North Grove Street,
East Orange, N.J.

Dear Mrs. Conner:

I have received your letter of 19 December 1944. . . . The great burden of anxiety you, and other parents, have been called upon to bear since our Army forces surrendered to the Japanese on Corregidor on 7 May 1942, and your added distress caused by this prolonged period without news regarding your son's whereabouts is fully appreciated. I sincerely wish there were some definite information I could furnish

you so that your concern might be lessened but it is regretted that no
report concerning Lieutenant Conner has been received. . . .

You, and other members of the family, have my sympathy during
this continued period of anxiety and it is my earnest hope that news
regarding your son's whereabouts may be received.

Sincerely yours,
Robert H. Dunlop
Brigadier General
Acting The Adjutant General

THE SOUND OF the plane triggered something deep within Conner. He'd been in exile so long and had poured so much energy into staying alive that he'd back-burnered the idea of MacArthur's men actually returning, perhaps to protect himself from the wounds of it never happening. But now came the sweet sound of propellers high overhead and, with it, rekindled hope.

The Japanese observation plane—"Photo Joe" as Americans called such aircraft—dipped low above the hideout. Disappointed, defiant, Conner didn't even bother to hide. Nor did he make the slightest effort to take down the flag. It was, of course, outlandish to fly an American flag on what amounted to the back porch of the Japanese-held Fort Stotsenburg. But as the two-year anniversary of his time in the jungle neared, Conner wasn't through being outlandish.

SOME GUERILLA LEADERS totally supported the Hukbalahap fighters. "It is my first conviction," wrote Second Lieutenant William Gardner in an April 7, 1944, message to Corporal John Boone, "that this organization is by far the most effective Anti-Jap organization in this area. Further, we Americans should do as much as we possibly can to aid them in maintaining their effectiveness." Lieutenant Ramsey hated the Huks and later said, "Any American who fought with the Huks was a renegade."

Conner's faith in the group had faded with time and experience, even if he would maintain an odd respect for particular leaders. Among them: Zambales Huk leader Rapido Sumulong, who basically wanted Conner dead. Indeed, as the 155th's power grew in the shadows of Mount Pinatubo, so did the Huks' apparent hatred for Conner and his men. In the lowlands, the Japanese were getting the better of the Huks, who wanted to move into the mountains for safety but couldn't because the Negritos would rebuff them. At first, the Huks decided to see if they could starve the Americans and their Filipino allies into leaving by halting food supplies to the mountains. Conner responded by rounding up Gyovai, Mailheau, and a handful of Negritos led by Kodiaro himself, and going to the lowlands to meet with Sumulong. The same Sumulong to whom Conner had once given thirteen rifles in turn for his men's cooperation and been double-crossed.

Conner knew the idea touched on the foolhardy, like playing catch with a live grenade, but he'd been through so much that by now there wasn't much fear left in him. He'd heard Sumulong had threatened to kill him. In advance of his visit, Conner had sent a note by runner: "I understand you want to kill me," he had written. "I am waiting." Impatient, Conner had decided to take the offensive.

In the lowlands, Conner's group hadn't been at the meeting long when Gyovai got suspicious. "The house was completely surrounded with guerrillas who had us under the cover of their rifles," Gyovai wrote. When the discussion was moved from the house to the Huks' headquarters, it got "hot and heavy," according to Gyovai, "as Clay was very much perturbed with [Sumulong] for taking the guns and not following, or joining, the USAFFE forces, but [continuing] to remain with the Huks." As the Sumulong-Conner exchanges escalated, Kodiaro whispered something to a Negrito messenger who'd come with Conner. The young man slipped outside and began to run away.

The two parties agreed to break and resume talks the next morning, which found them picking up right where they'd left off. "The discussions got hotter and hotter and it looked like we were in very deep water," said

Gyovai. "Clay was trying to convince Sumulong that Communism wasn't the way to go, which was very hard for Sumulong, who spoke very little English, and Clay, who spoke a limited amount of Tagalog."

Gyovai looked around. Sumulong's men, once again, were surrounding the open-air meeting hut. Meanwhile, however, the Negritos discreetly moved behind Sumulong and raised their rifles toward him, hiding just beyond some banana stalks. "I figured that at least if things got out of hand, Clay could handle a few inside, and I could take care of a few also," said Gyovai. "At least we wouldn't be totally wiped out without taking some of them along with us." Conner, too, realized what was happening. "We were trapped," he later wrote.

Sumulong's voice ratcheted up. Conner matched and raised him one, displaying what an interviewer would later call his "cocky brave, crazy brave" demeanor. Thirty or forty men, mostly Huks, pressed toward Conner. The noise level rose sharply, like a rumble of thunder portending the lightning to follow. Suddenly, in ran the Negrito who had slipped away the previous night. Breathless. Sweating. Spent. As if he'd run all night, which he evidently had. The debate suspended as the Huks turned to see what the Negrito was pointing to, in the direction from which he'd come. Were the Japanese coming?

From out of the jungle they emerged like an angry swarm of bees: two hundred Negritos carrying bolos, spears, blowguns, and rifles. Sumulong froze, his "home field" advantage suddenly gone. Conner exhaled. He realized a single command from him would decimate the Huks. Instead, the man who, a few years ago was quick to pull his gun in an attempt to settle a dispute, turned to his adversary, Sumulong, and made an outlandish demand that nobody would have expected, least of all Gyovai, who watched in wonder: Conner ordered Sumulong to prepare lunch for his Negrito friends—all 200 of them.

INSTEAD OF LOSING power—or his life—in the long and tense meetings with the Huks, Conner gained it. "[Sumulong] was a subdued rebel," wrote Gyovai. "He knew that if something ever happened to us, their lives would never be safe. The Negritos would come after them, one way or another." Conner, his men, and the Negritos returned to the mountains with a promise from Sumulong to cooperate with the USAFFE. Not that he and his men turned from hard-hearted rebels to choirboys overnight. "But he learned a lesson," said Gyovai. "He knew he couldn't enter the mountains and wipe us out. And if anything ever happened to us in the lowlands, he would have to answer to the Negritos."

The tribe's secret weapons in the mountains were balaise traps. They were made of razor-sharp bamboo spears that had been attached to the trunk of a bent-back, and thus spring-loaded, tree. When a boar or pig— or Japanese soldier—tripped a vine, the tree trunk released the spears. They seldom missed their marks. "I had great respect for the balaise," wrote Conner. "They were dangerous. We never ventured into an area [that had traps] unless we were with a Negrito guide."

The story spread of the Negritos coming to Conner's rescue from Sumulong. The more it was talked of, the more amazing it seemed. "The Negrito that went for help probably didn't get back up into the mountains until after dark," Gyovai wrote, "because it was a long and hard trip climbing the mountain, crossing the streams, winding up the jungle trails. And he had to also avoid the pig traps set along the trails so that he wouldn't trip them himself. After he arrived at one of the small clusters of Negrito huts, he informed them of what had taken place, and within a matter of minutes there was a singing of voices echoing through the mountains, carrying the message from one Negrito encampment to the other . . . asking them to meet at a certain place, probably carried on during the night and early the next morning until they were all assembled. I have to give credit where credit is due. Kodiaro Laxamana was probably responsible for saving our lives."

If Gyovai's respect for the chieftain increased, so did Frank's admiration for Conner. "My respect for Clay grew even more," wrote Gyovai, "but I didn't know whether he was courageous or whether he was crazy.

It didn't make any difference to him whether he took on one or a hundred, he always seemed to come out on top."

The Sumulong showdown won Conner and his men favor, but when word filtered to the Japanese soldiers in the lowlands, it also widened the target on Clay's back. If he was worried, Conner didn't share as much in an April 19, 1944, letter written—but only sent after the war—to his parents. He did mention that "my eyes are failing, probably due to the fact that I lost my glasses last April in a [terrific] Japanese raid in Tarlac." But also pointed out that "we expect the troops to arrive sometime this year, at least we hope so. I hope you know that I am well and able to make myself happy under the circumstances. I am having a lot of fun learning about life. I pray you are well."

MEANWHILE, THE JAPANESE-AMERICAN cat-and-mouse game began to intensify. Sergeant Bato, noting a weakness in the outer guard of Fort Stotsenburg, led a raid on the fort's supply dumps—a first for the 155th—and came home with fifty Japanese coats, several cases of canned goods, and grand stories of plundering the enemy for a change. "It was quite a sight," wrote Conner, "to see these Negrito 'Scouts' with loincloths and now, Japanese coats, carrying bows and arrows, returning through the mountains with cases of canned goods on their heads." For years, the guerrillas had been about defense. About hiding. About being the hunted. Now they were the hunters.

In retaliation, the Japanese increased patrols to the mountains in search of the Conner outpost. The balaise traps turned them around in a hurry—that is, those who hadn't already been skewered in their snares. "Once a man's hip is shattered through [by a spear] and he's hung on a balaise, that's the end of him," wrote Conner. The Japanese that day left six men behind to die slow, painful deaths.

TWENTY-FOUR

Stars on their Wings

September 21, 1944, to December 25, 1944

Time in the jungle since the Fall of Bataan:
Twenty-nine to thirty-three months

ON SEPTEMBER 21, 1944, Gyovai was gathering corn and Conner was resting on the porch of their log hut near Mount Dudu when they heard it: the drone of a plane. Or planes. Something sounded different this time.

"That's a heavy flight," yelled Conner, whose eyesight had never fully returned. "Are they Americans?"

The two scrambled up a hill, Conner trailing his buddy. The louder the rumble the faster Conner ran. At the summit, he saw it: smoke rising from Fort Stotsenburg, fifteen miles north-northeast. And heard it: the pounding of bombs. "They're Americans! They're Americans!" yelled Gyovai. "I can see the stars on their wings!"

Everything suggested Gyovai was right, but Conner couldn't comprehend it.

"Are you *sure*?"

"Yes. They're ours!"

The American planes were dogfighting with Japanese Zeros. "Those are American bullets," Conner yelled. "They can't kill me!"

Gyovai jumped, waved, and let out the loudest Tarzan scream he

could muster. Conner erupted into fist-pumping celebration that tran-
scended anything he'd mustered at Duke Stadium. The two waved arms.
Shouted. Hugged. "For the first time in three years," wrote Conner, "I
felt wonderful."

If anyone needed a visual symbol of the tables being turned, it came
not long after that when an American plane shot down a Japanese Zero.
The plane exploded into the side of a mountain after the pilot had bailed
out. The Negritos tracked the parachuting pilot. By the time he hit the
ground, he'd been stuck with so many arrows he looked like a pincushion.

BY LATE 1944, the lowlands in particular had become a cesspool of hopelessness. Civilians were publicly starving to death. Stinking corpses lay
unburied on the streets. Graves were being robbed for clothes and gold
teeth. But word of the American planes washed across Luzon like a cleans-
ing monsoon. Among the Filipinos and the Americans, nobody talked
about much of anything else. It was, they realized, now only a matter of
time, a fact that, naturally, triggered new Japanese patrols into the mountains with a vengeance. Things were getting hot. Conner, Gyovai, and
Mailheau headed for a new—and what would prove final—spot on
Mount Delijap. They called it Hidden Valley.

With renewed enthusiasm, Conner continued mapping Japanese
troop locations, movements, hidden caves and tunnels from which incoming troops would need to root out the enemy. "Our organizing activities
became almost feverish at this time," wrote Gyovai, "both with meetings
in the lowlands and in the mountains. Trips back and forth became
common—contacts with Colonel Merrill's headquarters, contacts with
other guerrilla units. We were on the go constantly and the work load
was pretty heavy."

On October 13, Conner was promoted from second to first lieutenant
on Merrill's recommendation. But when Merrill received a communiqué
from Conner signed "Major H. C. Conner Jr." Merrill greeted the surprising change in rank with anger and biting humor. "Congratulations on

your promotion," he wrote back. "How was it received by you?" On November 3, the Negrito messenger who had delivered the letter summoned Conner to a meeting with Colonel Peter Calyer, Merrill's deputy. Merrill, he told Conner, was trying to unite American guerrillas on Luzon and hone them for the return of American troops. Merrill wanted Conner to head up all guerrillas in Pampanga, but, as his previous message suggested, he wasn't thrilled about Conner's self-promotion. Never mind that Conner was hardly alone in such steps up in rank; it had, in fact, become commonplace among the few dozen American officers still alive in the jungles.

Conner wrote Merrill a six-page, single-spaced, typed letter, explaining that the Filipinos and Negritos placed a high value on rank, and he had made the change to further solidify the 155th's relationship with them. He apologized and said that if the brass considered him to have committed a court-martial offense, he would step aside and allow Merrill to choose someone else to head up the Negrito forces.

"I have always worked with the sole intentions of serving my country to the best of my ability and I would rather give my life than to suffer disgrace, if that is what I have brought upon myself. I want more than anything to do my part in helping to annihilate the enemy during the future campaign and I wish to be the first, if fate permits, to raise my flag over Ft. Stotsenburg."

Calyer, seemingly appreciating Conner's candor and commitment, replied that regardless of what Clay told others, he was, until further notice, a first lieutenant.

The incident did nothing to curb Conner's enthusiasm for the war effort, which was starting to get interesting with the anticipation of the Americans returning. He continued sending maps and updates on Japanese troop location, much of it gleaned from Filipino spies who worked at Fort Stotsenburg and adjacent Clark Field, and who drew intricate diagrams of troop locations, numbers of soldiers, and weapons available.

By mid-December, Conner, Kodiaro's daughter, Gyovai, and Mailheau had settled into the new Hidden Valley house built by Frank over-looking the Bamban River, not far from a knoll where they could watch the American bombings.

Aerial raids were occurring roughly every other day. Clearly, the American presence in the Philippines was more than a token flyover, but a prelude, it seemed, to bigger things to come. Oddly, though, the increased presence of planes gradually sent Conner—and to a lesser degree Gyovai—into an emotional tailspin. One day Clay told the others he needed to be alone. He then walked off into the jungle for three days by himself.

"Clay had become very depressed," wrote Gyovai. "We were [all] emotionally drained. After the return of our planes it was such a big relief to know that our forces were on the way back again, that . . . it was a big letdown for us as we realized that we were getting out from some of the pressure that we had been under. This was almost as big a battle for us as the strain of the past three years—or even more so."

To the outsider removed by time and place and circumstances, such a reaction might seem ridiculous, even disingenuous to the American flight crews who were risking—and, not infrequently, *giving*—their lives to the bombing of Stotsenburg in hopes of ultimately freeing men such as Conner and Gyovai. But after nearly thirty months, the act of survival had rooted itself into their lives with the thick persistence of bamboo roots. As much as the sightings of planes had initially buoyed Conner's spirit, the deeper reality of the future—and the idea of a sudden change in lifestyle—frightened him.

In the 1860s American South, it was not uncommon for freed slaves to stay put even when their proverbial chains were loosed. An oppressive routine, repeated over years, can engrain itself so deeply into the psyche that the oppressed forget how sweet the taste of freedom is. Caged animals, given enough time cowering within confinement, sometimes must be coaxed out of the home they've known for so long.

The Luzon experience had freed a certain adventurous spirit in Conner that a door-to-door sales job back in Jersey wasn't likely to adequately replace. Weirdly, the certainty of a predictable future may have suddenly emerged to be as worrisome as the uncertainty of his past.

ON DECEMBER 17, after Conner had returned from his contemplative retreat, he and Gyovai watched a burning U.S. Navy dive-bomber limp overhead like a wounded bird. It was losing altitude fast. Flames beat against its tail. The plane rolled over on its back, clearly out of control, and two men bailed out, their silk chutes popping open and floating down, soon lost in the jungle thicket as the plane exploded beyond.

Conner and Gyovai hollered to the Negritos with rough coordinates for the downed plane, which is where downed crews usually rendezvoused. Conner cautioned them to not harm the men, but to bring them safely back. By now, Conner and his men had built the trust of the Negritos, but Clay worried if they would extend the same respect to the two unknown men who had fallen from the sky—and who, frankly, wouldn't look anything like the ragtag, shorts-and-beard crew that Conner and his men had become.

"Americanos! Americanos!" Two days later, a forward guard of the Negrito "rescue platoon" burst into the house with news that the men had been found alive and were approaching. That the two hadn't been killed by Filipinos or Negritos—as were Japanese pilots who bailed—was a testament to whom the natives trusted. One pilot, Conner saw moments later, was clean shaven, wearing the crisp uniform of a navy officer, a lieutenant. The man behind him was taller and more slender, like Gyovai. They smiled at Conner and his men, though with smiles tinted by caution.

"Clay Hogan," said one, extending a hand.

"Bill McGrath," said the other.

Years later, Conner said the meeting carried with it a touch of uncertainty, in part because the two were surrounded by Filipinos and Negritos. "We just looked at them for a few minutes," he wrote. "I guess we must have seemed strange to them, with our heavy beards, barefoot, short pants, no shirt, and guns slung low on our hips. As I looked at them carefully, I could see they even questioned [whether] we were truly Americans." After three-plus years in the Philippines, Conner and Gyovai had been bronzed by the sun; the pilots look pasty white in comparison. And Gyovai's loincloth had them a touch worried. "I was a sight for sore eyes," he later wrote. "I had two-years' growth of whiskers. . . . [They] didn't know if I was American, Jap, Negrito, or what."

The two said they'd flown their Curtiss SB2C Helldiver from the aircraft carrier USS *Lexington*, the mere mention of which infused Conner and Gyovai with hope. A ship off Luzon!

Frank and a Negrito, King Tomas, went to fix the newcomers some food. Meanwhile, Conner engaged them in conversation, though it was marked by a certain awkwardness. What finally broke the ice was Conner learning that Hogan's full name was "Harry Clay Hogan."

"Hey, I'm 'Henry Clay Conner,'" he said.

Both, they came to realize, were twenty-six. And both were only children. "These series of coincidences sparked my imagination," wrote Conner. "I began to wonder if I was dreaming, and if it was really true all that these men were here."

"So, what's the latest song in the States?" Conner asked McGrath, who was from Plainfield, New York.

"'A Paper Dollie,'" he said.

"And Roosevelt is still president?"

"He was reelected last month for a fourth time."

Conner shook his head in amazement. Until Roosevelt, no American president had ever served three terms, much less four.

"And have the Japs or Germans invaded the U.S.?" asked Conner.

"Nope."

Everything back home, the two said, was pretty much the way it was when the soldiers had left in 1941.

"And when will the landing here be?" asked Conner. "When will MacArthur return?"

The two offered no insight, Gyovai believed, because "they weren't sure of me." If Conner was intrigued about life back home, the flyboys were no less intrigued by a handful of soldiers who looked as if they'd walked out of Defoe's *Robinson Crusoe*. "They asked us every conceivable question about our guerrilla activities; how we escaped from Bataan, and all the particulars involving hiding, running, fighting, existing—what we had eaten, how we had managed to survive in the face of so much sickness," Conner wrote. "Our very life and ability to exist was beyond their comprehension."

Like Conner, McGrath was a New Jersey boy, and the two compared notes about back home. Hogan was a graduate of the University of Wisconsin. Gyovai offered them fresh coconut bowls of horse-head soup, which the two politely declined, perhaps put off by a still-affixed eye of the animal. They settled instead for some sweet potatoes. When Gyovai gave each of the four of them a banana, Conner overruled the dispersion. He gave two each to the newcomers, none for him and Frank. In return, Hogan and McGrath thanked their hosts by passing out fresh packs of Chesterfield, Camel, and Philip Morris cigarettes, a swanky offering for guys who'd been rolling their own out of banana leaves.

In the days to come, McGrath and Hogan fit in nicely with Conner and his men, even if their jungle inexperience was a concern. "They didn't know beans from apple butter about survival in the mountains, and they were going to get themselves killed," Conner later wrote. He dispatched Crito to be their personal guide. Meanwhile, he secured supplies for the men from the Filipinos. And assigned them, along with other men, to mountaintop patrols: Delijap, Dudu, Dingauen, Cutuno, and Pinatubo— they would establish outposts on five mountains, night and day, per Merrill's request. The Americans were going to begin drops of supplies, radios, guns, ammunition, medicine—the works.

It was, frankly, monotonous duty and in the week to come resulted in very little; nothing seemed to be happening in the sky or at Fort Stotsenburg. It was Christmas. Conner called everybody in. "Between Christmas and New Year's," he wrote, "we just relaxed, talked about the States and grew to be great friends."

Across Luzon, most of the forty-eight provinces were, by now, controlled by guerrillas and not the Japanese. On December 28, a message came from Merrill: "Keep the reports and sketches coming and tell the boys they are doing a damn good job. It really begins to look like we might get out of the damn mess before we start to stumble and fall over our own beards and become grandfathers."

TWENTY-FIVE

The Return

January 9, 1945, to January 28, 1945

Time in the jungle since the Fall of Bataan:
Thirty-three to thirty-four months

HE HAD NO idea, the Filipino runner, that as he weaved through the jungle he was carrying history in his sweaty palms. Breathless, at journey's end, he handed the folded letter from Colonel Merrill to Conner. Clay unfolded it. The words of the letter itself were, initially, easily ignored. All he saw were the all-caps letters typed across the top: "THE TROOPS HAVE LANDED!" And at the bottom of the two-page letter: "IT WON'T BE LONG NOW!"

On January 9, American troops had landed on Luzon's Lingayen Gulf, about sixty miles north of the 155th Provisional Guerrilla Battalion's outpost. Word of such reached Conner and his men two days later. The troops pushed south, toward the Bataan Peninsula. For days, in Pampanga Province, Conner and the others listened for the sweet sound of American artillery; finally, on January 15, they heard it, from guns north of Fort Stotsenburg. Within a week, distant jungles crackled with the muted sound of rifles.

Conner sent out a group of Negritos to contact Bruce, whose guerrilla unit was north of the 155th and could more practically make contact with the incoming force. Soon, word got back that Bruce had, indeed, made contact with American soldiers surging south in central Luzon. It was as if buried miners had chiseled their way through to a glimpse of light. The Americans were now just north of the Bamban River and nearing the Fort Stotsenburg area, though they would be held up because it was being bombed.

Conner believed it imperative that the two downed pilots, Hogan and McGrath, get back to their squadron as quickly as possible. He sent them north January 21, with detailed maps of Japanese troop locations; when they arrived, they were to have orders sent back about how the 155th should proceed to link with the newcomers. Four days later, the pilots having safely returned to their units, runners arrived carrying orders for Conner's unit to leave the area—and with coordinates to connect with the 145th Infantry's 37th Division the next day. Conner's days as a guerrilla were about to end.

But Conner thought the transition back to the American lines was premature. An estimated twenty thousand Japanese troops stood between the 155th and the newly arrived Americans. What's more, his unit was the only obstacle standing between the Japanese and an escape for them westward, through the mountains, to the South China Sea. For Conner and his men to leave was to save themselves, perhaps, but to let the enemy off the hook. And perhaps invite a Japanese rout of the Filipinos and the Negritos.

Conner sent back a message: The 155th would hold out. Its work wasn't done yet. Merrill fired back that their area was going to be bombed soon—get the hell out. Now. Initially, Conner resisted. He ordered no nighttime fires that might give away their positions and make them vulnerable to American bombardiers who didn't know an American fire from a Japanese fire. But two days later when the earth started shaking around them, Conner and the others had no choice but to leave.

The arrival of U.S. troops had done wonders for recruitment of Filipino guerrillas, who flocked to Conner and other guerrilla leaders with gusto, eager to help finish off the Japanese—though scorned by some as "sunshine patriots," people who did nothing to help the Americans but were only too glad to join the victory parade.

Meanwhile, fleet-footed Filipino messengers were keeping Conner updated on the movement of Japanese troops. One such report caused him considerable concern. At Fort Stotsenburg, the Japanese were starting to move westward on the Pinatubo Trail, through a valley that, if not defended, could become a pathway for the enemy to reach the relative safety of the South China Sea some thirty miles away. The area was far from Conner's headquarters and hard to reach with bulk supplies, making it difficult to mobilize a force to defend it. Beyond that, it had been used so little in the last three years that jungle foliage was thick on it. Conner immediately ordered five hundred balaise pig traps rigged across the trail. The Filipinos and the Negritos got to work, planting sharpened bamboo spears in the ground, at an east-facing angle. The breadth and depth of this project was immense: Over a few weeks' time, hundreds of traps were spread over a three-mile span lined six traps deep.

As U.S. troops swept through, the Japanese troops that were flushed out of Stotsenburg headed west for the hills. When vines were tripped, the wooden lances were unleashed on whatever was in the line of fire.

Troops who survived the pig traps encountered an enemy that left the Japanese bewildered and, in many cases, dead: tiny black men—Negritos, of course—zinging arrows and blow darts at them. The small men flitted through the jungle ahead, beside, and behind the Japanese. Meanwhile, gun-toting Filipino guerrillas vented three years of oppression on their enemy. Later, Kodiaro would proudly proclaim to Conner that not a single Japanese soldier had made it to the South China Sea.

CONNER AND THE 155th had gotten maps to the air force with locations of optimum bombing targets: caves and tunnels in the Zambales that nobody else knew about. Merrill insisted Conner stop dillydallying and move the 155th east. Resigned to the inevitable, Conner obeyed—but, in turn, he ordered the evacuation of local barrios. If the Americans were going to steer clear of falling bombs, damn it, so were his Filipino and Negrito friends. Once civilian refugees were relocated to safety to the east, American guerrillas were to gather in the lowlands near Banaba, about ten miles south of Stotsenburg.

From that location, Conner sent word to the American commander in Angeles, about five miles east: The 155th could meet up with the American troops in that area the next day. It was now the end of January; it had been nearly three years since Clay had left the others and plunged into the jungle. Now, save some last-minute Japanese rally or some stupid, self-created mistake—say, falling prey to one of the Negritos' own pig traps—he and whatever stragglers had survived this bizarre existence would join the mass of troops that had returned to Luzon. Among them was a Corporal Charles Stotts, a British soldier who had recently wandered into the 155th camp. He had been captured by the Japanese in Singapore in 1941, escaped a Japanese-bound prison ship sunk in Subic Bay, and swum to Luzon.

From barrio to barrio, Conner and the others spread the word of the evacuation. The news sent the jungle into an awkward buzz, an emotional blend of panic, joy, and grief: panic because people were being flushed from their homes, if only temporarily; joy because this horrific war was finally coming to an end; and grief because the American soldiers had become, to the Filipinos and the Negritos, like surrogate sons—and to the soldiers, the natives had become lifelines. Suddenly, though all had eagerly awaited this reversal of fortune, people who had depended on one another were now having to part for good.

Rushed farewells. Occasional hugs. Overdue thank-yous. Conner's mind was a tangle of disparate emotions. Kodiaro, his daughter, Crito, and Mrs. Hardin. People who had given him and his men food when they were hungry, shelter when they were wet, hiding places when they were hunted. How could he have imagined that strangers thousands of miles from his home in America—people so different from the Duke and New Jersey folks he'd grown up with—could have come to mean so much to him?

Light began to fade. The tattered American flag that had been raised at their new location waved gently in a tropical breeze. Time, Conner realized, for one final tribute. Spread the word, he told a handful of Negrito messengers. The sound of *tambulies*—loud, then growing softer with each transfer of the call—reached deep into the jungle. Soon the people were gathered outside: to Conner's left were a few hundred Negritos armed, of course, with bows and quivers of arrows, always at the ready should the Japanese spring an attack; to his right were the loyal Filipinos with their rifles, including the man he would one day call the finest soldier he'd ever met, Sergeant Bato; and, directly in front were the ragtag handful of Americans with whom he'd been thrown together, as if they were drowning men who'd clamored onto the same life raft: his mainstays, Gyovai and Mailheau; a couple who'd joined him off and on nearly two years before, Decker and Campbell; and Stotts.

He scanned this clump of humanity, framed by jungle foliage, the darkened skin of the Negritos all but lost in the twilight; the hue of the Philippine Scouts almond; the once-pasty skins of the Americans now sun-scoured into browns and reds. Like him, many were fully bearded, hair covering faces imbued, for the first time since the journey began, with expectation. Of rescue. Of release. Of home.

Conner looked at the flag. It was the same flag that Sergeant Bato had taken from the hands of a gunned-down 26th Cavalry Regiment comrade nearly three years before and presented to the 155th. In accepting it, Conner had made a vow to Bato that someday it would fly over Fort Stotsenburg. Tomorrow, perhaps, it would.

"Attention!" Conner barked what would be his final order to this disparate collection of people.

At his command, the right hands of all snapped in salute before the flag was lowered for the last time.

PART FIVE

PEACE

TWENTY-SIX

Presentation of the Colors

January 29, 1945, to February 2, 1945

Time in the jungle since the Fall of Bataan:
Thirty-four months and twenty-one days

AT DAWN, CONNER checked his Bulova. Seven o'clock on January 29, 1945. The six Americans headed east for Angeles five miles away: Conner, Gyovai, Mailheau, Decker, Campbell, and Stotts. In a dry riverbed, the group began like the trickle of a high-mountain creek, just the Americans, their hopes as new and fresh as their clothes were old and spent. As always, Gyovai was barefoot. Mailheau, also without shoes, wore torn pants, a too-large shirt, and, atop his head, a beat-up straw hat.

By the time they reached the main north-south road to Angeles, the trickle had been fed by so many tributaries that the group had become a virtual river of humanity: three hundred Negritos and even more Filipinos. It was a veritable collage of colors and sizes, among the smallest a Negrito named Joe San Pedro, chosen by Conner to carry the American flag at the front of the column. A melding of people now paraded home in victory. The red, white, and blue—fringed in gold—hung from its bamboo pole. How long ago it had been since the day in Bataan when white surrender rags and T-shirts had hung from similar poles.

Soon, even Filipino civilians were joining the flow northward, though others feared that to do so was to join a second death march. Japanese soldiers, they warned, were thick along the road ahead. Snipers were hidden in the trees.

"You'll be killed!" someone shouted.

"Turn back!" said someone else.

Conner, knowing a patrol would be foolish to attack a force this size, ignored the warnings. After more than three years of living in defeat, the men were too close to victory. Too close to reconnecting. Too close to—

Suddenly, Conner heard the drone of a plane and looked skyward. It dipped lower, heading toward them, the pilot obviously homed in on this unlikely mass of people in the wilds. For an enemy pilot, it was a fish-in-a-barrel find. It could be a final venting over this unfortunate reversal of fortune, a victory that was slipping from Japan's grasp. Perhaps a heroic kamikaze crash as a final gift to the emperor. Conner exchanged quick glances with Mailheau and Gyovai. Hundreds of heads tilted to the sky. Whether the pilot saw the whites of the six men's faces or the red, white, and blue of their flag, he dipped the plane's wings back and forth in friendly recognition of the allies below. It was an American observation plane. Conner and the others whooped and hollered. Mailheau waved his straw hat. The Negritos and the Filipinos joined in the celebration.

The flow toward freedom continued. On occasion, Conner and the others would see a Japanese patrol in the distance, but when seeing the size of the units, the enemy troops slunk back into the jungle.

At mid-morning, the group reached the road from Angeles to Porac and headed north, Mailheau flanking Joe San Pedro and the flag to the left. Doyle, Campbell, and Stotts walked alongside Mailheau. Gyovai, all six-foot-two of him, was a comical sight next to San Pedro, not five feet tall. Both smiled broadly. Conner, in cut-off pants, flanked Kodiaro and Gyovai. With his whimsical bent, Crito, like a clown in a parade, zigzagged from side to side of the crowd lining the road, handing out cigarettes that the two pilots had given him for his assistance.

As the group neared Angeles, the song rose awkwardly from one of the Americans—nobody was sure who sang the first line—and the others spontaneously joined in: "California here I come, right back where I started from!" Over and over came the words from a 1920s Broadway musical that made reference to the San Francisco they'd left more than three years ago: *California, here I come / right back where I started from . . .*

It was silly. Crazy. At odds with nearly everything this battered bunch of soldiers had experienced since the Japanese bombers had descended on Luzon, and yet when the song ended, Conner couldn't help it. He cranked it up again. And again. And again. And the others showed no less enthusiasm, Mailheau and Gyovai—guys who, on more than one occasion, had bloodied each other's face—joining in with gusto. Meanwhile, the Negritos added their unique chant to the "California" mix. Conner and Gyovai wrapped arms around each other like schoolboys. Everywhere: wild joy as vibrant as the water cascading over the falls where Frank had once considered ending it all.

Then, through the dust that hundreds of feet had kicked up, Conner saw them ahead: a handful of tanks. Olive green with white stars on them. American tanks. They clanked with an ominous sound that reminded Conner of the Japanese half-tracks on the day when he'd buried himself in the mud to survive.

The tanks ground to a stop. Conner brought the column to a halt. The singing stopped. A pensive quiet settled over the scene. Slowly, one of the hatches opened on the lead tank. Then on others. When the tankers began popping up and out, Conner was taken by how neat and clean the men all were. How big. Thick. And, goodness, how *young*. Conner had been only twenty-two years old when he arrived at Scott Field in 1941; he was now twenty-six.

For a moment, the looks on the tankers' faces were of disbelief, as if the men could hardly fathom that the two groups of soldiers represented the same country's army. Below them on the road was a forever-stretching sea of black and olive faces: grimy soldiers, some bearded, most barefoot, a few in shorts, all leather-skinned, some no wider than a parking meter. And far older than many of those now standing atop the tanks.

The men of the 37th Division's 145th Infantry just stared; in this unchartered territory, nobody knew quite what to do or say. Conner stepped forward as the 155th's leader. A tanker climbed down from his perch and stepped toward Conner. The two men eyed each other; it was, remembered Conner, a bit like when he'd met the pilots, Hogan and McGrath. A touch of suspicion from both sides. Then, in a moment Conner would never forget, the tanker snapped a crisp salute to Clay.

"Welcome home, sir," he said.

The ice broke. Other tankers hopped down from their perches to greet the men, eye to eye. Handshakes. Back slaps. Smiles. "Get these men some food," said one of the tankers. In short order, canned food was being popped open and handed out. When a tanker lit a cigarette for Gyovai, Conner couldn't help but notice how the man's hand was shaking as he flipped open the lighter, as if the soldier was somehow awed by the opportunity. A few others in the tank crew, he noticed, turned their heads to wipe back tears that they didn't want seen.

Soon, trucks arrived. The 155th bid hasty but heartfelt farewells to the Negritos and the Filipinos. "With a tearful good-bye," wrote Decker, "they returned to their mountain home. They were a proud people and they looked let down as they turned to leave. After all, we had been together for over two years." Joe San Pedro approached Conner with the tattered flag, smiling large. Conner took the bamboo pole and nodded his head in thanks.

THE MEN WERE trucked about fifteen miles northeast, to Concepcion. Conner requested the opportunity for him and his men to meet with Lieutenant General Oswald Griswold. Request granted. Instead of a thatched hut, the U.S. brass, including Griswold, were living in a house that, relative to its surroundings, was a mansion.

It was January 29, 1945. The men sat down to their first true mess-hall meal since late 1941. Afterward, when escorted to Griswold's compound, they felt like paupers in the king's court; these, after all, were men who had slept beneath bamboo lean-tos, eaten monkey, and essentially worn the same clothes for three years. Now they were in an actual structure with floors and corners and electricity.

The man whom this finery surrounded, Griswold, was a fifty-eight-year-old lieutenant general who had graduated from West Point, fought in France during World War I, and swapped stories with MacArthur himself. A lieutenant approached Conner and his men with news: Griswold was moving elsewhere; the house was theirs. But he had a message for them, said the lieutenant: "Sleep well."

Conner and his men looked at one another in near-disbelief. But sleep well they did not. It was all too sudden. Too different. Too nice. The men tossed and turned on the softness of their cots. In the morning, one of Griswold's staff lieutenants heard commotion in the room.

"What the hell is going on in here?" he said.

Every man had abandoned his cot. They were huddled on the floor, wide awake.

"Don't mind us," said Conner. "We just aren't used to these creature comforts."

The lieutenant laughed. A debriefing with the lieutenant general would be held later that morning, he told them. Prior to that, however, they were served breakfast and given cursory examinations by an army doctor. They all were found to have tropical ulcers on their feet and fungus on their bodies. Mailheau hadn't yet healed from bullet wounds on his left foot and left knuckles. The doctor gave the men an assortment of ointments and powders.

Two others who'd eluded the Japanese soldiers in the jungles joined the six at Concepcion, too: Lieutenant Bruce and Sergeant Willard Bresler of San Antonio, Texas, who was recovering from a bullet wound to a leg and was still on crutches.

The men were fitted for new uniforms and boots. Gyovai took a few steps and winced. As if on cue, the others did the same. When escorted in to see Lieutenant General Griswold, the men all had their boots laced together and hanging from their shoulders. They were barefoot.

Word spread of a daring rescue of American soldiers and civilians from a prison camp in Cabanatuan, thirty-five miles to the northwest. Nearly five hundred Americans who'd been holed up in squalor since the end of what was now being called the "Bataan Death March" had been set free in what would prove to be the greatest rescue mission in U.S. military history.

The next morning, Griswold held a ceremony to honor the eight survivors who'd arrived in Angeles. In the middle of the compound head-quarters, hundreds of soldiers gathered. Conner stepped forward to make the presentation on behalf of his men. He handed Griswold the flag, finally home after its nearly three-year journey from Morong.

"Sir, we're proud to tell you," said Conner, "that this flag, despite the surrender, never ceased to fly over Luzon." His slightly revisionist history captured the spirit, if not the letter, of the law, though Griswold was astute enough to see beyond any such technicalities, to the unique moment this was. Conner, he would later note, had "tears in his eyes."

Griswold looked at the flag, then scanned the eight men in front of him. Lieutenant generals do not often grow misty-eyed. Griswold did, said witnesses.

"This," he said, "is one of the most touching incidents in the war. I accept the flag for the United States government in humility, in the pres-ence of the brave soldiers who carried it."

Applause broke out from hundreds of surrounding soldiers. At first, it jolted Conner; it was a sound he had not heard for years. Clapping. Then, it warmed him, revived him, wrapped him in the same kind of honor that, as a cheerleader, he had bestowed on the football heroes at Duke, but that, until now, he had never experienced himself.

In morning sunshine, the group of eight men posed for a photo: the thick-bearded Conner, front row left, on one knee; to his left, Stotts, Campbell, and Mailheau; and, standing behind, left to right, Gyovai, Bresler, Decker, and Bruce. The photo exudes a sense of lightness and relief, as if, instead of having been taken at the end of nearly four years of violence, disease, and despair, it had been taken at a fraternity party or following a sandlot baseball game.

"General," said Conner after the ceremony ended, "could I get a telegram sent to my folks back home?"

"Why, of course," said Griswold.

An aide of the lieutenant general's stepped forward with pencil and paper. Conner jotted a string of words and handed it to Griswold, who looked at the note.

"Dear Mother and Dad," it said. "Everything under control."

Griswold smiled, looked up at Conner, and shook his head.

IN EAST ORANGE, New Jersey, on North Grove Street, the doorbell rang at the home of Marguerite and Henry Clay Conner's apartment on Wednesday, February 1, 1945. Marguerite opened the door. There stood a reporter from the *Newark News Reporter*. A United Press dispatch, he told her, had arrived at the newspaper; her son had just marched out of the Luzon mountains carrying an American flag.

Marguerite collapsed on the spot. Hearing the commotion from elsewhere in the apartment, Henry Clay Sr. rushed to his wife's aid. He looked at the man on the doorstep.

"Is he—is my son dead?" he asked.

The reporter smiled. "Oh, no, your son is very much alive, Mr. Conner. That's why I'm here."

As Marguerite came to, the couple invited the reporter in. He asked if he could see Clay Jr.'s room They allowed him a look. "The room," he later wrote, "is typical of a young man's quarters with college pennants and pin-up girl sketches on the wall."

It looked just as it did when Conner had left for the Philippines more than three years before, as if he had never been gone, as if nothing had ever changed, as if nothing ever would.

TWENTY-SEVEN

Unfinished Business

February 2, 1945, to February 9, 1945

February 5, 1945

Red Cross Civilian War Aid:

Dear Sirs:

We have written the enclosed letter to our son although he was not a prisoner but as you can see by the enclosed United Press clipping he has returned to our lines and so we earnestly hope you will send him my letter. We know he will be worried about us too, especially me as I have had heart trouble and I want him to know as soon as possible I am alright. Also we do not want him to contact his girl as she is married.

Sincerely,
Mrs. H. C. Conner

February 5, 1945

Dearest Clay Jr.,

I don't need to tell you how supremely happy Dad & I are and so thankful to get the United Press report last Thursday that you came out of the hills. . . . Our daily prayers were answered and we know now miracles still do happen. We can hardly wait to see you. We believe you were conscious all the time of our intense love and faith and how much we need you to make life worth living and therefore you used all your courage and resourcefulness to somehow survive and fight your way back home. You sure are a hero to everyone we know but most of all to us.

Now I must tell you Mimi was married to a Lieutenant J. G. in the Navy last April. I hope you don't mind too much. I guess it was just meant to be that way. She didn't have the faith we did son and as I told you before you left, if she loved you enough she would wait for you but if she didn't, then you won't have missed anything. She met her husband in California in July 1942. She stayed there until Xmas when he must have gone to Africa and later he returned and they were married in April 1944. She seemed happy when she called me to tell me she was getting married so I told her we understood and felt sure you would too. Such a boy as you can always find a nice girl, Clay Jr.

Lovingly,
Mother

IN NEW JERSEY, Conner's folks spread the word that Clay was safe. Radio broadcaster Lowell Thomas told the nation of Clay exiting from the jungle with the tattered flag. Across the country, newspaper stories popped up about him and his vagabond men, a touch of triumph amid the still-lingering shock of the Bataan Death March. The horrific event had not made American newspapers until nearly two years after it happened. Thus, Conner's story and news of the rescue at Cabanatuan provided rare salve for the wounded home front.

Lute Pease, a cartoonist for the *Newark (N.J.) News* who would soon win a Pulitzer Prize, penned a cartoon showing "the flag that never touched the ground" coming out of the jungle. He dedicated it to Clay. The East Orange City Council sent Conner an official letter of welcome. Hearing of Clay losing his golf clubs on Luzon, an East Orange man bought him a set for $150. When word of Conner's safe return reached the Duke University campus, "everyone went wild," a secretary told Marguerite Conner. The folks at Schraffts, a favorite family restaurant of the Conners in Newark, "were all so overjoyed to hear about you," she wrote him. And, his mother noted, "Eliz. Ann Thomson can hardly wait to hear from you and she is now at Stephens College, Columbia, Missouri."

BACK IN THE Philippines, Conner had unfinished business. Griswold had loaned the men his personal jeep and, with Gyovai and Mailheau, Conner headed to La Paz. He had a score to settle with the Filipino mayor who had betrayed them in the incident at Lara. Two years had passed since the event involving these three and Eddie Keith; nobody, including the mayor, appeared to recognize the men, who now sported bushy beards and wore fresh army uniforms. The mayor was all smiles, welcoming them like old friends.

"I'm Lieutenant Conner," said Clay.

The mayor looked as if he'd been gut-shot. Some of the Filipinos started edging toward the door. Gyovai and Mailheau wouldn't let them leave. Conner asked for a piece of paper; he wanted the man to write out his own death warrant, complete with his signature: Pacifico Pascual.

The man's wife broke into tears. *Please, please, please . . .* Pascual hesitated, then slowly began to sign his name. His wife cried out for him to be spared. Others beyond her wailed. Family. Friends. *Please . . .* He had not wanted to betray the Americans, she said, but the Japanese forced him. If he had not done as they said, they would have killed everyone. Even the children. The woman fell to her knees, tugged on Conner's pants. *Please, please, please . . .* Her husband did not want to do it, she repeated, but he had no choice. *Please, no . . .*

Conner glanced at Mailheau and Gyovai, then back to the woman. In this instant, her anguish brought the entire war into fine, if unsettling, focus for Conner. These Filipinos, the people in this room—their country had been shredded, their crops ruined, their families threatened, their daughters raped. They had been awakened in the night by bayonets ripping through their floors, heard screams of their children in the darkness. It was a wonder, he thought, that they still believed in anything. Why should he give them one more thing—Americans—to not believe in? Why should he add to their misery? What good would it do anyone? At some point this war needed to end. Conner decided that, for him, that point would be now.

He took the paper from Pascual and crumpled it. The man broke down and wept. Conner motioned for Gyovai and Mailheau to leave. Conner took a final look at the man, then turned and left himself. The three drove down a few roads and Conner stopped. Gyovai and Mailheau immediately recognized it: the place of the ambush. Conner knew exactly where he was going, to a bamboo thicket the men had hidden in before they'd had to split up. To the place where he'd left Junko. But the stuffed monkey was nowhere to be found.

They turned to leave, going back through La Paz. They slowed to say good-bye to the mayor, who was outside. For some odd reason, Conner told him about Junko; told a man he had just about sentenced to death about a stuffed monkey.

"Oh, yes," said the mayor. "Little girl find. She take monkey. Now live in Manila."

Conner pursed his lips together and nodded. *Long live Junko.*

=======

CONNER AND HIS men were trucked north to a replacement depot on the Lingayen Gulf, where the Japanese invasion of Luzon had begun. There, he met the Americans who had been freed from Cabanatuan Prison Camp. Among the men was Captain Bert Bank, who had been at the Manila Hotel with Rocky Gause and Clay on New Year's Eve and who, during the surrender, had shouted across the radio, "The Japanese have broken through! Pull back! Pull back!"

"We talked, and he told me about all the men in the 27th who had died in Cabanatuan, and those who had been on the prison ship that was sunk on its way to Japan," wrote Conner. During the rescue, Bank was too blind to see his own feet and had to be led to safety by hand. "His eyes were weak," wrote Conner. "He had the same trouble as I had had. And he was a physical wreck. He said the worst thing of all was when the Japs really wanted to punish them, they'd put the men with bad cases of diarrhea in the upper bunks . . . and make them sleep with their pants off."

The two talked deep into the night, the stories enough to make any man want to catch the next ship back to Frisco. Not Conner. He wanted to return to Banaba. "Sir," he wrote to Colonel Merrill the next day, "I am sure you will understand my personal feelings about this situation. I wanted to personally complete the mission that was started two years ago. The people . . . were faithful in duty and were depending on me to relieve them. Now that I have been relieved I feel that I have not lived up to [the Negritos'] expectations."

"I had to find out if they were being recognized by the American troops," he later wrote, "if the Americans were feeding them, and treating them right. I knew the Huks would give them a bad time."

His permission to leave was denied—not by Merrill, who might have understood his attachment to the Negritos, but a Colonel Rawalli, who apparently did not. Conner mulled all that he had been through in Luzon. He didn't even know if his parents were still alive; neither had been the picture of health when he'd left and he hadn't heard back from them since sending his "all safe" telegram. Outside, a convoy was organizing to transport men south to Pampanga Province.

"Room for one more?" asked Conner.

THOUGH THE AMERICANS now controlled Fort Stotsenburg, the fighting was fierce to the west. Conner, technically, was AWOL, but when the 40th Infantry Division heard how well he knew the territory, he was quickly assigned to an intelligence and reconnaissance patrol; no questions asked. Forget the fancy name, their job was to root out Japanese soldiers, known to burrow down like ground squirrels.

Before heading out on patrol, Conner reunited with Democrito Lumanlan, who, if missing the guys from the 155th, was enjoying the victory-in-process. To higher-ups, Conner put in good words about Crito and about the Negritos, whose abilities and loyalties, he said, should be used by the Americans. Then he left on patrol.

Conner quickly emerged as a leader. He found caves and tunnels where soldiers were hunkered down. Hideouts tucked in steep ridges behind barrios. And, more than once, he cautioned the men in the platoon about the Negritos' pig traps. It was late February. Now carrying a machine gun along with his pistol, Conner was with ten U.S. soldiers when they came across a few thatched huts. One, in fact, Conner recognized as a place he had once slept.

"Hold on a sec," he said, leaving the cluster of other soldiers.

Except for the call of a bird and distant *tat-tat-tat* of a machine gun, all was quiet. Conner eyed the hut where he'd once stayed, and then started his approach. To his flank, something rustled behind the jungle cover. He spun.

Just an iguana.

He refocused, walked to the wooden ladder going up to the hut, and began climbing. Slowly. Cautiously. Nervously. One hand on the bamboo rail, the other on his weapon. At the top, he peered over the edge. His heart raced. Two Japanese soldiers were sprawled on the floor, dead or asleep.

He looked closer. Asleep. In an instant, the irony hit home. The tables were turned. For years, he'd been their prisoner, in essence. Now they were his.

"Up!" he shouted. "Get up!"

They scrambled to their feet and thrust their hands to the sky. One's hand bolted for a pocket. In the split second before he pulled the trigger, what flashed in Conner's mind was the Negrito who'd been blown to bits when a Japanese prisoner detonated a suicide grenade.

Clay's machine-gun fire dropped the two men in a bloody clump. He bent onto a single knee and carefully reached into the one soldier's pocket for the grenade. The pocket was empty. What he found, instead, was a surrender leaflet wadded in the soldier's lifeless hand, English on one side, Japanese on the other: "If you will deliver this to the Americans, they will give you safe convoy to a prison camp."

Conner looked up at the other men. Others stepped forward to search the bodies. A soldier held up something in his hands: photos of the men's wives and children. Conner looked away. Nobody said a word.

WHEN CONNER RETURNED to Fort Stotsenburg that night, Crito handed him something he hadn't seen in more than three years: a letter from home, postmarked February 5, 1945. His folks had gotten his telegram a few weeks ago; they knew he was safe. And were rejoicing. So was Clay. They both had bad hearts; it was good to know they were still alive and waiting.

The part about Mimi getting married did not bother him; both he and his former girlfriend had moved on with their lives, though in far different ways. Overall, however, the letter touched something deep within Conner, something that more than three years in the jungle had nearly made him forget. When he finished the letter, he knew it was time.

The horrific details of Cabanatuan, his shooting of the Japanese soldiers, the letter from his mother—all of it funneled into a single thought for Conner that, in the last few months, he had hidden from himself, as if he were afraid to leave this place that he'd loved and loathed.

"I wanted to go home," he wrote.

Musette bag packed, he stopped by to see Crito, who had been his provider when he needed food, his encouragement when he needed cheering, his eyes when he needed sight. A handshake turned into a hug. Then, a final exchange: A promise that they would see each other again. A thank-you from Conner. And parting words from a damp-eyed Crito.

"Good-bye, Mr. Clay."

TWENTY-EIGHT

Home

February 10, 1945, to April 9, 1945

10 February 1945

Dear Mrs. Conner:

It is a pleasure to inform you that that above named person ("Conner, Henry C., Jr."), previously recorded as missing in action in the Philippine Islands, has returned to military control. He is in weakened condition and requires rest.

Sincerely yours,
J. A. Ulio
Major General
The Adjutant General

AS CONNER WAITED to hear when and how he would be returning to the States, his mother continued writing him letters, as if to give release to her seemingly boundless joy. "We are just so excited about your being safe after all these years that we can't think about anything else," she wrote on February 11. "Life is worth living to us again and we are just counting time until you will be home again. We have tried to reach you in every conceivable way."

As for his father, she wrote: "All he can do now is go around saying, 'That's my boy!'" On March 1, Clay wrote back, having received that letter and another. "I was so happy I didn't know what to do," he wrote, continuing:

> First of all I noticed your name (Mother) on the return address and was momentarily worried about Dad's name not included. Hurriedly I opened the letter and scanned through for the news that I've been waiting for for three years. Tears came to my eyes to know that you were still there and that everything was the same as when I left. I always knew you would do more than your share to support the war and for that reason I was determined to fight it out in order that you would know I would never fail you.
>
> Best I should tell you a little about myself so you will be prepared when you see me. In general the same person all in tact thus far, eyes a little week [sic] which is noticeable, my hair is still wavy, usually not combed but that can be fixed in a hurry. There's a smattering of gray along the temples but that all adds up to the expectations of the crowds. After all, I'm supposed to be an adventurer. One thing I've added to my appearance is a [cigarette] in hand, however I think you can well understand that I had to do something to calm my nerves and there wasn't any chewing gum, laying around loose. By the way I've lost a little weight lately which makes me about the same as when I left the states, 145 lbs. About all those girls you mentioned, line me up with one for every night in the year for the next 40 months. Reserve a table at the place with the best band and turn me loose. Don't think I've forgotten you, make it a table for four, you and Dad and the gal and Jr. Something of a quiet party and (strictly) private. I'm bashful in a crowd, in fact I always was as you well know. Seriously I would like something like that. When we meet, it would make it

easier and wouldn't give us so much time to think about the past. I
am a firm believer in the tomorrow. What has happened yesterday is
a memory. What a memory.

By the way I haven't lost my sense of humor, at least that's what
the newcomers say and definitely I haven't lost my go gettem spirit.
High strung and hard to handle.

Just between you and me I have often hoped Mimi would be
married when this thing is over. I know the truth now and being a
little older and more experienced in the hard knocks I think any girl
I marry will have to have the stuff it takes to be like you have been
to Dad.

Well the light supply is nil and I haven't learned to use the brail
system so I'll call this one on account of darkness. All my love to you
two and thank God you are still all right.

Clay Jr.

Only days later, a heart attack felled Conner's father. He was in serious condition in a Newark hospital. "The doctor," wrote his mother, "says it is just a reaction to the strain of the last three years. When you get home it will speed his recovery quicker than anything else." Clay never got the message, however. Meanwhile, Marguerite Conner contacted Colonel George Herbert, asking for Clay's immediate return. A radiogram was sent to Luzon requesting as much. Again, word never got to the proper authorities or to Conner.

Instead of flying, on March 17, 1945, Conner headed for San Francisco aboard the USS *Capps*. It wasn't a first-class trip, but Conner did get a nice room up top, much to the chagrin of a particular colonel, who believed Conner was bunking a notch too high up for a first lieutenant. The two argued. The colonel won. Conner wound up spending most of his twenty-one days at sea in the ship's belly, not far from the annoying thrum of the propeller. Meanwhile, though, he had bet the man $100 that a look at his records would suggest his time and experience on Luzon justified the room. The colonel scoffed but shook on the bet.

The three-week trip home, with knowing only a few men on board, gave Conner endless hours for reflection. Pen in hand, he added new memories to his journal. The escape at Lara and Marco Polo. The Huks double-crossing him. Mrs. Hardin. Frank's Tarzan yell. The ambush in the church at Bacolor. Kodiaro. The way the jungle turned a soft orange-ish as the sun faded and the children's voices rose. Mailheau's Mickey Rooney stories. The day he and Herbert looked out at Subic Bay and pondered an escape by raft. The deaths of Herbert, Hart, Musgrove, Lawrence, and too many others to remember. Digging the graves for Dunlap and Porter. The sound of that first American plane. Two pilots dropping in for horse-head soup. And, of course, Sergeant Bato's flag.

Conner wrote it all down, then walked to the stern of the ship one evening, looked at the waters, and flung the notebook into the froth. To forget it all? To start anew? He never explained why.

Meanwhile, the ship churned toward home. As it neared the Golden Gate Bridge, Conner caught his first glimpse of America from the star-board side. To his flanks, hundreds of men pressed to the rail. Tired men. Some on crutches, some with heads bandaged, some in wheelchairs. And many, like Conner, hardened by war and far from the "mama's boys" they might have been on their way to the Philippines. Soon the colonel who had cost Conner his first-class accommodations nudged beside him. The two looked at the city by the bay at first, saying nothing to each other.

"I, uh, checked your record," the man finally said to Conner. "I owe you an apology."

As the ship glided beneath the bridge, the colonel reached inside his pocket. He slipped Conner a $100 bill.

IN SAN FRANCISCO, Conner's cousin, Marjorie, who'd watched him leave on that drizzly November day in 1941, and her husband, Max, greeted him with a long hug. They introduced Clay to his two-year-old namesake, Clay Maxwell Pamphilion, whom Clay Jr. held for a photo. It was April 8. By then, military authorities had realized their oversight in not getting

Conner home sooner, given what he'd been through and his father's grave condition. Mrs. Conner was assured that Clay would be flown home as soon as possible after he disembarked the ship. He was, courtesy of United Air Lines.

The next afternoon—April 9, the three-year anniversary of the Fall of Bataan—he arrived at LaGuardia Field in New York, where his mother was there to greet him. Clay's arrival, Mrs. Conner would later write, was "tonic" for her husband recovering from his heart attack, which Clay Jr. only learned about upon arrival. "Nothing could convince him that the boy wouldn't yet be a casualty in the Philippines but his actual appearance," she wrote. (Later, when Clay Jr. first met his father at the hospital, he was surprised at his attire. Though on oxygen and unable to leave the hospital, his father was, in honor of his home-from-the-war son, wearing a new suit.)

At the airport, Conner told a reporter from the *Newark Evening News* that next to the reunion with his parents, the most beautiful sight he'd ever seen was the Golden Gate Bridge. "But I was saddened," he said, "when I thought of those who passed it once and never will return."

A senator on hand had asked Conner how he was able to survive when so many others had not. Was it fate? God's will? What? Clay thought about the question, then realized something strange for a man who, regardless of what situation he had been thrown in, always seemed to have an answer.

"I had no answer for him," wrote Conner. "I wanted to know that myself. I knew I wasn't any better than the other men. I knew I hadn't done anything that they hadn't done. But somehow I had been spared, though thousands had died. I knew that I wouldn't be happy until I found the answer to this soul-searching question. I had experienced every pain, every hardship, every depravity. I had prayed, I had read, but there was still a longing within me to have an answer."

For now, it was time to resume the life that he had nearly forgotten he had, the life he had longed for and, perhaps, quietly feared. Less than three months before, he had been part of an unlikely band of disparate brothers, triumphantly carrying a tattered flag to its prophetic place of honor, surrounded by Negritos, Filipinos, and bearded, barefoot men like himself. At LaGuardia, in his dress browns and with his Bulova still ticking, he picked up his bag. His mother tucked her arm tightly around his, and, together, they headed for home.

EPILOGUE

PART I: BEYOND CONNER

Colonel Herbert
Casualty Department
War Dept.
Washington, D.C.

Dear Colonel Herbert,

Your call on April 4th saying we could expect our son home the first of the next week seemed like an answer to my prayer that he would reach here in time, for the [doctor] had just told me everything had been done that was possible for Mr. Conner and that all we could do now was to wait and hope. The [doctor] walked in and told the good news to my husband but he didn't rally for the better until the morning of the day Clay Jr. arrived home, but from that time on his recovery has been miraculous. Nothing could convince him that the boy wouldn't yet be a casualty in the Philippines but his actual appearance, and so Colonel Herbert we wish to thank you sincerely

for arranging to have Clay Jr. flown home immediately upon his
arrival in the States. Of course we are still giving him oxygen every
hour but he says Clay Jr. is his tonic and the [doctor] agrees with him.
   We will never forget how cooperative and kind you have been to
us in these past three years, Colonel Herbert, and again we wish to
say it has all been deeply appreciated.

Sincerely,
Mrs. H. C. Conner

ON MARCH 2, 1945, airborne troops parachuted onto Corregidor to crush an enemy garrison that was five times what was expected: Five thousand Japanese soldiers were entrenched in the tunnels honeycombing an island roughly the size of Manhattan.

It would take nearly a month to liberate Manila and would come at a huge cost. More than three-quarters of the "Pearl of the Orient" was destroyed; only Warsaw, Poland, suffered worse devastation during World War II. Fighting in Manila alone cost the lives of more than a thousand Americans, sixteen thousand Japanese, and a hundred thousand Filipinos. MacArthur may have fulfilled his three-year-old promise to return, but with the once-proud capital turned into a smoldering graveyard, he quickly abandoned the idea of a victory parade.

On Luzon, fighting continued in the mountainous northern regions until the two atomic bombs were dropped on Japan in August of 1945, to end World War II. Overall, World War II cost the lives of roughly 1 million Filipinos. All told, Filipinos suffered twice as many casualties in the war as did Americans, though they had a population only one-tenth as large. And yet, wrote Robert Lapham and Bernard Nordling in *Lapham's Raiders*, "when victory was gained at last, the Filipinos were the only colonial people in Asia who called it 'liberation' rather than 'occupation.'"

The United States, as promised more than a decade before, granted independence to the Philippines on July 4, 1946.

THE BATAAN DEATH March was judged by an Allied military commission to be a war crime committed by Japan. The Japanese had estimated about twenty-five thousand American and Filipino prisoners would be taken after the Fall of Bataan. Instead, three times that many—four, counting civilians—surrendered. Beyond that, the Japanese had woefully overestimated the condition the prisoners would need to be in to walk such long distances. Logistics broke down, as did any sense of nominal human ethics among many Japanese soldiers. The prisoners were herded, like cattle, for sixty-five miles, forced onto trains, and taken to what amounted to death camps. Stragglers were clubbed, kicked, bayoneted, and shot. The weak were left to die on their own. Seven to ten thousand died on the Death March; 1,565 Americans and 26,000 Filipinos died at Camp O'Donnell. In all, two-thirds of the Americans who surrendered on Bataan died in Japanese custody.

MacArthur and Roosevelt, historians would learn over the years, were both to blame for "help is on its way" promises whose fulfillment came so late for the men on Luzon. The Pacific fleet that would have sailed to the rescue was on the bottom of Pearl Harbor. Thus, the Bataan "defense," it would seem, was doomed to fail—and Washington knew that by Christmas 1941. Resources were being prioritized for the European Theater, leaving a distant outpost like Bataan on its own. In short, the Philippines were written off. Confided War Secretary Henry Stimson to British Prime Minister Winston Churchill: "There are times when men have to die."

THE 1944–45 YEARS in the Philippines marked the first time the U.S. Army had used guerrillas in Pacific warfare. "The reconquest of the Philippines," wrote Lapham and Nordling, "was different from any other Pacific campaign in that it was the only one in which large, organized guerrilla forces backed by a generally loyal civilian population made an important contribution to the defeat of the Japanese."

This, despite such guerrillas being unprepared for such an experience. In regard to his training, Conner wrote, "We learned how to wear a uniform; march; turn on a radio; but not how to fight a war."

"Even though they were in the military, the guerrillas were individualistic like hogs on ice," said Doug Clanin of the Indiana Historical Society, who interviewed dozens of such men. "But they weren't quitters."

"The remarkable fact," wrote Nordling and Lapham, "is not that many of them lost their lives and that most of the others bickered among themselves but that a considerable number of them did survive to form guerrilla organizations, badger the Japanese occupation forces persistently, and contribute appreciably to eventual Allied victory in the most extensive land campaign in the Pacific war, that on Luzon in 1945."

The 155th Squadron, in helping with the liberation of Luzon, supplied intelligence that helped define bombing targets for U.S. planes and helped root out enemy troops. From January 1 to March 3, 1945, the 155th was credited with killing 275 enemy soldiers. But its greatest legacy may not have been in soldiers killed—offense—but its protection of the Filipinos— defense—by the men's resolve to not quit. "They kept the spirit of the Filipinos alive," said Wayne Sanford, former chairman of the Indiana Historical Society's military history section. "And that was terribly detrimental to the Japanese. The Japanese were never able to gain the spirit of the Filipino people." Said one guerrilla: The respect the Japanese could not win through fear was won by the Americans "through love."

THE NEGRITOS' ABILITY to seal off the Zambales Mountains as an escape route for the Japanese was "critical" to the Americans quickly taking Fort Stotsenburg, said Sanford. With the return of U.S. troops, the warriors were attached to New York's 108th Infantry Regiment and won praise for their contributions in rooting out cave-dwelling Japanese soldiers and winning back Luzon. During the 1960s, the Negritos were the primary jungle survival instructors for Vietnam-bound pilots at Subic Bay Naval Base and for pilots at Clark Air Force Base. But in the decades to come, Filipinos stripped the giant mahoganies and wild game in the jungles where the tribes dwelled; the Negrito population dwindled to only a sliver of what it once had been. The Negritos looked to the Americans for assistance and were given land adjacent to Clark Air Force Base in return for providing security for the United States Air Force. There, they built huts from waste materials found in the base garbage bins and became scavengers, living off food thrown out by soldiers.

THE HUKBALAHAP (HUKS), the military arm of the Communist Party of the Philippines, fought a second war from 1946 to 1954 against the pro-Western leaders of their newly independent country. The insurgency was finally put down through a series of reforms and military victories by Philippine President Ramon Magsaysay, who, ironically, had served as a captain under Colonel Gyles Merrill, under whom Conner had also served.

OF THE 1,209 men who set sail on the *Coolidge* November 1, 1941, only 240—roughly one in five—survived the war. The bulk of them, 560, died on the Death March, in prison camps, or aboard "Hell Ships" while being transported to other camps.

Second Lieutenant Leroy Cowart, a twenty-year-old Atlanta boy and one of two soldiers who had driven cross-country with Conner before they boarded the *Coolidge*, survived the Death March. However, after being shipped to a POW camp in Fukuoka, Japan, he died of pneumonia on February 28, 1945, shortly before Conner sailed for home.

The other soldier, Second Lieutenant William Strese, a twenty-seven-year-old pilot from Durand, Wisconsin, was forced to Cabanatuan Prison Camp after the Death March. In November 1943, he sent a postcard to his parents that said, "Golden Gate in '48." (Though brutal, the Japanese allowed fortunate prisoners to send about two postcards per year, three lines on each.) But on December 15, 1944, about the time Conner was welcoming the two downed U.S. pilots to the 155th's Pampanga head-quarters, Strese and 1,619 other prisoners were en route to Japan on the SS *Oryoku Maru* when the ship was mistakenly bombed by an American plane and sunk. Nearly three hundred men, including Strese, died in the same Subic Bay that Conner had once said was so beautiful he could spend the rest of the war there.

Captain Damon "Rocky" Gause, the rugged Georgia man whom Conner admired so much and whom Clay had spent New Year's Eve 1941 with, proved true to his movie-star persona and escaped capture by sail-ing a twenty-foot boat to Australia, more than three thousand miles away. He returned to the United States—and to his wife—as a hero. He was sent on a war bonds tour, the government exploiting his adventurous escape by sea, but Gause was a combat pilot at heart. He appealed to the army air corps chief of staff, who granted him his wish to return to active duty. Home for just over a year, he held a newborn son in his arms for the first—and, it would turn out, only—time, then headed overseas. He died March 9, 1944, when the P-47 fighter he was piloting crashed south of London, England.

AFTER THE WAR, the few dozen American guerrillas found themselves neither fish nor fowl, neither soldiers who'd fought the enemy nor POWs kept prisoner by that enemy. Oddities for whom nobody was organizing reunions. In September 1945, a handful of Conner's men, including Gyovai and Mailheau, got together with Clay in New Jersey. Nearly forty years later, a series of small reunions were held in Indianapolis, where the Indiana Historical Society had taken a keen interest in the guerrillas of Luzon. Between those two bookends, the men rarely saw one another, though Conner and Frank Gyovai kept in touch and Doyle Decker revis-ited some of his war pals, too.

Gyovai, upon returning from the Philippines, spent three months in a hospital while being treated for chronic pleurisy, an inflammation of the lining around the lungs. But in July 1945 he returned to much fanfare in Red Dragon, West Virginia, where folks celebrated the man they dubbed "Jungle Jim." Until his return, most such gatherings at towns across America had been somber affairs, for soldiers who had died. And Gyovai's folks told a local newspaper they thought their son was dead, too. (They'd already lost one son to war, James, who was killed in France.) Now Red Dragon basked in the military version of the Prodigal Son: "He once was lost but now is found." A reporter at the *Verhovay Journal* penned a poem in Frank's honor, the final two verses of which made reference to the home cooking he had so often reminisced about on Luzon:

> Ma's baked the pies that he likes best,
> The chicken's golden brown
> And she has fancy dishes made
> That she brought up from town
> She says she'll have his favorites
> All spread in fine array.
> And my! but she moves sprightly since
> Frank's comin' home today!
> I hear the whistle as the train
> Comes 'round the little bend
> And folks are at the depot now
> With gifts and things, no end.
> I lift my face and give glad thanks
> Above, that I can say—
> Because He's made it possible—
> FRANK'S COMIN' HOME TODAY!

Conner was an honored guest at an all-town gathering in the Whites-ville High School gymnasium in honor of Gyovai. Five hundred people packed the stands. On the podium, Frank said, "This is my friend and

commanding officer. I did all the work, and Clay did all the thinking."
When Conner spoke of the heroics of Gyovai, "tears filled his eyes,"
reported the *Verhovay Journal*. "He was the most faithful friend I ever
had," Conner later said. "Without Frank, I may not have made it."

Gyovai moved to Aurora, Illinois, and spent most of his life as a mail
carrier. His first wife died in 1979—Conner had been a groomsman at
the wedding—and he remarried. He was the father of two daughters and
two sons, one of whom—six-foot-five Mike—not only played basketball
for Bobby Knight at West Point in the late 1960s but was called the
legendary coach's favorite player. In 1983, amid failing health, Frank
Gyovai and Conner got together for a final time. Clay remarked that
Gyovai had a "suitcase full of medicine." Frank responded: "No, Clay,
you're my medicine."

Only one of the other "Conner men" was still living as of January
2012—Bob Mailheau, ninety. After Conner shipped home, Mailheau
wrote to him, saying, "Gosh, Clay, I miss your company as though I've
lost part of my soul." Mailheau stayed in the service until 1955, then
became a banking executive before retiring to Palm Desert, California.

Joe Donahey returned to the United States with his Filipino wife,
Carazon, also a former guerrilla. He spent his entire career with the
military, retiring from the air force as a master sergeant at Chanute Field
in Illinois. He died of a heart attack in 1971. He was fifty-seven.

Doyle Decker raised a family and retired as plant manager of a paint
factory. He died June 12, 1992, and is buried in front of his mother's
house in Joplin, Missouri. He was seventy-seven. A son, Malcolm, wrote
two books related to the guerrilla experience on Luzon: *On a Mountainside* and *From Bataan to Safety*.

Bob Campbell reenlisted after the war and spent most of his life in
the army. He died April 13, 2000, in Claiborne, Louisiana. He was
eighty-two.

Gyles Merrill, the rough-hewn colonel with whom Conner worked
near the end of his time on Luzon, retired shortly after the war and died
in 1954 at age sixty-two.

Lieutenant General Oswald Griswold, who accepted the flag from Conner and called it "one of the most impressive incidents of my thirty-nine years of active service," retired in 1947 to the Broadmoor in Colorado Springs, Colorado. He died in 1959 at age seventy-three.

Tibuc-Tibuc, the traitor whose real name was Fred Alvidrez, was killed September 2, 1944, presumably by the Japanese to whom he'd transferred his loyalty and by whom he was ultimately double-crossed.

Although most estimates put the number of guerrillas who either eluded surrender or fled the Bataan Death March in the "few hundred" range, author Malcolm Decker's compilation shows only 103. According to his research, at war's end thirty-eight had died, been executed, or gone missing; twenty-nine were prisoners of war; and thirty were "guerrillas at liberty" such as Conner. (Decker was unable to determine the status of six.)

EVEN AS CONNER'S parents basked in their son's safe return home, both were struggling with health issues. Despite colon cancer and heart trouble, Marguerite Conner continued to be the same hands-on mother to Clay she'd always been, whether discreetly mentioning eligible young women who'd asked about him, writing to General Jonathan Wainwright to see if he could help Clay cut through red tape to get compensation for the Filipinos who had helped the 155th Squadron, or trying to convince Henry Ford III to make a hard-to-find convertible available to purchase for her "hero" son.

After the war, Conner found literally hundreds of letters from military personnel and parents of soldiers in response to letters his mother had written regarding his status. She had, he learned, made several trips to Washington, D.C., to lobby political bigwigs, believing that the boys in the Pacific were being overlooked while the U.S. fought the Germans in Europe. And she had worked at the Civil Defense Office and in the canteen for the USO, "hoping if I helped other mothers' sons, someone around the world would help mine." With Clay home, she regularly sent gifts and money to Mrs. Hardin on Luzon, thanking her for taking care of her son.

In July 1945, the Conners were surprised at what arrived in the mail: the package of letters Clay had written for them in the summer of 1943 and asked Crito to send home after the war. As promised, he was compensated for his efforts.

Although she had cancer, Marguerite Conner died of heart failure July 27, 1950, at age fifty-four. Six months later, her husband and son were driving to the cemetery in Indianapolis to see Marguerite's grave when Clay Sr. blindsided Clay Jr. with a question. "What do you think it takes to be a success?" he asked. Clay Jr. mulled it over. "If my sons grow up to think as much of me as I think of you, I will consider myself a success." Clay Sr. died the next day, January 10, 1951, of coronary heart disease. He was fifty-six.

Conner believed the deaths of both were connected to the stress of not knowing his whereabouts on Luzon; at one point, he learned, his father had even pressed the Red Cross to send him to the Philippines in search of Clay. Conner called his parents "victims of war."

CLAY CONNER JR.'S efforts to get American officers to utilize, respect, and retain Democrito "Crito" Lumanlan and Kodiaro Laxamana, were honored. Both not only played roles in the United States' retaking of Luzon, but were later commissioned as honorary colonels in the U.S. Army. After the war, Kodiaro, along with men from his tribe, helped with the security of Clark Air Force Base. He was featured in a *Life* magazine story in 1949. But in the same jungles where he and Conner had become friends, Kodiaro was gunned down by bandits in 1970 at age sixty-one. "As much as one man can love another, I admired and respected Kodiaro," Conner wrote in a newspaper letter to the editor after his friend's death. "I am alive today because of the faithfulness and love of the pygmy Negritos led by Kodiaro Laxamana and a faithful Filipino by the name of Democrito Lumanlan." At the request of his family, Kodiaro was buried in a

U.S. Air Force colonel's uniform, with his coffin draped by an American flag. He was accorded full military honors.

After the war, Crito became a special investigator for the United States Air Force and left, in 1963, to serve as chief of police in the fast-growing city of Angeles in Pampanga Province.

CONNER WORKED TIRELESSLY in an attempt to get compensation for Filipinos who had helped the 155th, but apparently to little avail. Because of the harsh conditions during the war years, IOUs had been scribbled on everything from brown paper bags to evaporated milk-can labels. Democrito Lumanlan risked his life for two years ferrying food and medicine through Japanese patrols for Conner and his men. But an April 29, 1948, letter to Conner from the War Department said that "a complete study of the entire matter shows that Mr. Lumanlan was not entitled to monetary compensation for his services."

Colonel Merrill empathized with Clay; he, too, knew how deserving the Filipinos and Negritos were. But records hadn't survived the war. Units were being deactivated. "I am rather at a loss as to advising you what to do," Merrill wrote.

Of more than a million claims, those from about 260,000 Filipino veterans and guerrillas were accepted as genuine, according to Lieutenant Robert Lapham, who did postwar work on Filipino compensation. Even assuming some claims were false, only about one in four Filipinos received renumeration for their efforts.

Meanwhile, while U.S. prisoners of war were given special benefits, U.S. guerrilla fighters were not, even if many suffered similar postwar stress. (In 1991, shortly before he died, Doyle Decker told his son, Malcolm, he still experienced "horrible" nightmares.) Starting in the 1960s and well into the 1980s, Private Leon Beck, who had escaped the Bataan Death March, fought the government for equal compensation for guerrillas like himself. "We suffered the same starvation diet, lack of medical care, diseases and illnesses as the POWs, plus the constant threat of the

Japanese Army during our entire time with the Guerrilla Forces, not counting our many fire fights with Japanese Forces." The government refused to compensate the U.S. guerrillas with the special benefits offered POWs.

Any account of Conner's good-byes to Kodiaro and his daughter weren't alluded to in anything he wrote and weren't mentioned by him or other men of the 155th in interviews. But a handful of people, including Mailheau and Decker, attested that, after the war, he didn't forget Kodiaro's daughter. "He made all sorts of financial arrangements and concessions for the girl and for Kodiaro," said Sanford.

CLAY MAXWELL PAMPHILION, the baby born to Conner's cousin Marjorie and named in his honor, is now sixty-nine and retired after operating his own public relations/marketing firm in Silicon Valley. He lives in Spain.

THE USS *COOLIDGE*, which Conner took on his journey to the Philippines, struck a mine off the small island of Vanuatu, east of Australia, on October 26, 1942. All but two of the 5,340 men aboard were able to safely disembark. The ship now rests in 70 to 240 feet of water and is popular for divers because of her accessibility, size, and relatively shallow position.

THE BATAAN PENINSULA, once rife with the litter of war is now sprinkled with vacation beach resorts. The Bataan Provincial Expressway now parallels the Old Highway that was the pathway of despair for thousands on the Bataan Death March. The waters of Manila Bay, where Conner watched Japanese planes strafe American soldiers trying to flee Manila by any floating craft available, are now plied by jet boats ferrying tourists to and from the peninsula. And to the north, Cabanatuan, home of the horrific prison camp, now touts itself as the "Tricycle Capital of the Philippines" and home of "Megacenter the Mall."

THE FLAG THAT was presented to Griswold at Concepcion ultimately was given to General MacArthur, according to a postwar letter from the lieutenant general. In the early 2000s, Malcolm Decker, author of two guerrilla-related books, searched "every possible museum and military memorial site" for the flag. He was not able to locate it.

PART II: CONNER HIMSELF

28 September 1945

Major H. C. Conner Jr.
174 North Grove Street
East Orange, New Jersey

My dear Conner:

Thank you for your letter of September 11, 1945, which has just reached me at my new headquarters in Sendai, Japan. It brought back vivid memories of that historic day at Concepcion, Tarlac Province, Luzon, when you and your men first made contact with the XIV Corps, and your formal presentation of the National Colors, 26th U.S. Cavalry to me for safe keeping.

The story of that flag is one of the most impressive incidents of my 39 years of active service. To me, it symbolizes the highest concepts of service, duty, and loyalty to the nation. I shall cherish always the honor of receiving it from your hands.

In my opinion the history of that flag in World War II will become one of the proudest traditions of the American Army. Rescued from the stricken hand of the regimental color bearer on the blood-drenched battle field of Bataan, it was at great danger successfully brought by

*loving hands through Japanese lines to the vastness of the Zambales
Mountains in Luzon. There, through more than three long years, it
was guarded, cherished and served by you and your indomitable
band of loyal patriots. With Japanese on all sides seeking to encompass
your destruction, with a price on your heads and in constant danger
from attempted betrayal by Pro-Japanese elements, nevertheless, on
clear days that flag was flown as a symbol of hope, liberty and
eventual victory. As you so aptly expressed it in your presentation to
me, "The American flag has never ceased to wave over Luzon."*

*May I express to you, to your men and to your family my best
wishes for all the nicer things in life.*

Sincerely,
O. W. Griswold
Lieutenant General, U.S. Army Commanding

FOR HIS DISTINGUISHED military service, Clay Conner Jr. was awarded a
handful of medals: Distinguished Unit Badge with three bronze oak-leaf
clusters; American Defense Service Ribbon with one bronze star; Asiatic-
Pacific Campaign Ribbon with two bronze service stars; Philippine
Defense Ribbon with one bronze star; and Philippine Liberation Ribbon
with one bronze star. He was promoted from first lieutenant to captain
on May 4, 1945.

"Lt. Conner was able to obtain valuable information regarding enemy
activity in the vicinity of Fort Stotsenburg and Angeles, and this information was sent forward to [headquarters] by all means possible," wrote
Colonel Merrill. "Regardless of who received credit for the information
received it is believed that this information was of great value to our Air
Force when the invasion of Luzon took place."

Post-traumatic stress syndrome was rarely talked of in relation to
soldiers returning from World War II. However, seven months after Conner got back, it was clear that the war had, in some ways, followed him

home. He was hospitalized at Santa Ana Army Base. "The [doctor]," he wrote to his folks, "thinks the tension has been too much. He thinks I should be resting instead of working. Guess the war was a little harder on me but I just can't seem to relax."

Because of his poor eyesight—he could see peripherally but hardly anything straight ahead—Conner was found incapacitated for military service and was relieved of active duty on April 17, 1946. He left, officially, having been promoted to the rank he'd once promoted himself to: major.

FINISHED WITH THE army, Conner went to see Elizabeth Ann Thomson, the daughter of his family's close Indianapolis friends, who now attended an all-women's school, Stephens College in Columbia, Missouri. She had been fourteen when he last saw her. By eighteen, she had blossomed into a beautiful young woman. The two were married June 25, 1946, at Tabernacle Presbyterian Church in Indianapolis, the reception being held at Meridian Hills Country Club. He was twenty-seven, she was nineteen.

The first of four sons, Henry Clay Conner III, was born April 21, 1947, followed by Jack Thomas Conner on April 12, 1949. Ardé Bulova was so impressed with Conner's feats—and, of course, with Clay's Bulova watch surviving the war—that he had Clay head up a new division in which disabled veterans built timepieces. Conner didn't like the routine or his performance. He left Bulova within a year to launch the Conner Insurance Agency in Indianapolis.

CONNER'S EYESIGHT NEVER returned to what it had been; he could drive but was legally blind. In 1953, the Veterans Administration—after nearly eight years of Conner pressing his case—granted him 60 percent disability.

Spiritually, Conner realized, his vision was similarly impaired, even if to admit it took something that did not come naturally for him: humility. He acknowledged that reading the New Testament in Luzon had encouraged him, but wrote that "I had all the religion I needed." In 1951, when invited to a weekend men's retreat in Ohio, Conner initially chaffed, but later went, if for no other reason than to appease the friend who had invited him.

He was surprised to find—and, frankly, dubious about—a handful of men who said they'd built their lives on the promises of Scripture. "I thought that was rather a narrow viewpoint," he wrote. "The Bible certainly was a good book, but after all, this is the age of reason and logic, and broad-minded, calculated thinking."

What he couldn't as easily dismiss was the peace of mind these men seemed to have found. Not by, he said, "being good." Not by going to church every Sunday or memorizing Bible verses. They had tried that, he wrote, "but there was still a vacancy—an emptiness until they had surrendered their lives to Christ."

Conner knew of such emptiness; indeed, it was one thing to scrawl "everything under control" at the bottom of a letter, another to actually feel such serenity. Years removed from the squalor of war, he felt like a man sitting at a virtual banquet of food and yet still hungry. "I should have been joyful, too," he wrote. "I had experienced a war of killing, hatred, and sickness, and yet I had lived through it. I had a beautiful wife and wonderful sons. I had a good business, and I was respected in the community. I seemed to have everything that a man wanted. And yet, where was the peace that these men knew?"

At the retreat, a soldier who, like Conner, had fought in the Southwest Pacific shared that he, too, was struggling with such emptiness and that he, too, had found peace in Christ. "And I realized that God, to me, had never been the reality that these men knew Him to be," Conner wrote. "I had always taken God or left Him as I needed Him or didn't. But these men seemed to live with Him, commune with Him, and enjoy His presence. That I didn't have. And then I prayed, and I asked Him to come into my life and be as real to me as He was to them. And I surrendered all I had. And when I got up from my knees, I knew I had found the answer."

The answer, he believed, to the question the senator had asked him when he arrived home at LaGuardia Field six years before about why he had survived. "I knew the joy of living, the joy of surviving, the reason for it all was in God's plan. He had chosen me to go forth and to give Him the credit and glory for having watched over and protected me."

CONNER'S FAITH GREW; he attended Central Baptist Church, started sharing his guerrilla-to-God story in speeches, and rose to international director of the Christian Businessmen's Committee. His business grew; Conner Insurance blossomed into one of Indianapolis's premier agencies. His family grew; James Hilton Conner was born June 4, 1952, and Thomas Hamilton Conner January 18, 1955, giving him and Elizabeth four sons.

A year later, Conner was in Los Angeles, headed out for dinner in Hollywood with friends, when a man popped out of a studio with a wired microphone in hand and a movie camera operator at his side. It was television show host Ralph Edwards. Clay Conner's war story was about to air in front of the nation on the Emmy-award-winning program *This Is Your Life*. After Conner was gently cajoled into a studio, Edwards brought on stage a handful of people who had been instrumental in Clay's life, including his Duke fraternity brother Bob Stivers, his close wartime pal Frank Gyovai, downed pilot Clay Hogan, and Lieutenant General Oswald W. Griswold.

Conner was visibly moved by the surprise visits. At show's end, Elizabeth and the four boys joined Clay on stage. Edwards announced that $1,000 was being donated for medicine to help the Negrito tribe that had helped Conner. Despite this emotional onslaught, the biggest surprise for Conner was the appearance of a small Filipino man whom he had not seen since leaving Luzon eleven years before, Democrito "Crito" Lumanlan, now thirty years old. A handshake turned into a hug with the young man who'd virtually kept Conner alive with his risky runs for food and medicine.

A week after the program aired, Conner got a personal letter from Edwards. "We have not had a show that has received any more wonderful comments than yours," he wrote. Conner received more than one hundred letters himself. "You make us proud to be Americans," wrote Warren Hull of Scarsdale, New York.

The program made good on its promise to send $1,000 worth of medical supplies to the Negritos. But Kodiaro sold most of the supplies for something he believed they needed more: four caraboas and a plow.

ON THE TWENTY-FIFTH anniversary of the Fall of Bataan, April 1967, Conner and Gyovai joined 160 others for a trip back to the Philippines. Gyovai, in marginal health and hardly financially flush, wasn't going to go, but Conner talked him into it.

Once in Luzon, Conner made it clear to Gyovai that this would be no Grayline Tour. He immediately went to see Faustino del Mundo, aka Sumulong, the head of the Huks and the man Conner had had the showdown with until the two hundred Negritos saved the day. The man who had threatened to kill him. The man who, in 1967, was known to many as a ruthless gangster running the Communist show. Now forty-eight, Conner talked and laughed with the Huk leader. Sumulong gave Conner a souvenir ball cap. A *Life* magazine reporter, hearing of the meeting, tagged along for a story.

Conner and Gyovai then met up with Crito, who, since 1963, had been chief of police in nearby Angeles. "It was," wrote Conner, "one of the most joyous moments of my life to renew that old acquaintance." Ironically, though, Crito was losing officers right and left to men suspected of doing the murderous bidding of Sumulong, as if the jungle wars of World War II had never gone away.

Along with Gyovai, Crito, and others, Conner toured a few of the areas where they had lived during the war. A Philippine newspaper article said Conner "was amazed at how the once-dense forests . . . had disappeared." After the group had lunch that included fried chicken, French fries, hot peppers, and drinks, Gyovai said: "During my last stay here, we always dreamed of having such meals."

"The . . . men spoke of how they worked their security system for that area by placing Negrito families on the mountains," the paper reported. "They told how fear ruled many a man's life. They talked and they remembered. At about half past three they climbed the hill overlooking the creek, took a last glimpse and headed back."

Later, when the *Life* magazine story came out, Conner was furious. Sumulong, he contended, was not the Communist devil the reporter made him out to be. Conner apologized to Sumulong in writing and closed the letter with "Your cap is hanging in my closet and is the prize souvenir of my trip."

Conner wrote President Ferdinand Marcos, pledging to help end the divisiveness that Communism was causing in the Philippines. "I have never been completely happy since returning to the states as I have always felt I could somehow contribute to the well being of the Philippines," he wrote. "I am confident that given the authority and cooperation, I could greatly assist you in my desire to help strengthen the Filipino people."

Nothing came of Conner's offer. But he soon found another way to help. On October 23, 1968, Democrito's wife, Jo, wrote Clay and Elizabeth to say she thought her husband's life might be in danger because of the Communists. "I am so worried about [Crito]," she said.

Conner wrote Democrito and invited—no, insisted—he move to the United States; Clay would see about getting him a job in Indianapolis. Democrito dragged his feet. But in January 1970, a group of rifle-toting men shot him in the arm as they whisked by in a jeep. Democrito left for the United States the next month, and his family later joined him.

Conner ran interference for him, using his friendship with war buddy and escaped-from-Bataan POW Edgar Whitcomb, the newly minted governor of Indiana, to get Democrito a job as a special investigator with the Indiana State Patrol. He convinced Whitcomb, in fact, to allow Crito to stay in a spare bedroom at the governor's mansion. Twenty-five years removed from their World War II days, the role reversal involving the two men emerged as both stark and almost comical: the young man who had helped Conner survive in Crito's rural jungle now being helped by Conner to survive in Clay's urban jungle.

WITH HIS INSURANCE agency thriving, Conner bought twenty-five acres of land in Indianapolis and spearheaded the development of a Lexington-type spread, the kind he'd seen so many of in his father's home state of Kentucky. He called the family compound "The Conner Pony Farm." His four sons spent summers putting up, and painting, miles of four-board fence, their father occasionally barking an order in Tagalog. Ever the dreamer, Clay envisioned those four sons and their families someday each having a house on the land and grandchildren playing in the fields.

Now in his late forties and early fifties, Conner continued to lead Bible studies, seminars, and retreats, even as remnants of Luzon stayed with him. Once, when a son, Tom, sneaked in after curfew, he was stunned to find his father at the top of the stairs in boxers and a T-shirt, his gun strapped around his waist—and loaded. "I thought you were a burglar," said Clay Conner Jr. "OK, good night."

Meanwhile, he channeled his other passion—or at least his obvious passion—into the past and the future: the past by beginning to dabble a bit in research about his family's history, the future by encouraging his sons to become more responsible young men, even though there was every indication they were exactly that. "We were," said Jim Conner, "his soldiers, his men in training."

Conner once became so disenchanted with Jack that when the young man returned home one evening he found his belongings stacked in the driveway, ready to be moved elsewhere. Conner was slightly more diplomatic in dealing with Jim, a freshman at Indiana University, but, even then, his letters had a sort of spit-polish formality to them, as if Jim had better straighten up or be court-martialed. "I am definitely not interested in helping you to look like everyone else or be one of the gang," Conner wrote. "Your potential is far above average, and you should strive to act the part. Upon your graduation in 1974, I want your classmates to remember you as the best-dressed kid on campus, not just Jim Conner."

Despite such rigid standards, despite his devotion to Bible studies and prayer, despite dozens of men attesting that it was Clay Conner who "led me to the Lord," he nevertheless lived with a latent thirst for adventure that rumbled deep within him like tremors beneath Mount Pinatubo.

IN 1973, CONNER, at age fifty-five, sold the insurance agency to his four sons. Jack, twenty-four, had been working at the agency for two years and Clay III was, at twenty-six, a stockbroker with a local investment firm. Jim was still a junior at Indiana University and Tom still a junior in high school.

Even if it had been his idea to sell the business and even if having his sons take it over brought him a certain fatherly pride, Conner was, for the first time since high school, a man without a mission. There was no Huk leader to go nose-to-nose with. No survival of his men to ensure. No business to start. If he was still the swashbuckling adventurer—at least in his own mind—Libby was Queen Elizabeth. And their marriage, after nearly thirty years, had become as rote as the four turns at the Indianapolis Speedway. For Clay, there was no Kodiaro to win over. No return letter from President Marcos, pleading with Clay to come to the Philippines and quell the rise of Communism. Not even a pony farm to establish.

Like the biblical King David, Conner was a warrior who suddenly found himself without a war.

THE INK HAD hardly dried on the June divorce papers, when, on December 23, 1975, Conner married a woman who worked at the agency, Cheyanne Huffer. She was twenty-nine years old, a year older than Clay's oldest son. Conner was fifty-seven.

Conner's new direction mirrored the enigma that he had long been. What was different about this tactical offense was those wounded by the friendly fire. If trying to build bridges to the Negritos with a tribal union involving the chief's daughter was done for the greater good, his sudden divorce and remarriage seemed only about Conner, and felt, to family and friends, like something Clay despised more than anything else in the jungles of Luzon: betrayal.

Conner left his church out of shame; many, though not all, members essentially shunned him. Elizabeth, jolted to her bones, moved to Florida. His wounded sons tried to make sense of a man whose expectations were so high—and yet who, in their eyes, had stooped so low. He asked his sons' forgiveness. In different ways and at different times—though never simply or easily—Clay III, Jack, Jim, and Tom granted him that forgiveness. In the following year's Christmas letter to Jim, Conner thanked his son for a present and said, "the carefully chosen words in the letter gave me deep satisfaction. Your love and appreciation for me as your father is the most rewarding gift one can receive. You see, a father is never sure of his course in guiding the life of his son. He may have good intentions but his humanities get in the way, causing many regrets which he hopes will not affect the life of his son adversely. Your words of love have resolved that question in my mind."

When Clay married Cheyanne, she had a four-year-old son, Ty. In 1979, the two had a son of their own, David. The birth rejuvenated Conner, who was now sixty-one. But in a letter to Jim, he lamented that these nevertheless had been difficult times for him. He was experiencing heart problems; his mother had died at fifty-four, his father at fifty-six, of heart-related ailments. His betrayal of Elizabeth and the boys ate at him like a malaria parasite; this, remember, was a man who, when called on the carpet for a self-promotion in Luzon, had written: "I would rather give my life than to suffer disgrace."

"It was as if everyone else forgave my father," said his oldest son, Clay Conner III, "but he couldn't forgive himself."

IN THE SUMMER of 1983, Conner sat with Clanin and Sanford for a handful of lengthy interviews for the Indiana Historical Society, some of which included Crito and Gyovai. In one, Sanford asked about shooting the two Japanese soldiers, one of whom Conner had thought might be reaching for a suicide grenade. "You wouldn't know how many nights I lived with that," he told Sanford. In another interview, Clanin said: "Did you ever have a feeling that this is kind of an idealistic Robinson Crusoe existence there—that you would have really liked to have stayed there?"

"I was tempted to stay," Conner replied. "I would have stayed there, had I not been an only child, and I felt a definite responsibility to my folks. I didn't even know if they were alive. And when I got this first letter and found out they were, I knew that it would be impossible for me to stay there with any kind of personal happiness. So, I intended to go home, and find out what it was all about, and try to work my way back. It didn't work out that way. I felt like I could have done a lot with those Negritos. And if I had devoted my life to them—I thought that would be worthwhile. I honest to God really loved them. When Kodiaro died, I cried for a week."

IN OCTOBER, CONNER left on a two-week car trip to research family history across the South. On the last leg of the trip, he was in Mount Sterling, Kentucky, exploring the roots of his father's family tree, when the heart attack hit. The man who'd survived countless brushes with death in the wilds of the Luzon jungle died in the sanitized emergency room of Mary Chiles Hospital on October 26, 1983, at 6 P.M. It was almost forty years ago, to the day, that he had walked into the Negrito camp and, in the best bumbling Tagalog he could muster, introduced himself to Chief Kodiaro by saying, "*Magandang hapon. Kumusta ka?*" He was sixty-five.

THREE DAYS LATER, Conner was buried at Crown Hill Cemetery in Indianapolis, next to his parents. The *Indianapolis News* headlined its obituary, HENRY C. CONNER WAS WAR HERO. But in offering a eulogy at Conner's memorial service, a friend of Conner's, Jack Brown, said that Clay's war experience was only part of this deep but flawed man. His real impact on the world, he said, went well beyond his military career and his business achievements to "a record written in lives," in particular to the four wonderful sons he had raised.

> Clay had many sides, but because he limited his circle of close, intimate friends, many did not have the privilege of knowing the real Clay. We all are aware of his brilliant military records. Because of that military background, some may think of Clay as "Major Conner," unbending, unyielding, or, perhaps, even unloving. But those who really knew him, his wife, his children, his grandchildren, his truly close friends, knew that beneath that military exterior was a compassionate, loving man.
>
> When Clay was behind the lines in World War II, he was sustained by the hope of the return of the American forces. Without that hope, as he stated many times, he would have perished. Because of that experience, after his conversion, he often described Ephesians 2:12 as the most desperate verse in the Bible. What does it say? It tells us that, "a man without God is without hope in this world." But Clay wanted men to have hope in this world, so that wartime experience, centered in hope, was a compelling force inducing the evangelistic ardor which dominated Clay's life for so many years.

He then made a veiled reference to Conner's late-in-life detour. "The last decade of Clay's life was lived in utter dependence upon God's grace. He realized, as few do, that God's love is shown in His grace to you and to me. Henry Clay Conner Jr. was a living example of God's grace to men. Clay knew that even as David is a beautiful example of God's grace almost three thousand years ago, Clay's life illustrated the grace of God to all men today."

He paused. "Clay Conner," he said, "was a precious friend. I have known no one like him."

"[Crito] loved him like a brother," said Jo Lumanlan, Democrito's wife, who is still alive. "Clay saved our lives." And saved the lives of the men closest to him—Gyovai, who called Clay "the best, most faithful friend I ever had," and Mailheau, who said, "Truly speaking, I've never had a better friend."

"I suppose you could say he saved our lives as well," said one of the man's sons, Jim Conner. "Each one of us came to know the Lord through Dad. He was a hero to us and, yes, we saw him fall off his pedestal, saw him at his worst, but, to a man, we're glad God gave him to us as our father. As a kid, I can still hear him singing that '*Paru Paru Bukid*' song to us that he used to sing with the kids on Luzon."

FOURTEEN MONTHS AFTER the passing of Clay Conner Jr., his war pal Frank Gyovai—his body patched with not one but two pacemakers—died of a heart attack on December 21, 1984, in Aurora, Illinois. He was sixty-four. The local newspaper obituary made no mention of his time on Luzon. Shortly before his death, Gyovai had attended the first-ever reunion of the 155th, in Indianapolis. The entire day was dedicated to Conner, who had once written: "It was a grand experience and, truthfully, I wouldn't have missed it for the world. It was an epic adventure."

Cheyanne Conner remarried nine months after Clay's death and moved with her new husband and sons to Texas.

Democrito Lumanlan retired after more than thirty years as a criminal intelligence analyst with the Indiana State Police. He died December 3, 2008, in Indianapolis. He was seventy-four.

———————

TODAY, ALL FOUR of Conner's sons—Clay III, Jack, Jim, and Tom—live with their families on the Conner Pony Farm, their houses on a grassy hillside through which a creek tumbles. Together—and with help from some of their now-adult children—they run the Conner Agency that their father began in 1949. Elizabeth Conner, eighty-four, lives in a condominium only minutes away. Beyond their four sons, Elizabeth and Clay Conner Jr.'s legacy lives on in twelve grandchildren and seven great-grandchildren, the younger ones of whom sometimes play in the farm's fields just as their great-grandfather had once imagined.

AFTER FIVE CENTURIES of dormancy, Mount Pinatubo, a volcanic peak in whose shadow Conner spent much of the war, erupted in 1991. Its blast was ten times the magnitude of the 1980 eruption of Washington's Mount St. Helens. Nearly one thousand people were killed and forty-two thousand houses destroyed. The fallout further splintered the nearly decimated Negrito tribe. The jungle where Conner and the others lived during World War II was essentially buried in ash, lost for all time. The eruption left an eery legacy for the men of the 155th Squadron, a legacy reflected in a verse from the Book of Genesis that Clay Conner Jr. knew well: "For dust you are and to dust you will return."

AUTHOR'S NOTES

ON OCTOBER 26, 1983, in Anderson, Indiana, World War II researcher Doug Clanin wrote a letter to Clay Conner Jr. about two books the pair hoped to collaborate on regarding guerrillas in the Luzon jungle. Then sixty-five, Conner was looking forward to fulfilling his dream of writing a book on his war adventures. It wasn't to be. He died that very day.

I have no way of knowing how similar *Resolve* might be to a book Clanin and Conner would have written. But without doubt the main ingredients for whatever literary meal I've served up came from those two men and from Wayne Sanford, who, like Clanin, doggedly pursued the guerrillas' experiences on Luzon in interviews for the Indiana Historical Society.

Conner was the two researchers' first subject. The former guerrilla leader was initially reluctant to grant an interview when Clanin called him one morning in June 1983, but ultimately agreed to meet later that day. "By the time I arrived, he'd already had a friend in state police intelligence check me out," said Clanin.

The investigator was Democrito Lumanlan, Conner's pal from Luzon, now with the Indiana State Police. After the interview, Clanin shared his enthusiasm about Conner with Sanford, chairman of the historical society's military history section. "This was virgin territory for everybody," said Sanford. "I had never heard of anything on Luzon beyond the Bataan Death March."

The Conner interview was the first of 373 that the two researchers would do on the subject of guerrillas in the Philippines; at the Indiana Historical Society, the Sanford/Clanin Philippine Resistance Records, 1910s–1987 (M 0863), span more than twenty lineal feet and include more than one hundred thousand pages.

CONNER, THEIR FIRST interviewee, was a compulsive chronicler. "He was always writing," Lumanlan said after the war. Conner captured his war experiences in letters written while he was on Luzon and later sent to his folks in New Jersey, as he had requested, by Crito; in a fifteen-page piece he wrote with a ghostwriter for the August 1946 edition of *True* magazine; in "Survival," a 528-page unpublished transcript of taped recollections he recorded in May 1956; and in lengthy interviews he did with Sanford and Clanin for the Indiana Historical Society in 1983.

He saved practically everything from his war years: personal letters to him and from him, military correspondence, records, postcards, newspaper articles, photos, a Japanese flag from a downed pilot, his Colt .45—even the brown-covered, pocket-sized New Testament given to him by the soldier named Edwards in the early goings. With his late-in-life interest in genealogy, Conner wrote and organized profiles of his and his parents' families dating back generations.

With all this as the informational foundation for the book, *Resolve* undoubtedly reflects Conner's bias—just as books by others about their Luzon experiences reflect their biases. This is not an all-encompassing treatment of guerrillas on the island, but a book about one man's war, essentially through his eyes. At times, Conner's written and oral recollections are tinted with a certain Hollywood sheen. It could have been no other way, for a quixotic man who was an unabashed adventurer; in the words of Clanin, "an action-figure living out his life's experiences."

Robert Lapham, in his book *Lapham's Raiders*, called Conner "one of those complex, compulsive characters about whom colorful stories accumulate and circulate."

"He was an absolutely remarkable individual," Sanford said. "Intensely courageous. Intelligent. Emotional. Sensitive. He reminded me of a modern day Robin Hood.

"You could believe everything he said, even if it was a bit more dramatic than someone else's interpretation. That's just how Clay saw the world. The blues were bluer, the pastels brighter. But you never got the impression that he was spinning you."

Indeed, after *True* magazine published the piece by Conner, Colonel Gyles Merrill, then retired, lauded Clay's story: "In addition to being well written," Merrill wrote, "it is the most accurate account I've seen of the conditions as they existed."

The dialogue in *Resolve* is not contrived; instead, it's how Conner—as recorded in his own writing and in interviews—remembered the conversations playing out. And, in a few cases, how people with him remembered such exchanges. For example, the Manila-Hotel-on-New-Year's-Eve conversation between the waiter, Conner, and Damon "Rocky" Gause came from Gause's journal, as reported in *The War Journal of Major Damon "Rocky" Gause* (New York: Hyperion, 1999).

That same night, Conner and Gause met a nurse, Helen Summers, whom Clay mentions in his taped transcript, "Survival." Going through Conner's letters, I was surprised to find correspondence between this same nurse and Clay's mother, Marguerite, regarding Clay's status in the Philippines. And further surprised, while reading the memoirs of a chaplain, *Days of Anguish, Days of Hope* (Longview, Texas: StoneGate Publishing, 2011), to find another Summers-Conner connection: In tiny Mariveles, where Clay is on the same afternoon, a heartbroken Summers boards a boat for Corregidor after just having been told by the chaplain her fiancé was killed in battle.

The challenge for writers of history is putting together thousands of such informational puzzle pieces to create one large image, to fashion from disparate happenings one unified story. That job was made easier for me by firsthand accounts from those in the Luzon jungles. Beyond Conner's recollections, I relied heavily on memories either shared in interviews with or letters to Clanin and Sanford from: Democrito Lumanlan, Frank Gyovai, Bob Mailheau, Doyle Decker, Joe Donahey, Albert Bruce, Eddie Keith, Vernon Fassoth, Leon Beck, Francis Grassbaugh, Albert Hendrickson, Blair Robinett, Winston Jones, Edwin Ramsey, and Pierce Wade. Conner, Gyovai, and others also had drawn pictures and maps that provided me context to their experiences.

If *Resolve* contains nothing in the way of specifics about the tribal union between Conner and Kodiaro's daughter—other than that it occurred—it's because I could find virtually no additional information, not even the woman's name. Mailheau and Decker both attest that the union took place and that it sealed the Negrito-155th bond tighter; beyond that, it seemed journalistically imprudent to assume specifics for which I had no supporting facts.

A HANDFUL OF books added particular depth and breadth to Conner's story. *Operation Plum: The Ill-Fated 27th Bombardment Group and the Fight for the Western Pacific* (College Station, Texas: Texas A&M University Press, 2008) by Adrian R. Martin and Larry W. Stephenson offered keen insight into Conner's journey from Savannah (Georgia) Air Base to Manila in late November and early December 1941; *Tears in the Darkness* (New York: Picador, 2009) by Michael Norman and Elizabeth M. Norman describes pre-surrender Bataan in chillingly real detail; and *On a Mountainside* (Las Cruces, New Mexico: Yucca Tree Press, 2004) and *From Bataan to Safety* (Jefferson, North Carolina: McFarland & Co. Publishing, 2008), both by Malcolm Decker, contributed considerable detail about the 155th Provisional Guerrilla Battalion, of which Decker's father, Doyle, was part.

The finest books about guerrilla warfare on Luzon are Chris Schaefer's *Bataan Diary* (Houston: Riverview Publishing, 2004, which outlined the Luzon guerrilla operations well, and Robert Lapham's and Bernard Nordling's *Lapham's Raiders* (Lexington, Kentucky: The University Press of Kentucky, 1999), from which I dipped often.

Photographs and illustrations from *They Drew Fire: Combat Artists of World War II* by Brian Lanker and Nicole Newnham (New York: TV Books, 2000) and *World War II* by James Jones (New York: Ballantine Books, 1975) helped me get a keener sense for the nuances of war in the Pacific jungles.

The *Indianapolis News*, the *Newark Evening News*, the *Charlotte (North Carolina) Observer*, the *Raleigh (North Carolina) Times*, the *Cincinnati Enquirer*, the *Manila Time*, the *Verhovay (West Virginia) Journal* all contributed news I used, much of it provided by the United Press and Associated Press wire services. I also gleaned information from *True*, *National Geographic*, *Life*, and *Modern Maturity* magazines.

Beyond that, I feathered in data from myriad sources: dozens of copies of official military correspondence, some restricted, between Conner and other officers, particularly Colonel Merrill; War Department letters; Western Union telegrams; Army Amateur Radio System radiograms; v-mails; military records; military newsletters; travel vouchers; ship publications; court affidavits; state vital statistics; state and military medical records; military medical board depositions; travel itineraries; and dozens of personal letters, particularly between Conner and his parents.

The end result is a story that, more than seventy years after it unfolded in the jungles of Luzon, I'm privileged to tell.

BOB WELCH
EUGENE, OREGON
JANUARY 2012

ACKNOWLEDGMENTS

DOUG CLANIN said Conner was a man of "moxy." True. But what saved him in the jungle, Sanford pointed out, was humility. His willingness to realize he couldn't do it on his own. He needed help, sought it, and got it from the Filipinos and Negritos. "If he hadn't humbled himself," said Sanford, "he and his men never would have survived."

Likewise, I wouldn't have survived this project had I not had help from a number of people. Thus do I humbly thank:

• Clay Conner Jr.'s sons, Clay III, Jack, Jim, and Tom, who, after an initial setback, refused to quit in their quest to have their father's story told. They dug deep, often into painful memories, to help me better understand their father. And worked diligently with me on editing the manuscript, twice when I visited them in Indianapolis and through countless e-mail exchanges, phone interviews—and prayers.

• Bobbi Conner, Tom's wife; Christine, Jim's wife; and Jana, Jack's wife. Each, in her own way, offered unique insight into their father-in-law and made some great "catches" when editing the manuscript.

• The Indiana Historical Society, which had the foresight, back in the 1980s, to encourage Clanin and Sanford's research on the guerrillas on Luzon. Thanks, in particular, to Paul Brockman, director of manuscript and visual collections, who helped me on my visits.

• Chris Schaefer, author of *Bataan Diary*, whose deep understanding of Luzon during World War II and whose willingness to read the manuscript for errors were invaluable. Schaefer took countless hours combing the book to rid it of mistakes. I take full responsibility for any that remain.

• Malcolm Decker, whose father served with Conner as part of the 155th Provisional Guerrilla Battalion. He was helpful because of his keen knowledge of the unit. Decker has written two books on guerrillas on Luzon, *On a Mountainside* and *From Bataan to Safety*, so he was particularly empathetic to my late-night e-mail requests for information.

• Bob Mailheau, the only member of the 155h still alive. Not only did Mailheau, at age ninety, allow me time to interview him, but he did so even as his wife, Anne, was in her final days.

• Elizabeth Conner, Clay Conner Jr.'s first wife; Jack Brown, one of Clay's closest friends; and Sydney Jackson, a daughter of Clay's cousin Marjorie Pamphilion, all of whom contributed insight into Clay Conner Jr.

• Pat Gariepy, a fellow author who lent his World War II expertise to the book's original edit.

• Vicki Silverthorne, a counselor whose insight into how people's pasts shape their futures, helped me understand Conner's personality nuances.

• Jeff Wright, my supervisor at the *Register-Guard*, whose flexibility with my schedule saved me time and again. ("As long as I get three columns a week . . .")

• Tom Penix, Sophie Penix, and Greta Penix, whose advice helped me make a key decision on content.

• Paul Neville, a longtime friend whose encouragement while on noontime walks helped keep me going.

- Marianne McNally, daughter of Easy Company soldier Don Malarkey and the person who served as a liaison regarding her father writing *Resolve*'s foreword.

- Toni Susemichel, of the Back Door Quilt Shop in Greenwood, Indiana, who gave me laptop power when I was in dire need of it.

- Leon Sterner, of Yachats, Oregon, who offered me a port in the storm— literally—when my printer wouldn't work in a final writing session on the coast and allowed me to plug into his.

- My Beachside Writers Workshop students, whose keen questions regarding the book convinced me to press forward on the project.

- My agent, Greg Johnson, who played matchmaker with the Conner sons to bring the five of us together.

- My friend Jane Kirkpatrick, a novelist whom I'd often think about when my alarm went off at 5 A.M. If reluctant to rise, I'd remember that Jane had already been at her keyboard for an hour.

- And, finally, my wife and best friend Sally, who continues to be the wind beneath my often-flailing wings—and whose three- and four-word Post-its on my computer offered some of the most inspirational writing I've ever read.

BIBLIOGRAPHY

Ambrose, Hugh. *The Pacific*. New York: New American Library, 2010.

Asprey, Robert B. *War in the Shadows: The Guerrilla in History, Volume One and Volume Two*. Garden City, New York: Doubleday & Co., 1975.

Bradley, James. *Flyboys*. New York: Little, Brown and Company, 2003.

Bradley, James. *The Imperial Cruise*. New York: Back Bay Books, 2009.

Costello, John. *The Pacific War 1941–1945*. New York: Perennial, 1981.

Cronin, A. J. *The Keys of the Kingdom*. Chicago: Loyola Press, 1941.

Gause, Damon. *The War Journal of Major Damon "Rocky" Gause*. New York: Hyperion, 1999.

Guardia, Mike. *American Guerrilla: The Forgotten Heroics of Russell W. Volckmann*. Philadelphia: Casemate Publishers, 2010.

Hedges, Chris. *War Is a Force That Gives Us Meaning*. New York: Anchor Books, 2002.

Keith, Bill. *Days of Anguish, Days of Hope: Chaplain Robert Preston Taylor's Ordeal and Triumph as a POW in World War II*. Longview, Texas: StoneGate Publishing Co., 2011.

Knox, Donald. *Death March: The Survivors of Bataan*. New York: Harcourt Brace Jovanovich, 1981.

Leckie, Robert. *Helmet for my Pillow*. New York: Bantam Books, 1957.

Levy, "Yank." *Guerrilla Warfare*. New York and Washington: Penguin Books, 1942.

Linderman, Gerald F. *The World Within War*. New York: The Free Press, 1997.

Manchester, William. *Goodbye, Darkness: A Memoir of the Pacific War*. New York: Back Bay Books, 1979.

Martin, Adrian R., and Larry W. Stephenson. *Operation Plum: The Ill-Fated 27th Bombardment Group and the Fight for the Western Pacific*. College Station, Texas: Texas A&M University Press, 2008.

Norman, Elizabeth M. *We Band of Angels*. New York: Pocket Books, 1999.

Norman, Michael, and Elizabeth M. *Tears in the Darkness*. New York: Picador, 2009.

Ramsey, Edwin Price, and Stephen J. Rivele. *Lieutenant Ramsey's War: From Horse Solider to Guerrilla Commander*. Washington, D.C.: Potamac Books, 1990.

Schaefer, Chris. *Bataan Diary: An American Family in World War II, 1941–1945*. Houston: Riverview Publishing, 2004.

Sides, Hampton. *Ghost Soldiers*. New York: Doubleday, 2001.

Sledge, E. B. *With the Old Breed*. New York: Ballantine Books, 1981.

The U.S. Army Survival Manual: Department of the Army Field Manual 21-76. Berkeley, California: Ulysses Press, 2009.

Whitcomb, Edgar D. *Escape from Corregidor*. New York: Henry Regnery Company, 1967.

Wise, William. *Secret Mission to the Philippines*. Lincoln, Nebraska: iUniverse.com, 1968.

Zinn, Howard. *A People's History of the United States*. New York: Perennial Classics, HarperCollins Publishers, 1999.

Zuckoff, Mitchell. *Lost in Shangri-La*. New York: HarperCollins, 2011.

INDEX